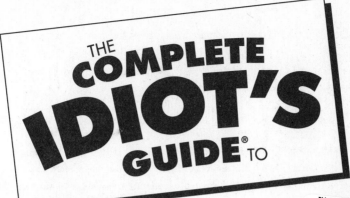

THE
COMPLETE
IDIOT'S
GUIDE® TO

W9-BMH-110

Low-Cost
Startups

by Gail Margolies Reid, CPA

ALPHA

A member of Penguin Group (USA) Inc.

For my mother and father, whose entrepreneurial spirit laid the foundation for my own low-cost startup.

ALPHA BOOKS

Published by the Penguin Group

Penguin Group (USA) Inc., 375 Hudson Street, New York, New York 10014, USA

Penguin Group (Canada), 90 Eglinton Avenue East, Suite 700, Toronto, Ontario M4P 2Y3, Canada (a division of Pearson Penguin Canada Inc.)

Penguin Books Ltd., 80 Strand, London WC2R 0RL, England

Penguin Ireland, 25 St. Stephen's Green, Dublin 2, Ireland (a division of Penguin Books Ltd.)

Penguin Group (Australia), 250 Camberwell Road, Camberwell, Victoria 3124, Australia (a division of Pearson Australia Group Pty. Ltd.)

Penguin Books India Pvt. Ltd., 11 Community Centre, Panchsheel Park, New Delhi—110 017, India

Penguin Group (NZ), 67 Apollo Drive, Rosedale, North Shore, Auckland 1311, New Zealand (a division of Pearson New Zealand Ltd.)

Penguin Books (South Africa) (Pty.) Ltd., 24 Sturdee Avenue, Rosebank, Johannesburg 2196, South Africa

Penguin Books Ltd., Registered Offices: 80 Strand, London WC2R 0RL, England

International Standard Book Number: 978-1-59257-994-5
Library of Congress Catalog Card Number: 2009934676

12   11   10   8   7   6   5   4   3   2   1

Interpretation of the printing code: The rightmost number of the first series of numbers is the year of the book's printing; the rightmost number of the second series of numbers is the number of the book's printing. For example, a printing code of 10-1 shows that the first printing occurred in 2010.

Printed in the United States of America

Note: This publication contains the opinions and ideas of its author. It is intended to provide helpful and informative material on the subject matter covered. It is sold with the understanding that the author and publisher are not engaged in rendering professional services in the book. If the reader requires personal assistance or advice, a competent professional should be consulted.

The author and publisher specifically disclaim any responsibility for any liability, loss, or risk, personal or otherwise, which is incurred as a consequence, directly or indirectly, of the use and application of any of the contents of this book.

Most Alpha books are available at special quantity discounts for bulk purchases for sales promotions, premiums, fundraising, or educational use. Special books, or book excerpts, can also be created to fit specific needs.

For details, write: Special Markets, Alpha Books, 375 Hudson Street, New York, NY 10014.

Publisher: *Marie Butler-Knight*
Editorial Director: *Mike Sanders*
Senior Managing Editor: *Billy Fields*
Senior Acquisitions Editor: *Paul Dinas*
Senior Development Editor: *Phil Kitchel*
Senior Production Editor: *Megan Douglass*
Copy Editor: *Emily Garner*

Cartoonist: *Shannon Wheeler*
Cover Designer: *Bill Thomas*
Book Designer: *Trina Wurst*
Indexer: *Tonya Heard*
Layout: *Ayanna Lacey*
Proofreader: *Laura Caddell*

Contents at a Glance

Contents

Introduction

At some point in their lives, most Americans consider the idea of starting their own business. For some it is a passing fancy. For others the idea is more of a recurring dream. In either case, it is always hard to overcome the barriers we put up for ourselves and just do it. So many things can go wrong. So much negative thinking …

> *"I don't have the money!"*
> *"Who will pay my bills?"*
> *"How do I get started?"*

Often it's hard to get past the most obvious hurdle: *"What should I do for a business? I don't have any special skills or knowledge to offer in the open market."*

That is exactly why we have written this book: to help you identify an idea that clicks for you—to bring you to your "Ah-ha!" moment when you realize that starting your own business is within your reality. Here's the advice that lays the groundwork for your success:

Start small, start slowly. There is always the possibility that your startup will turn out to be the Microsoft of the twenty-first century. We certainly don't want to hold you back. But that's not what this book is about. We've stayed faithful to a business model of a home-based startup that requires an upfront cash investment of $1,000 or less. This includes equipment, supplies, and marketing materials. When you stick to a low-cost startup concept, you don't have all that much to lose. You can expand your business as you generate more cash than you need to pay your bills.

Build a solid foundation to avoid future problems. We provide you with a basic understanding of how to set up your business and the administrative responsibilities you have to handle from the very beginning of Chapter 1. We keep it simple, but encourage you to put together a business plan and *use it*—as a guide and yardstick to help you stay on track.

We focus a great deal of attention on marketing your startup, both in the beginning and throughout the life cycle of your company. You can have all the talent imaginable but if you cannot sell your services or products you will never succeed on your own. Another way to say this: "Know yourself and your limitations."

The statistics are in your favor. Yes, that's right. Everyone starting a small business has a 50/50 chance of survival. If you follow the recommendations in this book, you will improve your odds of success dramatically.

Here's what to keep in the forefront of your mind—the secret to keeping your eye on the prize. Every day, millions of Americans wake up, have their coffee, and walk into their home offices to start their work days. No commute, no traffic, no boss controlling how their day unfolds. They have headaches and glitches for sure, but they also get to decide who they are going to work with, what time to break for lunch, and which afternoons they will knock off early to go watch their kid's soccer game. And the real kicker? They are making a living running a profitable, home-based, low-cost business.

Today can be the day you look yourself in the mirror and ask, *"Why not me?"* Reading this book will give you the ideas and tools you need to answer with a resounding, *"Yes, it's my turn now."*

How to Use This Book

Most of this book is dedicated to identifying a variety of business ideas that can be started from home for under $1,000. In addition, we have included several chapters that cover the basics of laying the groundwork for any home-based startup.

Part 1, "Getting Comfortable with Working for Yourself," zeros in on common-sense, basic business tenets underlying all successful businesses. Here we expand on the concepts underlying "low-cost." Also included are chapters on doing your research, outlining a business plan, and setting up your home headquarters.

Part 2, "Home Maintenance," jumps right into an entire range of business ideas centered on recurring services for residential homeowners. These include everything from assisting homeowners with buying or selling a home to everyday household chores.

Part 3, "Home Makeovers," highlights interior and exterior design, renovation, and landscaping. These businesses focus on larger, one-time projects that help homeowners take their homes to a new level.

Part 4, "Personal Touch," covers a variety of one-on-one services. Everything from baby nurse to elder care is covered, along with other services that help individuals take care of themselves, their loved ones, even their pets.

Part 5, "Hospitality Beckons," digs into the latest "here to serve you" business ideas. This section highlights food, event, and travel services.

Part 6, "Business Goods and Services," explores several business-to-business concepts that allow you to transition your past job experiences into a livelihood of an independent, self-employed businessperson. We end with different ideas for selling products from your home.

Each chapter includes different types of boxes of information intended to call your attention to various important details.

> **Success Story**
>
> Real life snapshots of startups that share some of the secrets of their successes.

> **Bonus Point**
>
> These boxes share insider tips and best practices with the intent of helping you to hit the ground running.

> **Snags**
>
> These are words of warning, often based on experiences of seasoned businesspeople. If you heed the advice you can avoid the pitfalls encountered by others.

> **def•i•ni•tion**
>
> We've made a point to include definitions for terms that have specific meanings when used in referring to small business startups.

Acknowledgments

Thank you to Gordon Warnock and Andrea Hurst at Andrea Hurst Literary Agency for seeing the potential for me to write this book. Thank you to my senior acquisitions editor at Alpha Books, Paul Dinas, for his patience and guidance in getting me through the process of writing my first book (and letting me live to tell the tale). I am grateful for the support from my good friend and "behind the scenes" editor, Phyllis Mueller, who held my hand through the early stages.

A huge thank you to all the home-based business owners across the United States, too numerous to name, who shared their stories with me so I could bring authenticity to this guide.

And lastly, a very special note of gratitude to Matthew, Rose, and Samantha, who are my biggest champions and continue to support my choosing to say, *"Why not me?"*

Trademarks

All terms mentioned in this book that are known to be or are suspected of being trademarks or service marks have been appropriately capitalized. Alpha Books and Penguin Group (USA) Inc. cannot attest to the accuracy of this information. Use of a term in this book should not be regarded as affecting the validity of any trademark or service mark.

Part 1

Getting Comfortable with Working for Yourself

Most of us struggle with the decision to take the leap into self-employment. Some of us get pushed off the cliff; in fact, the newest label for this group is "enterpreneur by necessity." When the economy slows in a major way (the last several years have been officially coined the Great Recession for a reason), the number of startups spikes accordingly. After all, no matter what your background or heritage, you are living in the United States, home to the American dream of small business ownership.

Part 1 of this guide focuses on the basics of building a solid foundation for any startup. We cover general business topics that apply to every idea in this book. We define the concept of a startup and clarify exactly what we mean by low cost, so we are all on the same wavelength for the rest of the book. There's a chapter on investigating your competition and there's a lengthy discussion about the importance of marketing. Finally, we give advice on how to go about setting up your office and managing your taxes and recordkeeping systems.

1

What Exactly Do We Mean by Startup?

In This Chapter

◆ Startup and startup costs defined

◆ Home-based businesses

◆ Why now is a good time to start your own business

◆ Matching the right business idea to your talents

You've decided to start your own business. You have many skills and talents but have always worked for someone else. Maybe you've ventured out on your own but it didn't work out, or your idea wasn't as winning as you had hoped. You are willing to work hard but you don't want to risk a lot of money. What can you start right now?

If you've been searching for an idea that feels right—that you can get excited about—this book is just for you. Our goal is to present business ideas that can be implemented for under $1,000 in startup costs. Moreover, we have selected proven business concepts that are viable in today's marketplace. Many people are making good, solid incomes through their ownership of and work in these businesses. Even with all the gloomy news about our current economy, the business opportunities included here are thriving across the country.

We used three criteria in our idea selection process. First, the idea had to be low cost. Second, it had to have solid potential earning power—a minimum of $35,000 a year in income to the owner at full capacity, working full time (and most have the promise of much more). Last, the ideas had to have the potential for a decent cash flow within three months or less before scaling up to a decent cash flow. So if you're ready to begin work, we've got a great resource to help you through the startup phase.

What We Cover in This Book

When we talk about a startup, we're describing a fledgling business that's just starting up. Technically, the term "startup" refers to the time period from when you decide to start a business and the day you are ready to begin *operating*.

def•i•ni•tion

When used in the business world, **operating** means to run or conduct an ongoing business. Operating a business includes everything from sales to administration and all the other processes that are required to deliver your service or product to your customers. When a company goes out of business, it ceases operating.

Once you decide on a direction and are ready to take action, you are creating a startup. Your initial expenses—the money you spend to get your business operating— are your startup costs. To a certain extent, every business has some of the same startup requirements and costs, from purchasing necessary equipment and acquiring a local business license to designing your business cards and printing your first marketing materials.

The Case for a Home-Based Startup

Working out of your house allows you to minimize your capital investment in your new business venture. The beauty of working from home is that you can get your business up and running without a big initial investment and without committing yourself to long-term overhead costs. It's a practical, down-to-earth approach to starting a business for someone who does not have much money to invest in a startup. You can gain a lot of ground and reach your break-even point much more quickly if you are not burdened with the high startup costs and responsibilities of leasing commercial space.

A big financial commitment for any business is a multiyear lease for office space. Even if you form a corporate entity, a landlord typically will require a small business owner to personally sign for the lease term. The monthly rent may not seem huge, but when multiplied by the 24 to 60 months of the lease term, the total expense you're locked into is significant. If you have a home-based business and decide to close, either to return to work for someone else or to relocate to another part of the country, you will not be tied to a lease.

Large corporations also understand the economic advantages of home offices; today, many corporate employees work from home to avoid time-consuming commutes, and the companies they work for use Internet communication and cellular telephone service to avoid the high fixed costs associated with having all company employees under one roof. These are the same reasons it makes perfect sense to start a home-based business.

Working from home isn't for everyone. Many people find it socially isolating and miss the company and camaraderie of colleagues. Others find they don't possess the self-discipline to get their work done during the business day and feel like they're working all the time. Working from home is for someone who is ready to venture out on his or her own and live the flexible and independent lifestyle available to the self-employed.

Establishing a startup from home is for those who want to be in that group of businesses that succeed after the first year and keep on succeeding year after year.

Why This Is the Right Time for You

Periods of recession, especially when accompanied by high rates of corporate cutbacks and business failures, have always seen a jump in the number of small business starts. This Great Recession is no exception. As the economic cycle begins to trend upward, forecasters predict we will enter a new economy, propelled by the self-determination of individuals using technology to expand their reach into the world marketplace. We are already seeing post-mortems on many of the nation's industrial keystones of the last century: manufacturing, auto making, and giant big-box retailers. As our society reshapes itself for the twenty-first century, small businesses will lead the innovation.

Graph of historical peak during recessionary periods.

(Courtesy of the U.S. Census Bureau)

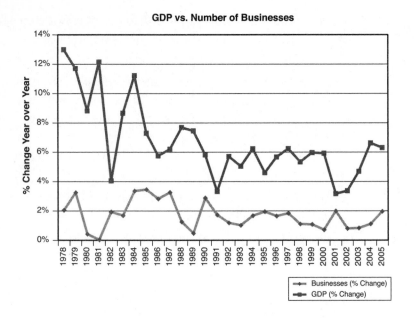

GDP vs. Number of Businesses

Bonus Point

By following the marketing and planning recommended in Chapter 3, you can build a business that generates the revenue you need to support yourself and your family. What's more, you have the potential to create something of your very own that will forever release you from the fear of being the next victim of a company's layoffs or the whims of your boss.

The big ideas of this new economy are being hatched right now, in the basements, dining rooms, and garages of people just like you. Some of these concepts will require venture capital and corporate support. But you don't need money to make money. Unlike the dot-com startups that defined the 1990s, most new twenty-first-century businesses started by individuals will be built with determination, a little bit of cash, and a lot of hard work. Using the ideas and guidelines in this book, you can start your own home-based business with ultra-light startup costs.

Truly, you have little to lose and everything to gain.

Matching Your Talents to a Winning Business Idea

You may already have a viable business idea, and are reading this book for reinforcement and advice. You'll want to focus on the guidelines for setting up your business: organizing your office, creating a marketing plan, and streamlining your recordkeeping. You can also consult the chapter that best relates to your specific business idea and modify the advice to suit your needs.

If you are determined to launch a startup but can't settle on a business idea that would work best for you, the following statements might help steer you in the direction that's right for you.

- You have specific skills learned from previous jobs that you can sell in the marketplace as an independent contractor.

- Your previous employment experience has shown you a need in that industry that is not being met.

- You enjoy providing services or products related to your former employment.

- Your previous experience has provided you with a strong network of contacts you could use as a base for launching your business idea.

- You have a hobby or passion for something that can be translated into earning power.

- You enjoy helping others. You have raised children, cared for elderly parents, taken in stray animals, or sold a home.

- You are comfortable enough using the Internet to help others obtain services or sell goods.

- You are tired of working for others.

- You are in a job that seems to be going nowhere.

- You have been laid off in the last year, or have made it through numerous rounds of layoffs and don't want to wait around for yours.

- You are discouraged by the lack of job prospects in this down economy.

- You believe in the American dream of small business ownership.

Success Story

Debbie D. loved making personalized gifts for her friends to commemorate special occasions. She developed a specialty of painting designs on ceramic plates, usually matching a favorite animal or item for a specific friend. When she started using friends' college mascots and icons to personalize their gifts, the feedback was so positive and the demand became so great that she started her own small business. Today she operates a very successful small company from home, supervising the design concepts but outsourcing the manufacture of the items.

The following statements capture three different ways to approach making a decision on a business idea that you can be passionate about.

- ◆ You have a skill in a field you enjoy but can no longer secure a job as an employee for someone else. You are ready to work as a freelancer and enjoy all the benefits of being your own boss.

- ◆ You need to uncover a special, somewhat hidden talent that you take for granted. For example, your sister who never fails to stop and rescue stray dogs on the road would be a natural at taking care of other people's pets. Or your best friend Linda, who knows the layout of every retail clothing store like the back of her hand, has an uncanny ability to select striking outfits for you when she takes you shopping.

- ◆ You have the personality and the perseverance to succeed in your own business. You just lack an idea that will spark your inner passion. Who knows—your hidden talent may be a knack for making money.

Reading the various chapters in this guide will give you the opportunity to ponder many potential business ideas. You only need to choose one. Launching a startup takes hard work, but it isn't difficult. Many Americans already make good livings by working on their own from home. By following the guidelines in this book, you can easily join their ranks.

Chapter 2

How Low Is Low-Cost?

In This Chapter

- ◆ How much money do you need?
- ◆ Can you afford this?
- ◆ Startup costs vs. recurring annual costs
- ◆ Sources of financing

Question: How much money do you need?

Answer: $1,000 or less

Anyone who has ever had to budget—and that's practically everyone—knows that it's more work not to spend money than to simply buy what you think you need. When it comes to the true essence of a startup, most of what you need is available for free. (We know this sounds trite, but keep reading and you'll see what we mean.) A big budget isn't necessary. Really.

Low-Cost Startups: A Winning Formula

A low-cost startup is characterized in the business world as having low *barriers to entry*. All the business ideas in this book have low initial expenses—$1,000 or less for startup costs. And they're good money makers.

Gradual growth at minimal expense is a pervasive theme of this book. It may surprise you to learn that many people are able to go out on their own with very little seed money. Remember, our goal is to generate income for one person—*you*. You are not trying to build an international, multimillion dollar company (at least not initially).

def•i•ni•tion

Barriers to entry are obstacles in the path of a startup that make it difficult to enter a given market. Typical kinds of barriers include high-dollar upfront investment, crowded and highly competitive markets, and sophisticated skill sets needed to attract customers.

This is everyone's dream of starting a business: their idea will hit the jackpot, their timing will be spot on, and their business will become something big. But even though it would be terrific to start the next Better World Books, when you launch a low-cost startup, you don't need sales in the millions to achieve success.

Success Story

In 2002, three former college roommates held a local book drive for charity. It was a huge success that made them realize they could generate a good revenue stream selling used books. Being Internet-savvy young men (and having no money to fund a startup), they built their own website and began selling used books online. Today, their company, Better World Books, is a global organization with sales in the seven figures.

What We Include in Startup Costs

The key ingredients of any startup business are:

- A great and workable idea

- A written, straightforward business plan

- The ability to implement the plan

- Attention to details

- Follow-through and persistence

Our $1,000 budget for startup costs includes all the purchases necessary to get you to Day 1 of operations. This comprises equipment, licenses, marketing materials, and supplies. Some people set out to buy the best of everything when starting a new business. They are under the misguided impression that having the "best" is necessary to be successful.

This could not be further from the truth. The telltale sign of impending startup disaster, as evidenced by the dot-com era, is spending investment capital on fancy new equipment and facilities, when less expensive or secondhand options are good enough to get you started and when working from home will work just fine.

Some of your startup costs will be for items or services that you'll need to replenish periodically as long as you run your business. These include supplies, marketing costs, insurance, and your business license. Once you are fully operational, any cost you incur is considered an annual expense. Review Chapter 4 to learn how to set up a simple bookkeeping system for tracking costs and keeping receipts. It is important to review your expenses regularly, to make sure that you are not exceeding your budget because of waste or inefficiencies.

How Much Money Can You Afford?

If you spent $20 on this book, more likely than not you can come up with the $1,000 to cover your startup costs. Yes, you may have to use your charge card or get a loan or take cash out of your Christmas account, but you can manage it. The larger, more costly question is how to cover your living expenses while you get your business started and ramp up your revenue to the level of income you need to support yourself.

If you have savings you can use to cover your household expenses for at least three months, you have a solid cushion. For those of you who haven't put as much away (outside your retirement accounts), your first few months will be challenging, but manageable. Since one of our criteria for the ideas in this book is a quick ramping-up period, you should be able to manage with your early sales, tight reins on your spending, and perhaps some extra use of your credit card.

Success Story

Joanne D. began cleaning homes in the early 1990s to support her family. Her only startup costs were a good vacuum, business cards, and flyers. She was good at it and soon had a full schedule of business. She saw that if she hired someone to help her clean homes, she could do each one in half the time and double her business while only adding a portion of the original costs. Joanne is still in business today, with three cleaning crews and hundreds of customers. In 2008, her small company grossed over $300,000, with Joanne earning a six figure income.

Should You Quit Your Job?

If you are currently employed, evaluate your resources and determine whether you can afford to quit your job immediately. Quitting may not be necessary just yet. Many successful businesses are begun by people during the off hours from their full-time jobs, which they keep until they have enough money coming in from their new venture. This decision is entirely dependent on your personal finances and your tolerance for risk.

Have You Already Been Laid Off?

If you are already unemployed, there is nothing to stop you from proceeding full tilt with your business idea. Do exercise caution if you are collecting unemployment compensation. Be sure to educate yourself about your state's requirements to continue collecting unemployment. If you need that weekly check to survive until your business is underway, you need to pay attention to the rules and stay within the parameters of eligibility. If the FAQ section of your state's Department of Labor unemployment page isn't crystal clear on this topic, make a call or visit the unemployment office to clarify any questions you may have.

The Three C's of a Startup

In thinking about startup costs, we have made certain assumptions about items you already own that can be used to start your business. These include the following everyday technology tools that are commonly owned by most Americans.

A Home Computer

To follow the recommendations in this book, you will need to have a basic home computer or at least have access to one. That's because a critical phase of each startup is researching the competition. For many business ideas, you will also need to use the Internet to source the equipment you will have to buy in the startup phase. You may even decide to create and print your own business cards and marketing materials.

Resist the temptation to indulge in a fancy new laptop—make do with the computer you already have. Other options, at least in the beginning, are a friend or relative's computer or your local public library.

A Cell Phone

Every business needs a phone number, and many of the business ideas in this book require you to be on the go. You will initially be responsible for making and receiving all your business calls. It's common today to use a cell phone as a primary business number, and the cost is more reasonable than landline business service. You can certainly get a business line for your home office, but this is an optional expense that can be postponed—perhaps indefinitely.

 Bonus Point _____

Phone companies charge a lot more for a business line than a residential phone. For the cost of one business line that gets you a "free" listing in the business directory, you can maintain your own website—a better use of your marketing dollars.

A Car, Van, or Truck

Not all businesses in this book require a vehicle, but many of them do. Some will require a truck or van. If you need to acquire a vehicle in order to get started, we have presumed that the vehicle will be purchased with a loan or leased with a minimal down payment. We have not included the ongoing cost of the monthly loan or lease payments in the startup costs. Instead, you should consider the payments expenses to be paid out of the cash flow of the business.

Sources of Financing

Companies of all sizes depend on borrowed money to start a new business. If you follow news reports on the recent business climate, you may have the impression that there are no loans to be had anywhere for anyone. Right now the credit market is tight and until the economy rebounds, it will be difficult to get large loans.

However, borrowing up to $5,000 to purchase equipment you need for a business is not impossible. If you choose to buy new equipment, you will have access to lenders through reputable manufacturers or wholesale companies that will offer a revolving credit type of loan for a decent interest rate. If you have an excellent credit rating and a good relationship with your local bank or credit union, check to see whether a bank loan is possible. Arranging your own financing through your bank or credit union could save you money in fees and interest over the loan term.

Charging Startup Costs to Your Credit Card

Using a credit card for business expenses requires the same commonsense approach you should take with using a credit card for your personal expenses. If you have several cards, select the one with the lowest periodic interest rate. That way, if you decide to pay off the charges over a few months, you won't be charged exorbitant interest on the unpaid balance.

> **Snags** _____
>
> Just because you have more than $1,000 in available credit on your card doesn't mean you should veer from the budget for a low-cost startup and spend a lot of money. The whole point of keeping startup costs to a minimum is to avoid future debt if your business idea does not work out or if you change your mind.

Borrowing Against or Using Your Retirement Savings

It is never ideal to take money from funds set aside for retirement, but, depending upon your age and circumstances, this may be the right time to put these funds to use. The taxes on withdrawing $1,000 from a retirement account are minimal. Regardless of your age, if you are still an active employee, you may be able to borrow against your account and postpone any taxes indefinitely.

These factors vary significantly from employer to employer, so be sure to review all the paperwork in your retirement plan file. You can also talk with your company's benefits department so you understand exactly what the consequences of the transaction will be.

Friends and Family

Many businesses get started with loans from family or friends. If you know someone who would be interested in bankrolling your business—maybe someone who has always encouraged you to go out on your own—there is nothing wrong with asking for a loan. As an act of good faith to the lender, it is always best to write up a brief promissory note to be signed by both parties with a stated interest rate. You should put some of your own money into the business, too. Most lenders want to see that their borrower has "skin in the game."

Avoid the temptation to offer a private lender a stake in your business. If you are doing all the work, you will eventually resent sharing your profits with an investor who's sitting on the sidelines. Moreover, it is likely that in the first few years you will be making only enough to support yourself and your immediate family. If you have to split your profits with a nonworking partner, you will not be happy.

Bank Loans

Even during good economic times, it is highly unusual for a bank (or the Small Business Administration) to approve a business loan for a brand new company, so a bank loan—even a small one—is not really an option for a startup business.

What is feasible, even in current times, is applying for a loan that is fully guaranteed by the individual starting the business (you). If you have excellent credit and/or assets that can be used as collateral (such as nonretirement savings accounts or home equity), there is a chance that you could borrow money from a bank for starting your business in the form of a personal loan. To do this you would either provide your personal guarantee (you promise to pay off the loan if the business cannot meet the obligation in the future), or pledge personal assets to the bank for the loan term.

Keeping It Low Cost and Legal

People dread dealing with the Internal Revenue Service. They worry that they will make some mistake when filing their various taxes that will cost them dearly in penalties and interest. As a result, they feel compelled to consult both a lawyer and accountant before they start their businesses. While good professional advice can always add value to a startup, this book is intended to get you started without the cost of professional services. If you read the "Paying Your Taxes" section in Chapter 4, we explain that if you keep your records in order and follow basic advice, you should have no problem staying in the good graces of the IRS.

If you need assistance, there are resources you can avail yourself of. It is possible to go to an IRS office in your area and get help directly. Certified Public Accountant (CPA) professional associations often run volunteer programs for working with the public; you can check on this by calling your state society of CPAs. See the Appendix for links to Service Corps for Retired Executives (SCORE) and Small Business Development Centers (SBDC), two organizations that provide free services to startups.

Choosing Your Type of Business Entity

Many new business owners believe they must form a legal business entity before they take steps toward launching their business venture. The perception is that a corporation, partnership, or Limited Liability Company (LLC) will protect them from potential legal liability.

Although operating as one of these formal entities can be a good idea, it is not necessary. What it can be, however, is expensive. It costs several hundred dollars to incorporate and many more dollars over time for all the legal paperwork and tax returns that have to be continually completed and filed in order to keep the corporate entity intact.

Operating as a Sole Proprietor

Any of the business ideas in this book can be started as a *sole proprietorship*, which is the only no-cost operating structure. It's the simplest to launch and manage.

def•i•ni•tion

A **sole proprietorship** is a business owned by an individual who is personally responsible for its debts. A sole proprietorship can operate under the name of its owner or it can do business under a trade name. Either way, it is not a legal entity separate from the sole proprietor owner.

There are no legal formalities for opening a sole proprietorship other than acquiring the proper business licenses. No, you can't put "Inc." after your company name, since that denotes a corporation. But everything else is exactly the same, only less complicated. Chapters 3 and 4 provide more details on operating your business as a sole proprietorship.

Chapter 3

Do Your Homework

In This Chapter

- Writing your business plan
- Finding the gap in your marketplace
- Revenue and cost worksheets
- Developing your marketing plan

Before you line up your first customer, before you spend a dime on equipment, before you decide what to print on your business cards, you need to have a plan. Why? Because the fastest, easiest path to creating a successful business is following a clear, realistic, and well-thought-out business plan. The amount of planning required depends on the kind of business and the amount of your initial investment. Simple, low-cost startups like the ones described in this book require very basic, concise, simple business plans. You don't need to complicate this process with fancy software or by reading in-depth books on the subject.

Writing a business plan is nothing more than using your common sense to guide you in spending your startup dollars. The rest of this chapter takes you step by step through the business-planning process. If you do your "homework," which will be assigned in the rest of this chapter, you will end up with a suitable business plan to launch your business.

A business plan is comprised of several straightforward individual analyses which, when assembled into one document, can provide a comprehensive step-by-step guide to navigating the startup phase of your business venture. Looking at each component separately demystifies the process and breaks it down into clear, simple steps.

Researching Your Market

Use basic market-research techniques to obtain objective feedback on your business idea. This will help you make sound decisions based on facts and your understanding of your market, not on gut feelings or intuition. Researching your market gives you valuable information and insights about the people or businesses to whom you will sell services or goods. For example, certain business ideas are going to be more suited to one area of the country than another. Similarly, if you live in a metropolitan area, you will want to identify the geographic and demographic areas within your city that have the greatest need for your service or product.

Devise an effective and systematic method for organizing and analyzing the data you collect. This may sound complicated or intimidating, but it's really no more difficult than researching any type of major consumer purchase, like you would if you were buying a car, contemplating a major home repair, or choosing a new appliance.

Your goal is to answer this simple question: is there sufficient demand in your area for the service or product you want to offer? A "yes" answer means you move ahead, a "no" means you try another idea that will get you a "yes."

To determine that the level of demand is sufficient, follow these steps:

1. Survey individuals and search the Internet for opinions from potential customers in your area. Develop a list of no more than 10 pertinent questions to be asked of interested parties, such as:

   Do you currently use this service or product now?

   If not, what would entice you? Price? Added value?

   How much would you be willing to pay for XXX?

   If I added something would you be willing to pay more?

2. Make a list of all the people you can think of who might want your service or already have someone fulfilling this need. Contact these individuals by phone or e-mail and ask them to complete your brief survey. Make an appointment (30 minutes is long enough) to telephone the person, read the questions, and

jot down the answers. (The telephone approach is easiest on your interviewees and avoids making them feel put upon. Even if you are not well-acquainted with someone, it is likely they will give you a half hour to talk over the phone.)

3. After you complete your surveys, consolidate the responses onto a single worksheet. Use a scale of 1 to 5 to rate each person's response to each question, 1 being a low or lukewarm answer and 5 the most enthusiastic. Then calculate your average rating and determine an overall score.

If your respondents confirmed your intuition that this is a good business idea by a score of 80 percent or more, there is a strong reason to move forward. If your idea rates less than 80 percent, it would be prudent to rethink your idea and either modify it or create something else that garners more enthusiasm from your group of participants.

Sizing Up Your Competition

Study your competition and use this information to define the basics of your own business. This will help you finalize your decision about moving forward with your business venture. Simply Google businesses in your area that offer competitive services and study their websites. See what they offer and what they charge for their service or product. If prices are not included on the website, call and play "secret shopper." Pretend to be a prospective customer and ask the questions your customers would ask. How much is it and what do I get? Is there a guarantee if I am not satisfied? Do you have insurance? How long have you been in business?

Understanding the alternatives your potential customers can choose from allows you to tailor what you offer to fill in your competitors' gaps. By going beyond the rest of the pack and differentiating yourself, even in a small way, you set yourself up as the first choice for customers in your market.

When McDonald's entered the restaurant market in the 1950s, it created the entirely new concept of fast-food dining. In the 50-some years since opening its first restaurant, the market has been flooded with hundreds of competitors. Some have long since faded from memory, but others developed enormous market share by improving

Bonus Point

Some of the best ideas in business have been copied from competitors. By taking the time to study their ads, brochures, and promotional materials you can improve on what other companies offer.

on the McDonald's concept. The competition's response to market demands has re-defined customers' expectations of fast food, and in the last decade forced McDonald's to improve the nutritional value of their menu.

You can learn the most about your prospective business idea by talking with someone who is already doing it. This is your best source of information for your business plan. Other small business operators are often very generous with their stories and advice, having learned many lessons the hard way themselves. Their input will improve your chances for a successful startup and rapid growth. You can e-mail some of the businesses you found through your Internet research. You can also ask one of your new vendors, such as an equipment salesman, banker, or insurance agent, if they can introduce you to someone else in your industry.

Here are some other easy methods for investigating your competitors:

- Scrutinize competitors' websites in your geographic area. Study the way they organize their business. Use their pricing to come up with your own.

- Research services provided by the national companies and learn from their best practices, which are the methods the most successful companies use. You may find checklists and other tools that you can incorporate into your business. An example of this is the "What we do" checklist on the Mini Maid website.

- Look for blogs, articles, and websites that give you insight into the needs of your prospective customers. Use your research to create a unique offering for your services (flex hours, customization for client needs, and so on) to differentiate yourself from the competition.

Defining Your Startup Costs

It is vitally important to control your cash as you get your business off the ground. To do this effectively you have to start out with a defined budget for both your startup costs and your continuing expenses. Most startups have similar kinds of expenses as they prepare to enter the marketplace.

We've already stated you're going to have a total startup cost of $1,000 or less. Now we are ready to define those costs and give you tools for applying your budget to your business idea.

Your Startup Costs Worksheet

In Chapter 2 we detailed the Three C's, items we assume you already own (a cell phone, a computer, and a car or truck) and will use for your business, at least in the initial stages. Typical items included in startup costs are equipment required by a specific business, initial inventory of supplies, insurance premiums (or at least an initial payment on a policy), and as much marketing as you can afford.

Here's a simple template you can use to create a budget:

Startup Costs

Description	Cost
Equipment:	
Purchase or	$_____
Down payment	$_____
Initial Supplies	$_____
Total Equipment and Supplies	_____
Marketing Materials:	
Business cards	$_____
Flyers	$_____
Car magnets	$_____
Internet	$_____
Total Marketing Costs	$_____
Business license	$_____
Insurance:	
Annual premium or	$_____
Initial payment	$_____
Grand Total Startup Costs	$_____

How to Budget for Your Startup Costs

Here are some helpful tips for filling in the budget blanks:

In the first subsection of each business idea presented in the remaining chapters of this book, you'll find estimated costs for equipment for that business idea. This will give you a starting point, but you should do your own research to find equipment most suitable to your needs at the best price.

Many businesses require specific supplies. This could be vacuum cleaner bags (for a housecleaner) or warming platters (for a caterer). Include your initial purchase of such industry-specific items in your startup costs, since you will need them on hand for your first customers.

Marketing materials can be purchased from a variety of providers, or if you have a good computer and printer in your home office and the skills to generate attractive printed materials, factor in the cost of the ink, paper, and card stock you will need. If you prefer to outsource these tasks, check the prices at a local print shop. (To find one, try a quick web search of your zip code. See the Appendix for website links.) Because graphic design has become more digitized and accessible, printing services have expanded to include all kinds of graphic design support. You should be able to purchase business cards, a flyer, and car magnets for around $200. You can also hire freelance marketing help. A web search will bring up a range of freelance marketing professionals in your area.

There are many alternatives to the high cost of designing, building, and hosting your own website on the Internet. Many industries represented in this book have web-based marketing companies that provide soup to nuts marketing support. For as little as $99 down plus a per-lead fee, you can belong to a network referral source that will send you leads on interested customers. Some referral networks will bundle a webpage of your very own on a pay-as-you-go basis. The Appendix has links to a few of these sites.

Bonus Point _____

If you pursue an idea for which network referral marketing is not available, look into doing a low-cost website on your own. With so many IT professionals unemployed right now, it is possible to get help with a basic website for a rather small investment. You can also find websites that offer guidance on designing your own site. There are monthly hosting fees to consider, but these costs are minimal, often less than $10 per month.

Most home-based businesses are required to have a business license issued by the municipality in which the owner lives. Most local governments have websites that explain business licensing requirements for your area. Sometimes called a "business tax return" or "permit," these are all essentially the same. Read the instructions carefully. These license fees or taxes are usually based on anticipated revenue. Be sure to use a low, conservative projection of your first-year revenue to keep your fee to the minimum. If you exceed your estimated revenue, you will have a chance to make a catch-up payment in the following year. But if you overestimate your revenue and pay a higher license fee than you need to, it is difficult (or not possible) to request a refund of an overpayment on a business license.

There are many good reasons to have business insurance. Although insurance coverage is not always required by law, it is an investment in the future of your business. The primary types of insurance for businesses are liability, workers' compensation, health, employee bonding, and property and casualty. For many businesses, especially service-oriented ones, insurance may become the single largest annual expense. Sometimes when cash is tight it is hard to pay for something that is not absolutely necessary to daily operations. But there is no better way to protect your investment of hard work and hard-earned money than to cover yourself for potential risks and threats specific to your industry.

A good insurance agent can save you a lot of time and money, so find someone in your city who works with small businesses and is knowledgeable in this field. There are websites where you can request insurance quotes listed in the Appendix.

> **Bonus Point**
>
> A review of professional-association websites is a great place to start to educate yourself about the insurance needs for the business idea you are interested in. They will also have checklists of qualifications for becoming a member, and insurance coverage is a common prerequisite. Frequently a major benefit of membership in an association is access to the insurance at reduced fees.

Using Your Own

Certain business ideas, especially those that develop from hobbies, give you the opportunity to put your personal assets to use in your business. Some examples are a vacuum cleaner for a cleaning business, a lawnmower for a yard service, and a personal toolbox for a handyman. If you already own an item and it is paid for, you do not have to include it in your startup costs. If it has a limited useful life, say a residential mower being converted to business use, you will need to consider budgeting for replacement equipment at a future date. This amount will appear in your budget for annual expenses in the year you expect to buy the replacement.

There are tax advantages to converting personal assets to business use because they become tax deductible. In addition to industry-specific equipment, this would apply to your cell phone, computer, and anything else that you use regularly to conduct your new business. If this applies to you, it would be a good idea to read up on tax deductions for small businesses or to follow up with a professional.

Business Use of Your Vehicle

The costs associated with operating your vehicle for your business are no different from those of a commuting employee. To calculate how much of your vehicle expenses to allocate to your business, it's easiest to start out with your total costs. (If you have more than one vehicle, choose one to use for your business and include only the costs for that vehicle.)

For tax purposes, you have the option of using a mileage rate times your business mileage to arrive at an amount you can deduct on your tax return. For cost purposes, use the actual cost method by completing the table below for an accurate accounting of your vehicle cost. This is an important step that will reinforce the idea of limiting your geographic range for conducting business to maintain higher profitability.

Estimated Annual Vehicle Expenses

Items Required for Vehicle	Annual Expenses
Car loan or lease payments	$_____
Insurance	$_____
Gasoline	$_____
Repairs and Maintenance	$_____
Subtotal Annual Expenses	$_____
Less: _____ percent of personal usage	
	$_____
**Total Cost of Business Use Year 1	$_____

Notify your car insurance agent that you are now using your vehicle for business and no longer commuting. This may impact your current insurance premium. To estimate your gasoline costs, project your annual mileage and calculate your annual costs based on the current price per gallon of gas.

The proportion of your driving that is personal will depend upon whether you will be driving to customer sites to deliver services or products or working predominantly in your office each day. You will have to guess your percent of personal use in the beginning. After a few months of tracking your business mileage, you will see a pattern emerge based on your total miles for the period divided by your business miles. If you have more than one vehicle, you can dedicate one to purely business use and use 100 percent of the cost in your expense calculation.

The seasoned business owner of a housecleaning company solved this problem with a great idea for controlling her transportation costs. She decided to accept new customers only if they were inside a specified geographic area. She posted a map of her city on the wall and outlined the area where she wanted to do business. When prospective customers called for a quote, her first question was "Where do you live?" If the caller lived outside her bid zone, she politely made a referral to a friendly competitor in that area.

Snags

You will always have a tug of war between not wanting to turn down work and the economics of taking on that work. As your own boss, you have to determine your costs of doing business and your break-even point every time you accept an order from a customer. Your transportation costs, even for use of your personal vehicle, are an important factor to consider when you are in business for yourself.

Ongoing Annual Costs Worksheet

Before you determine how much you will charge your customers, lay out your continuing expenses for the next 12 months. Any expenses you anticipate from the time you start operating through the end of your first year should be included in your annual budget. These projected expenses include ongoing supplies, Internet access fees, cell phone bills, vehicle expenses, and business taxes, among others. You can use or modify the following worksheet for budgeting your annual costs.

Costs

Items Required	Annual Expenses
**Vehicle	$_____
Insurance	$_____
Marketing	$_____
Business license	$_____
Supplies	$_____
Telephone	$_____
Internet	$_____
Training and certifications	$_____
Dues and memberships	$_____
Total Expenses Year 1:	$_____

**Enter the total from the vehicle expense worksheet.

These categories will vary somewhat with each idea and the degree to which you expand your business. Use this format as it works for you, adding or deleting categories as necessary.

Projecting Your Revenue

Anyone who has put a business plan together will tell you it is much easier to project expenses than it is to estimate revenue. First, you need to think about all the factors that will influence your cash inflow. For example, during the ramp-up period—the first few months after you open for business—you will be building a customer base. It will take you some time to reach full capacity and maximum revenue. You'll have to work against persistent negative thoughts like, "No way I'll ever do that much business," just as you have to keep a realistic perspective to prevent yourself from overreaching and overestimating your success in the early stages.

The best way to project revenue is to think in terms of three scenarios: best case, worst case, and what you really think might happen. Make an agreement with yourself to use your best guesses and admit that you really don't know exactly how things will work out. Then you will be ready to crank out some numbers.

The worksheet for revenue projections provided later is meant to make this process as painless as possible. You'll estimate revenue based on an hourly rate or on a per job or per project basis. The sections on business ideas in each chapter will give you a starting point for pricing based on our research. If you use our basic information and do your own market research more specific to your particular situation, you should be able to make realistic projections.

Pricing Strategies

The best place for a new small business to be—pricewise—is in the middle of the pack. There are leaders in your field who charge the highest prices, and other companies that compete with low prices. If you start in the middle, you avoid head-to-head competition with the industry biggies and the struggle for profitability that comes with rock-bottom pricing.

Steve D. owns a window cleaning business in a large metropolitan area. When a prospective customer inquires about his prices, he uses the opportunity to educate the customer about his business. He welcomes prospects to compare his pricing with that of his competitors, but lets them know in advance that his prices are in the middle range. He explains that he is a small company but he carries top-level insurance to protect his customers and his employees. Many of his low-priced competitors don't have insurance, he points out, and this is something most customers don't think about when they hire workers for jobs in their homes. With this said, few prospects ask him to come down in price because they understand the value his company provides and why he charges what he does.

Snags

A word of warning for the new business owner: be careful to not focus on competitive pricing. It is very common in business for potential customers, especially other small business owners, to hone in on your price. Many times you will get leads to customers who already have the product or service you are offering, but want an opportunity to "bid it out" and look for a lower price. As a newbie in the marketplace you will be tempted to take all work that comes your way. You may even be pressured by good negotiators to give them a deal. Our advice: stick to your price.

Sometimes even the best worded responses to prospects looking for a price discount won't close a sale. As a new business owner, you are going to have moments of doubt in your pricing and whether you should make an exception and give a price reduction to get a sale. When this happens get out your benchmarks and projections. Look at how much more work you will have to do if you lower your prices. Experienced business owners have learned the hard way—it usually is not worth it to be the low-priced option. You have to work harder for your profits (more hours) and truthfully, customers who are most interested in price are often not the best customers.

Pricing Strategies Comparison

	Column 1	Column 2
Price per job	$250	$300
Jobs per week	11	9
Weekly Revenue	$2,750	$2,700

In the preceding simple example, a 20 percent increase in price per job ($50 more in Column 2) yields a 20 percent reduction in the number of jobs (and hours) the business owner needs to complete in order to make virtually the same amount of money. You don't need as many customers (which can translate into less marketing costs, transportation costs, etc.) if you can manage to charge a slightly higher price for each job you do.

Solo vs. Team Approach

A big decision for any startup business will be whether to work solo or to increase revenue by hiring a team. There are pros and cons to each approach. If you need to start bringing in money right away, it's usually best to go solo, at least until you have enough work to offer part of your pay to a helper or partner. Working by yourself also helps you decide if you would prefer company. To calculate the different income potentials from a solo versus a team approach, you need to consider both the added potential revenue (more customers, more hours billed) and costs (pay, supplies) of adding a second person. In many instances, it adds at least 50 percent to your personal take-home pay if you expand to a team.

If you decide on the team approach from the beginning, you will have to research whether it's common in your area to pay your helper as a contract worker or an employee. Make sure you are in compliance with federal and state employment laws. If it's commonly accepted in your part of the country to pay a worker in your industry as a nonemployee independent contractor, you are on good footing to do so. Treating helpers as independent contractors when possible reduces paperwork and is more straightforward than having your own employees. If you determine that you need to consider your helpers legal employees, you will have to learn the proper procedures for *running a payroll*.

Revenue Worksheet

You can use this worksheet for projections based on an hourly rate or on a per job or per project basis. Use the lines that apply to you, and scratch out those that don't.

How much you charge will be determined from your research of your competition. You decide how much you want to work. This method of estimation is appropriate for people who are seeking full-time work as well as those who may be downsizing to a part-time schedule. It can also be useful for those who want to supplement income from an existing job with income from self-employment.

The table below shows a sample calculation of annual revenue. You can follow the formulas given to project your own earnings.

Revenue

Working hours per week	40
Less estimated travel time	-5
Hours to be billed per week	=35
Vacations/Holidays/Sick weeks	6
Working weeks per year	46
Rate per hour	$25
Rate per job	$N/A
Revenue per week	$875*
Total Revenue Year 1:	$40,250**

Hours to be billed each week (35) X Rate per hour ($25)

**Revenue per week ($875) X working weeks per year (46)*

Figuring Your Monthly Payment

Your monthly payment for any equipment you purchase with a loan will depend upon the amount you finance and the compounding interest rate. Many times the financial institution will provide a loan payment amount and schedule for your use. If not, you can use one of many simple financial programs available on the Internet to do your own calculation (see the Appendix).

You will need to know the amount borrowed (principal), the interest rate of the loan, and how many months you have to repay the loan (loan term). All this information can be found on the loan document (promissory note).

Basic Marketing Techniques

It is quite possible to grow your market on a small budget. You should have already included marketing materials in your startup budget. You will not have enough money to pay for traditional advertising, but don't worry. The following recommendations for no- or low-cost alternatives have helped many small businesses get off the ground.

Drumming Up Your First Customers

Here are some easy techniques to attract your first customers:

- **Craigslist:** Check your local Craigslist website for help-wanted listings for your business category. You'll still need to launch a marketing effort, but as you are ramping up you can start generating money right away by snagging the low-hanging fruit there for the picking on Craigslist.

- **Word of mouth:** Get out your Rolodex and contact everyone you know. It will take some time to get the word out but you will find many of your early customers through personal contacts.

- **Flyers:** Print up a brightly colored flyer and post it at local supermarkets, schools, churches, and recreation centers. In many suburban neighborhoods it is accepted practice to leave flyers tacked to individual mailbox posts.

- **Local advertising:** Neighborhood newspapers, newsletters, bulletins, and websites are an inexpensive way to get your name known in your area. Familiarize yourself with the promotional media in your target area. Study the other businesses that advertise in them and follow up by calling some of the current advertisers and asking them how much business they get from their ads. Use the results of this research to test different options to see what works for you.

◆ **Networking:** Sole proprietors often join a business group as a way to market their business. Every community has myriad networking options. In addition to outright networking events that are open to the public for a fee, endless groups of small business people meet regularly to help each other with referrals. Check out our list in the Appendix for national organizations you are likely to find in your region.

Bonus Point _____

Make a habit of asking every potential customer how he or she heard about your business. It is surprising how few small companies do this. Make the most of your advertising dollars by understanding what marketing efforts result in gaining new customers.

Expanding Your Customer Base

Customers who are pleased with your services will refer friends and neighbors to you. As an incentive, you can offer a discount to a customer who refers a friend who actually uses your services. Another marketing trick that gets people's attention is offering a guarantee—if a customer isn't pleased, the service is free. But watch out! This can backfire if you encounter unpleasant customers, but normally it's a way to get your foot in the door when you are just getting started and compensating for not having references.

Look for other good locations to post your flyers: churches and synagogues, apartment and condominium club houses, supermarket bulletin boards, and fitness centers are just a few suggestions of places that get a lot of foot traffic on a daily basis.

Polishing Your Reputation as a Marketing Strategy

Present yourself as professionally as possible to help accelerate the growth of your income and customer base. Return calls promptly, make appointments, and show up on time. Carry your business cards and give them away like crazy. Invest in advertising magnets for your vehicle. The first impression you create really does make or break your customers' purchasing decisions.

Bonus Point _____

Little things can go a long way to differentiating yourself from the competition. Simply wearing a T-shirt or collared shirt with a company name and logo will not only impress your current customers but also bring you new business.

Online Marketing

There are marketing options available on the Internet for a fixed monthly fee. The most widely used method currently is *search engine optimization* (*SEO*).

The direct costs of this technique are billed at pennies per click and can be kept to a minimum by setting up a monthly budget with the SEO provider. What can be very expensive, however, is setting up a website that maximizes the benefits from SEO. If you have the IT skills to do this on your own, or have someone who is willing to help you at low cost, this could be a very helpful boon to your marketing efforts. Books about SEO can provide you with more details on how to make the most of this. (Check the Appendix for a reference guide on SEO techniques.)

As we mentioned in the section on Internet options, membership in a network that includes an online presence as a benefit can be a cost-effective online marketing choice for a new startup.

def•i•ni•tion

Search engine optimization (SEO) improves the volume of traffic to a website from search engines via increased search results (hits). Typically, the higher up a site appears in the search results list, the more visitors it will receive from the search engine. To achieve search results where your company's frequently at the top of the list creates a stronger web presence.

Bonus Point

Always get permission from the people you would like to be your references in advance. Let them know when to expect a referral call. This courtesy will set you apart as a professional.

References

Many new customers will ask for references. Until you have a list of satisfied customers, a good strategy is to prepare a short list (three is sufficient) of character references. They can be business contacts, former employers, teachers, or your pastor. Once you have been in business a few weeks and have some satisfied customers, you can ask them if they would be willing to serve as references.

Offering Something Different

By the time you begin work on your marketing plan, you should have done a good bit of research on your competition, the ins and outs of the business idea that you want to pursue, and your marketplace. You can give yourself a competitive edge right from the start by using this preparation to come up with a new idea or even just a small twist on the norm to differentiate yourself.

People often start businesses that fulfill a need of their own that they could not satisfy in the existing market. One of the best exercises you can do is to put yourself in the place of your customer by shopping around with competitors, acting out the role of a potential customer. What does your competitor do that impresses you? You can learn to avoid a competitor's behavior or tactic that you don't appreciate. Even better, get some feedback from potential customers by discussing your startup ideas with others. By listening to the voices of your imagined or potential customers and identifying their unfulfilled needs, you can create a business that provides a unique customer experience and really sets you apart.

Success Story
When John D., a CPA, started his practice in 1986, he gained several new clients because they needed representation dealing with inquiries from the IRS. John realized that fear of the IRS was a major reason people hired CPAs. He came up with an unusual offer: he filed a Power of Attorney with the IRS for every one of his clients. While most CPAs wait until their client has received a notice before taking this action, John knew that with a Power of Attorney on file he would receive duplicate notices as a matter of protocol. When his clients called with concerns about an inquiry, he was able to reassure them because he had received the notice as well and was already handling it. This simple action made John the kind of CPA everyone hopes to have, and brought him a lot of positive word of mouth referrals.

Putting It All Together

Now it's time to find your big idea. Read the rest of this book as a discovery process. Be open to the ideas presented and give some thought to which idea might excite you enough to keep you going in the tough patches. Once you identify the idea you think is right for you, get to work in a systematic fashion by going through the steps outlined in this chapter. The completed budget worksheets will give you a working budget that can be your operations manual as you work through the startup phase.

To complete your business plan, you need a hypothetical, realistic projection of revenue to use as a *benchmark*.

Having benchmarks allows you to continually measure your progress. It's the same idea as goal-setting; you need to be able to measure how you are doing, whether it's by

def•i•ni•tion

A **benchmark** is a standard measurement or yardstick used to evaluate one's performance as an individual or company.

using number of total customers, number of new customers per week or month, revenue dollars per day or week, or dollars earned per hour.

Successful business owners stick to a budget and develop benchmarks to chart their progress. Don't fool yourself into thinking you can rely on your gut instincts and pure moxie—that's why the majority of business startups fail. Adhere to the attitude that you can't afford to wing it, get into the good habit of reviewing your budget and target revenue week by week, and watch your business grow into a successful startup. Once you succeed in the startup phase, you'll be on your way to a sustainable income stream, and anything will be possible for you.

4

Nuts and Bolts of a Home-Based Business

In This Chapter

◆ Creating your work space

◆ Keeping up with your paperwork

◆ Taking care of the tax man

Setting up your home-based business in a professional manner sets a tone that will resonate throughout your startup phase. Successful home-based businesses share several critical characteristics: a well-lit, comfortable office that is separate from the rest of your residence; a well-organized filing and recordkeeping system that is kept up to date; and procedures that ensure that all of your paperwork is processed in a timely fashion. It is just as important to bill your customers promptly as it is to pay your taxes on time.

With all the inexpensive technology available today, it is possible to run a sizeable business without letting on that you are actually conducting business from your house. For example, if you have partners or employees, you can even use a sophisticated but inexpensive phone system that allows all calls to come in to a central business number, then be transferred automatically to one of a dozen different employees, each working in the comfort of his or her own home—at no extra cost to the company!

Your Home Office

Establishing a true home office can provide you with the stability you need to accomplish your tasks with efficiency and competence. You don't need to add a wing to your house, build out a fancy space in your basement, or remodel your den. Just meeting a few basic requirements provides you with the organization and privacy you need to run a professional business.

Privacy

In a perfect world, you would create your home office in a room with a door you can close. You will appreciate the privacy when you are on the phone with vendors or customers. You don't want chiming doorbells, ringing telephones, barking dogs, or talk from family members interrupting you when you are trying to conduct business.

If a dedicated room is not an option, try using a portion of a room that is somewhat out of the everyday flow of your household—a corner of your living room, dining room, or guest room perhaps. Avoid being close to high-traffic areas like the kitchen or entryways if at all possible.

Organization

You will find it much easier to be productive in uncluttered surroundings with enough storage space for your files. Office-organization specialists encourage home-based business owners to set up their workspace with filing cabinets and supplies close at hand. You also will need a reliable system for scheduling your projects. This can be as simple as a large wall calendar or an appointment book from an office supply store, or you can use a PDA or the calendar software that comes with your computer.

Necessities

You won't have much money in your startup budget for furnishing and decorating your office (that can come later as you establish yourself), but a couple of items are essential from the start. The biggest investment you should make is in a comfortable chair that is the right height for working at your desk. The second must-have item is the fastest Internet connection you can afford. You won't want to waste time or lose potential customers because you have an outdated connection to the web.

Recordkeeping 101

Whether you maintain your business's financial records using a computer program or keep them manually, there are certain key procedures you can put in place to ensure you are an ideal client for your CPA and never get caught off-guard by the IRS. Follow these rules and you will never have a problem with accounting for your revenue or expenses.

- Open a separate checking account for your business. This makes it much easier to track and capture your business expenses. Be sure to write in your deposits, too, and keep a running cash balance. Record any online banking transactions in your check register. Get paper copies of your bank statements and file them chronologically in a labeled file.

- Acquire or designate a credit card that you use only for business. Make a separate file for those statements.

- Your bank and credit card statements—along with your check register—will become the major source documents for creating your accounting records. You can do this yourself with a software program like QuickBooks accounting, or hire a bookkeeper or CPA to create your books for you.

- Keep a mileage log in your car and record each trip you make for business, along with the mileage and purpose of the travel. If you have recurring customers, you can use your calendar to keep track of your appointments and make a one-time record of the mileage. Even though you are tracking your actual vehicle expenses (see the Estimated Annual Vehicle Expenses worksheet in Chapter 3), your mileage log documents your business use of your vehicle. Calculate the percentage of business use by taking your business miles for the year and dividing them by your total annual miles. Keeping a log in conjunction with an appointment calendar will give you exactly what you need for budgeting and for preparing your income tax return.

- At the end of each year, put all your paper files in a box, label it with the year, and file it away after you file your tax return. If you have been using software programs to keep your calendar, accounting records, or anything else related to your business operations, make a backup on a storable medium (CD or memory stick) and keep it with the stored paper records for that year.

- Keep your records for seven years for tax purposes.

Snags

Many new business owners struggle to keep books using a computer program. Since they are usually occupied during business hours with customers and generating revenue, they end up spending many midnight hours hunched over their computers trying to get their books in balance. This is not the best use of your time. Concentrate on building your business and use the preceding simple recommendations to keep your documents organized. At the end of the year, you can hire someone to help you handle the accounting and tax work—while you stay focused on bringing in more business.

If you have money left over in your checking account at the end of the week or month, you are making a profit. But in general if you are running a simple business, paying your bills on time, and making timely deposits of your customer cash receipts, your checkbook balance should be an accurate reflection of your profit. The money in your business checking account isn't all for your use, however, since periodically you will have to pay a portion of it in income taxes (and possibly sales tax).

Paying Your Taxes

As an employee of a company, you probably took it for granted that each time you received a paycheck it would be the same amount (unless you are paid on commission), and that all the appropriate taxes were withheld from your pay. For years you may have been filing your annual tax returns earlier than your self-employed friends because your returns were simple and all of your income was reported on a Form W-2. Quick, easy, and clean. You've come to expect a refund each year.

That's not the way it works when you're the boss and paying your taxes becomes your responsibility. Paying taxes can be the most painful task the newly self-employed individual faces. As a business owner, you are responsible for remembering the dates when taxes have to be paid, and for putting the money aside so you have it when it's time. If you can't handle this responsibility, than launching your own startup is not for you.

How Much to Budget for Income Taxes

Though we are all accustomed to having taxes withheld from our pay, many people aren't conscious of the portions that are Social Security and Medicare taxes. When you work for someone else as an employee, your employer pays half of these taxes, matching the amount that you pay.

When you are self-employed and operate as a sole proprietor, you pay both the employer's share (your company is the employer, even if you are not incorporated) and the employee's portion of Social Security and Medicare taxes. When added together with your federal income tax and your state and local taxes (if applicable), your tax bill might be a significant amount of money.

If you are going to set aside all or most of your tax money as you earn it, you will want to save 30 percent of your revenue for your taxes. Yes, this is correct—30 percent. Your individual situation—whether you are single, married, own a home, have a spouse that works, and so on—affects the specific amount, but 30 percent is a reasonable ballpark figure.

How to Pay Your Taxes

Handling money responsibly is work, and it takes getting used to. (This is why self-employed people hire professionals to help them with money matters.) But if you are comfortable with numbers and being responsible for your money, then you will be able to handle most of these tasks yourself.

As a sole proprietor, you are not required to run a payroll just for yourself. You can pay yourself when you like, as much as you like, and as often as you like, but you need to pay your income taxes as you earn your money throughout the year.

Self-employed individuals are required to make quarterly tax payments using IRS forms called 1040-ES (they can be downloaded from the IRS website, www.irs.gov). Known as estimated tax payments, they functionally accomplish the same thing as withholding from a paycheck. The due dates for estimated tax payments are April 15, June 15, September 15, and January 15. See the Appendix for resources available to help you with all the details of taking care of your tax payments.

This is not difficult once you get used to the process. What gets people in trouble is waiting until April 15 to pay the entire amount they owe because having to pay all at once can be overwhelming. Making estimated tax payments four times a year is sensible and smart. We can't stress this enough.

Sales Tax and Other State and Local Taxes

If you are selling a product or even a service, your revenue may be subject to sales or other taxes, depending on your state of residence. Certain local governments levy different taxes on businesses, too. Since every locality is different, the burden is on you to research the various taxes your business will be required to pay. Remember, "I didn't know" is not a valid excuse for nonpayment of taxes. As the taxpayer, getting this information is your responsibility.

Snags

Ever known people who had past-year tax returns they still hadn't filed? Ever wonder how they got themselves into that predicament? Well, they usually wait until their return is due and then realize they don't have enough money to pay all their taxes. So they put off filing. And they keep putting it off. Soon they are waking up in the middle of the night wondering if tomorrow is the day they are going to get a letter from the IRS with a demand for payment. Don't let this happen to you.

Although it is possible to use government websites to access tax information, this is important enough for you to seek out professional guidance in the form of a phone conversation or personal meetings with people who can help you. Every state has a Small Business Development Center (SBDC), a nonprofit service funded by the federal Small Business Association and state university systems, with several offices in every state. Their main mission is to provide free business consulting to new startups and existing small companies. Take advantage of this free service.

You may be able to attend free workshops with a small business focus in your city or town that give you access to people who can educate you about taxes for your particular business idea in your specific area. Don't assume that everyone knows everything: be sure to exercise due diligence to ensure you have complete information.

Using a Professional Tax Advisor

We have offered many suggestions for accessing free advice in helping you establish how and when to pay taxes. If you've worked with a CPA or tax preparer in the past, then you have a relationship with someone who can guide you through the tax requirements. Usually a professional will gladly talk with you briefly by phone or answer a few e-mails without sending an invoice. Some will accept an invitation to lunch in exchange for sharing some insights with you on setting up your business. Although it is always helpful to consult professionals if you have concerns specific to your situation, the advice in this book is intended to keep you on the right path until you get past the startup phase.

Part 2 Home Maintenance

We jump right into the heart of the matter with ideas for fundamental services that are part of the fabric of everyday life. There is no more straightforward business concept than residential housecleaning. For years, people in need of work have been able to fall back on cleaning as a consistent source of income. (And in today's marketplace, there is very good money to be made as a maid!)

For those who prefer working outside, we put together a chapter on several ways to build a revenue stream and a customer base that keeps growing. The chapter on concierge services includes businesses that help people maintain their property and protect its value. We discuss professions targeted to helping people sell their homes and realize as much profit as possible in our chapter on home-resale services. All ideas fit into the schematic of working for homeowners on a regular, recurring basis.

Chapter 5

g

g

ıct cleaning

yman specials

rk, there is no faster route to profitable
l home maintenance. No matter how many
ling their services in the marketplace, there
s to entry are practically nonexistent, and

In this chapter, you will learn about four home-maintenance services with
low barriers to starting a profitable home-based business. These services
do not require a formal education, prior experience, or extensive training.
As a result, you can get started almost immediately—and start generating
income very quickly.

Housecleaning and Maid Services

Estimated startup costs: $500–$700

Estimated first-year revenue: $30,000–$50,000

There are many different ways to approach housecleaning, but in general the tasks involved include dusting, mopping, cleaning kitchen and bath surfaces, removing trash, and vacuuming. A customer who pays for housecleaning or maid service expects to come home to a completely clean home on the day your service is done.

Many national maid-service companies, such as Mini Maid and Maid Brigade, publish their cleaning checklists on their websites. This helps them be very clear with their customers about the work to be performed. You can use these lists as valuable tools when you are defining the services you are going to offer and are planning your cleaning method.

Housecleaning professionals assert that theirs is a very easy business to start and to quickly ramp up to a full schedule. Take Bill, a former trucking-industry executive who was known among his friends for his immaculate home. After being downsized, he decided to start a housecleaning business. Within two or three months, his calendar was full of appointments just from word of mouth. Although he did a one-time flyer distribution during his first year, he always had more customers than he could handle for the more-than-10 years he ran his business.

Equipment and Supplies

Many cleaning companies ask their customers to supply their own general cleaning solutions and supplies. This will cut down dramatically on your startup and recurring costs. Make a checklist of supplies you prefer to work with and provide it to your customer when you accept a job. Ask that they purchase all requested supplies prior to your start date. Then monitor the supplies each time you clean and remind your customer when it is time to replenish a particular product.

The only equipment you will need is a good vacuum cleaner—one that can handle both carpets and floors. While most homeowners own vacuum cleaners and may offer theirs for your use, many successful housecleaners prefer to use their own higher-quality vacuum. If you don't already own one you would want to transport, there are hundreds for sale and comparison on the web. We've budgeted $400 for a vacuum in the startup costs, assuming you will need to purchase one.

Estimating the Time Commitment

Be sure to budget a sufficient amount of travel time between jobs if your business plan includes cleaning more than one house per day. Jobs will vary in time required based on how neat the homeowner is and how clear the surfaces are to start with. (Wouldn't it be great if you could charge per "tchochke" for dusting time?)

A good formula to use is one hour for every 500 square feet of home. Accordingly, a typical 3-bedroom, 2-bath home of 2,000 square feet will take you 4 hours. If you charge an hourly rate of $20 to $25, you would earn $80 to $100 per customer on average. It will be up to you to decide if it makes sense to schedule two houses in one day.

Once you factor location into your scheduling, you may find it works out to your benefit to do two homes in a day if they are located close by each other. Over time as you gain experience at projecting your hours per job and become familiar with traffic patterns in different neighborhoods you will boost your bottom line with improved scheduling efficiency.

Pricing and Payments

Many cleaning companies give estimates over the phone, so it's a breeze to get several quotes in an hour's time. You can do this via e-mail, too. Either way, you can easily derive competitive pricing for your services. Some people are fine with pricing based on an hourly rate; others are more accustomed to being quoted a price by the job.

One of the best aspects of housecleaning is the collection process. Whereas most other businesses bill and collect later for their services, home cleaning companies get paid by cash or check the day services are rendered.

Snags

Be cautious about adding more work for customers without a corresponding additional charge. You can choose to include a small task that really won't take much extra time. But for the larger ones that will add up to an hour to your schedule, be ready to quote something extra for yourself (like $25 extra to clean a refrigerator).

Special Requirements

Certification programs for maid service providers are few and far between. Some new websites focus on *green cleaning* and offer online certification courses for less than

$100 per class (see the Appendix). Depending upon the value folks in your region place on environmental friendliness, green cleaning might be a smart way to attract the notice of new customers. You should also check with your local municipality to see if you are required to have a business license.

def•i•ni•tion

Green cleaning involves using plant-based, chemical-free cleaning products for cleaning surfaces in homes and businesses. Examples of these products include nontoxic, all-purpose cleaners that are also biodegradable. These products are readily available at natural food stores and sold through dozens of commercial websites.

Carpet-Cleaning Services

Estimated startup costs: $700–$800

Estimated first-year revenue: $60,000–$100,000

Carpet-cleaning equipment has come a long way over the last decade, and buying one machine can give you the capability to clean all types of floor surfaces in addition to rugs, wall-to-wall carpeting, and even upholstered furniture. Most residential customers only need their carpets cleaned once or twice a year. As a carpet cleaner, you will make more money from each customer per visit than you will make from regular housecleaning, but you will need to build a much larger base of customers and spend more time scheduling appointments.

At first blush, carpet cleaning may not seem seasonal, but demand for services is higher at holiday times, with a second, smaller busy season that varies by geographical location—during the spring in warmer parts of the country, and summer in the cooler regions—correlating with pollen season and the times of year that people tend to keep their windows open.

Equipment and Supplies

Carpet-cleaning equipment is expensive, priced anywhere from $2,000 to $5,000 for the initial purchase. The good news is that many equipment wholesalers target their sales to new businesses. That provides two important benefits: good equipment financing (our startup costs include a down payment only, estimated at $500) and lots of how-to manuals and telephone support from the sales rep.

Take the time to shop your options and find a sales rep who is willing to help you get started. Request the names and phone numbers of the sales rep's other recent customers and call them before you make your purchase. It's not just your capital you want to protect: you want to lay the foundation for rapid success.

You will also be able to purchase cleaning solutions from these companies, although you are not required to buy supplies from your equipment company. This market has lots of competitors. The supplies for this business are not expensive, but you need to consider them in your overall budget.

Estimating the Time Commitment

Before servicing your first customer, try out your new equipment and build some technique by cleaning the carpets in your own home and those of a few friends and family members. Once you get a procedure down, make a point to clock your time. When you're starting out, you can reasonably expect to clean carpets in at least two homes per day, building up to three as you gain experience and your schedule fills up. Calculate your time per square foot per room, and add in time for travel between jobs.

If you add some commercial jobs to your schedule, you should try to fit these smaller, more frequent jobs around the residential jobs on your calendar. They will take less time and bring in less money per job, but with much more regularity.

Many a small carpet cleaner has gotten a boost in regular business from landing a movie theatre chain or a locally owned restaurant franchise. One carpet-cleaning professional we talked to expressed regret at having abandoned his commercial marketing efforts in the early years of his business. As he looked back on his 30-year career, he wished that he had stayed with the commercial customers. In the long run, he would have experienced much less stress over tight cash during the slower times of the year.

Pricing and Payments

Carpet-cleaning companies price their services by the job. Although pricing will vary across regions, it is common for customers to be quoted a per-room charge of $50, with a 3-room minimum per job. Hallways are quoted at a lower flat fee, say $15 to $20 each, and stairways per step at $2.50 each.

Upholstered furniture is usually priced at $19.95 per chair or ottoman, $29 per loveseat, and $39 for a sofa. Not all fabrics benefit from cleaning. You can make a customer for life if you learn when to tell them not to waste their money cleaning a

During the slower times of year it is common for carpet cleaners to make calls and encourage customers to book a semi-annual appointment. This is frequently accompanied by a small discount to sweeten the deal. You can also offer "one room free" to customers who refer their friends and neighbors.

cotton-covered sofa. Take the time to go over the materials that benefit from your equipment and cleaning solutions.

Like housecleaning, carpet-cleaning businesses get paid upon completion of the job. This should be clearly stated to the customer when you schedule the appointment. Although most companies accept personal checks, many also take credit cards. You will need to determine whether it is worth the cost of a merchant account to process the credit cards. The upside, especially if you are going to do commercial accounts that expect to be billed monthly, is that you can keep the credit card account on file and charge it automatically on the first or last day of the month.

Special Requirements

Carpet cleaning requires no special licensing other than a general business license. There are many different regional and national carpet-cleaning associations that can be good sources of information, training, and support. Two of these are Professional Carpet and Upholstery Cleaners Association (PCUCA) and Professional Carpet Association (PCA). The Carpet and Rug Institute offers some classes on carpet cleaning and a great deal of information on new carpet fibers and innovations in the industry.

Air-Duct Cleaning

Estimated startup costs: $200–$300

Estimated first-year revenue: $50,000–$80,000

Air-duct cleaning generally refers to the cleaning of various heating and cooling system components of forced air systems, including the supply and return air ducts and registers, grilles and diffusers, heat exchangers, heating and cooling coils, condensate drain pans (drip pans), fan motor and fan housing, and the air handling unit housing.

The recommended frequency for having home air ducts cleaned is every five years, unless the homeowner has a particular need (like allergies) for getting it done more often. This is a growing business with increasing consumer awareness for the value of the service. Some companies offer deodorizing and mildew reduction by spraying chemical solutions through the duct system. When researching your competition (see Chapter 3), determine whether you want to offer these additional services.

The main challenge for air-duct cleaning as a startup business is that, although the revenue potential and cost models are very comparable to carpet cleaning, and the cost of equipment can be less than $1,000, the ramp-up period is much longer because you need a base of approximately 1,500 customers to have a full appointment schedule for one service person or team. Therefore your marketing efforts can cost a great deal more and take much more time than housecleaning or carpet cleaning.

Equipment and Supplies

Many air-duct cleaning equipment wholesalers are accessible via the Internet. These companies offer support to startup companies similar to what we covered in carpet cleaning. The equipment is a self-contained unit, not unlike a large vacuum cleaner, that is brought into each customer's home. With list prices starting at $995, lease payments over 12 months would run less than $85 a month. Equipment companies also carry the solutions you will need for add-on mildew reduction and deodorizing.

Estimating the Time Commitment

We recommend the same practice procedures for carpet cleaning in order to get a feel for how long it will take you to clean the ducts for a typical residence in your service area. Most air-duct cleaning companies schedule two homes per day, allowing a half day for each job. Use this frequency and the budgeting template in Chapter 3 to calculate your potential revenue.

Pricing and Payments

Most air-duct companies charge their customers based on square footage of the house and the number of heating and cooling systems used. The average fee ranges from $350 to $500 per house.

This business has the same payment protocol as carpet cleaning. You would also enjoy similar benefits from establishing a merchant credit card account as discussed above.

Special Requirements

Several states (see the Appendix) require a specific license in order to access the air conditioning system in a consumer or business location. These include Arkansas,

California, Florida, Georgia, Michigan, and Texas. You should check your state's licensing website to be certain your state has no licensing requirements.

National Air Duct Cleaners Association (NADCA) offers two types of courses to become an Air System Cleaning Specialist. One class is offered online and can be taken at any time as a self-study course. You can also take more in-depth all-day webinars. All NADCA members must be Air System Cleaning Specialist (ASCS) certified. Check out the website (link found in the Appendix) for more detail.

Handyman/Handywoman Services

Estimated startup costs: $125–$250

Estimated first-year revenue: $30,000–$50,000

If you're handy with tools, lots of people need your help around the house: two-earner households with limited time; people who don't have the skills, tools, or patience to maintain their own homes; elderly or disabled people who can't physically do the work—the list goes on and on. To start this kind of business, you need the skills and tools to repair things that commonly break around the house, and a vehicle to transport yourself and your tools to customers.

Bonus Point

Online referral services can help you get business in your area without having to set up a website. Check out the offerings in your area by searching for handyman services on the web.

Many handyman service providers include everything from basic appliance installation and repair to ceiling fan and flat-screen TV installation, and even light plumbing work.

Equipment and Supplies

If you are enough of a handyman to be considering making a living at it, we are assuming you already have a large toolbox. There are no major pieces of equipment required to be a professional; most handymen rely on the most basic tools to make their repairs.

Estimating the Time Commitment

Your biggest challenge is going to be predicting how long it is going to take to make a repair. It's common to make an unplanned trip to the hardware store for a part or tool you didn't anticipate needing. In the beginning it will be hard to charge customers for all your time, and as you start out, you will have to make it a high priority to create protocols for handling the unexpected.

The best defense against running into time constraints with customers is to deal with this issue upfront. Avoid the murkier and more time-consuming kinds of repairs. As you get enough jobs under your toolbelt, you will feel more comfortable scheduling two to three calls per day, which should allow you to bill about 6 hours per day at your hourly rate.

Pricing and Payments

The business model for handyman services is similar to housecleaning; your startup costs will also be similar. The hourly rate ranges from $20 per hour in rural areas with high unemployment to $45 per hour in large metropolitan cities and high-end resort areas. You may want to set a minimum fee. Be sure to let customers know you'll be charging them for trips to the hardware store or home improvement center to buy materials.

Make it clear that payment is due upon completion of the job. If you agree to a project that will take more than one day, be sure to clarify the payment terms in advance of starting the work.

Special Requirements

Almost every state has licensing requirements for certain systems work. Be careful to confine your work to areas that do not require licensing. Repairing a lamp or electrical outlet is one thing; rewiring a circuit box is something entirely different. Generally, electricians, plumbers, and general contractors will require a professional license. If you have any questions about licensing, check your secretary of state website under the professional licensing tab.

Chapter 6

Outside Work

In This Chapter

- ◆ Putting your green thumb to work
- ◆ Cool pools and hot spas
- ◆ Scaling the heights of window cleaning
- ◆ Common add-on services to expand revenue in the off-season

Several types of outside home-maintenance chores are fertile markets for building a steady income with little startup costs or experience required. Although these businesses run the gamut from sole proprietorships to large regional companies, there is less competition from national franchises than there is for housecleaning and carpet cleaning.

There is plenty of opportunity to differentiate yourself if you are willing to work hard and seek out your own continuing education. A willingness to learn as much as you can about these industries will help you expand your customer base and expand the breadth of your service offering to your existing customers.

Lawn and Yard Maintenance

Estimated startup costs: $750–$1,000

Estimated first-year revenue: $40,000–$60,000

The market for lawn- and yard-care customers has stopped growing in recent years due to the cooling off of the housing market. Nonetheless, an enormous base of homeowners are still as committed as ever to keeping up with the Joneses. The last two decades saw nonstop growth in suburban housing, expanding the neighborhoods of single family homes complete with private lots and neat lawns. Many of these homes have been built in subdivisions governed by homeowner associations that require each property owner to maintain his or her home's exterior to specific standards. These expectations, coupled with an aging population grown weary of mowing their own lawns, have given a boost to lawn-care and yard-maintenance professionals.

There are several components to this line of work, which is considered to be part of the "Green Industry." Unless you have worked in this business previously or have developed a broad range of skills as part of a hobby or caring for your own home, you are best off starting out with the simpler side of yard care, such as mowing, edging, and leaf blowing. Many more yard chores have the potential of increasing your revenue. Most experienced lawn-care professionals advise building up your service offerings as you expand your knowledge base. Once you get started offering the basics, you will have the opportunity to observe other common problem areas in your customers' yards, educate yourself on the proper remedies, and offer those services as an add-on to your basic maintenance fee.

Equipment and Supplies

You can use many tools sold at everyday hardware stores as part of a lawn-care business. In order to keep startup costs to a minimum, the following equipment is recommended as a starter kit. You will not be able to afford the best commercial equipment at the beginning; you will have to settle for good-quality items meant for sale to individual homeowners. As you build your customer base and use the equipment, it is likely you will want to upgrade to a *zero turn, self-propelled mower* and add more specialty items like pruners and hedge trimmers.

The prices in the table on the next page should cover the initial purchase of equipment to fill your truck or trailer.

Lawn and Yard Maintenance Startup Equipment

Items Required	Dollars
Good quality residential mower	$700
Weed whacker and edger	$150
Blower	$150
Total startup costs	$1,000

Estimating the Time Commitment

How much time you spend on each customer will vary with the work you do each visit. A good estimate is one hour per yard plus travel time. Your ability to cover several customers in a day will depend on the size of the property and the distance between each customer. Concentrating your marketing efforts in one or two neighborhoods and lining up several houses on each street can make a huge difference in your weekly revenue by limiting travel time and increasing time available to service customers.

Successful lawn-maintenance companies acclimate to working long hours during the spring, summer, and fall. They maximize their income during the warmer months and put money aside for the slower winter months. Some may take on a side business in winter; delivering firewood and Christmas tree delivery and removal are just two examples of work that utilizes the company truck, gets the company name into new neighborhoods, and provides a service likely to be needed by existing customers.

Pricing and Payments

Many resources are available for helping you to price your customer bids. The Internet is full of websites with lawn-care guys selling "how-to" manuals that will take you through all the significant frequently asked questions that you need to answer as you go through the startup phase (see the Appendix). Manuals available for download for less than $50 will provide estimate formulas, sample forms, and other advice. You can easily use the websites of other competitors to obtain estimates either by e-mail or phone.

The recommendation from other lawn professionals is to base your pricing on an hourly rate. The range of pricing goes from $30 per hour in areas with high levels of competition to $1 per minute or $60 an hour in higher-income areas with more particular homeowners. Most experienced lawn-maintenance professionals advise estimating prices based on your time, and then quoting the job at a flat rate.

As you gain confidence in your skills, you can add to the basic service with seasonal or less frequent maintenance tasks. Some appreciated add-ons include shrub pruning, mulching, weeding flower beds, over-seeding in spring, and leaf removal in fall.

Using the team approach outlined in Chapter 3, adding a helper can boost your revenue to twice as much and significantly increase your take-home pay, depending on how much you pay your helper. Say you average $50 per customer and handle 30 customers per week. That would bring in $1,500 per week in revenue. If you can add 20 more yards per week, another $1,000, with a helper who earns $10 per hour or $400, that bumps your share to $2,100 per week ($1,000 more in revenue less $400 paid to your helper). That will be reduced by additional travel and gas for increased equipment usage, but is an excellent way to increase your busy season revenue and save some cash for the slower, colder months.

Yard services frequently bill their customers monthly either by mailing or hand delivering an invoice when service is rendered. Asking customers to leave a check on their service day is a good way to keep up your cash flow. Another option is billing customers in advance for service on the first of the month. A merchant credit card account would work well for billing customers automatically when service is rendered or at the beginning or end of each month. Another benefit of billing charge cards is that you can have an agreement with the customer to add on extra fees as you see the work is needed, either for supplies like seed, weed killer, and mulch, or for more occasional services like pruning and ant control.

Special Requirements

When doing yard work, proper safety gear may not be required by law but it is a necessity to avoid personal injury. It is inexpensive to purchase sturdy shoes, safety glasses, and hearing protection.

Some states, cities, or counties require that you have a business license in each municipality in which you perform services. This sounds expensive, but each fee is limited to the amount of business you do in the specific locale. You want to stay aware of these requirements to avoid excessive penalties for noncompliance. You will also want to use the map rule discussed in Chapter 2 and decline a customer who will cause you to incur additional business license fees because they are across the line into a county or city you are not yet licensed to do business in.

Pool and Hot-Tub Service

Estimated startup costs: $625–$700

Estimated first-year revenue: $35,000–$50,000

According to experienced pool and hot-tub professionals, this industry requires a level of skill and knowledge of chemical compounds and mechanical equipment not easily acquired on your own or as you go. Certification programs are available through the Association of Pool and Spas Professionals (APSP) that will give you a basic understanding of pool and hot-tub maintenance, but will not take the place of on-the-job training. There is also a great deal of information online. If this industry appeals to you, it's worth it to hire on with a respected pool company for a season and learn the ropes before setting out on your own.

On the other hand, if you already know about pool and spa maintenance, perhaps from owning and taking care of your own pool or hot-tub, this could be your ticket to a lucrative career. According to the International Aquatic Foundation, there are over 4.5 million in-ground residential pools and over 5 million residential hot-tubs in the United States—and the majority of owners rely on an outside service to perform maintenance. This makes pool and hot-tub servicing a great market for a newcomer, especially in the parts of the country where it is warm enough to keep a pool open all or most of the year.

Equipment and Supplies

Pool and spa maintenance require more chemicals than equipment. The positive side to this is that you don't have to start out with a warehouse full of chemicals. It will be more cost effective to buy in bulk, but when you are starting out it is always prudent to limit your quantities of supplies on hand. The equipment list is found in the table on the following page.

Pool and Hot-Tub Maintenance Startup Equipment

Items Required	Dollars
Skimmer	$75
Vacuum	$350
Test kit	$50
Chemical starter kit	$150
Total startup costs	$625

Estimating the Time Commitment

Regular pool maintenance is typically a one person per customer job, so any employees you hire will need their own truck and equipment. If you don't have the capital to cover the additional expenses for a full-time helper (the extra vehicle, salary, insurance, and equipment), you will want to go the solo route. You will have to plan well to be able to get to every job you schedule on any given day. With travel time and planning for additional services such as adding chemicals, scheduling an hour per customer is reasonable for a beginner. As you gain skills and customers, it will be easier to add new business from the neighbors of existing customers, which will boost your revenue without adding much additional travel time.

Even with heated pools and customers who keep their pools open all year, the business is going to be highly seasonal. As you grow, you will be able to extend the busy season, but initially anticipate that you will have four to six months a year of much slower business. The ramp-up time in warmer, more densely populated areas (like suburban Florida, California, and other southern regions) is going to be a lot quicker than in areas like New England and the Pacific Northwest. The more foliage your area has, the more likely a homeowner will be to outsource the pool cleaning.

Success Story

Servicing both pools and hot-tubs is a great way to balance out your revenue throughout the year. Hot-tubs are used most frequently in the cooler months. Daryl G. added hot-tub servicing two years after he started his pool cleaning business. By the end of his fourth year, he was working year round and earning $25,000 more a year just from fall and winter hot-tub maintenance.

Pricing and Payments

Pool services are priced monthly and include weekly visits to customers. Maintenance involves skimming and vacuuming the pool or spa for debris, checking chemical levels, and adding chemicals as needed. In most areas, monthly fees range from $160 to $220 depending on the density of the area (which influences how much time you spend in transit) and the affluence of the zip codes. Chemicals are added onto the weekly fee based on whatever is required each visit.

It is important to establish a minimum fee from the start and to quote your fees as part of your initial call to a prospective customer. This will avoid wasting time making on-site bids to homeowners who aren't willing to pay the standard rate for your services.

In addition to weekly maintenance during warmer months, many of your customers will close their pools for the off-season. This protects the pool from storm damage and eliminates the need to continue maintenance when the pool is not usable. The fees for opening and closing a pool are invoiced separately, and usually run between $150 and $300 at the beginning and end of the season. You will need to schedule additional time with each customer for these longer service calls. You will also need to consider a temporary helper (a teenager is adequate) to help you manage the large, heavy pool covers.

Special Requirements

While there are no special licensing requirements for pool technicians, you'll need experience in the field to develop repair skills. Equally relevant is that it can take several hours to make an on-site repair. Both these factors make offering repairs as a sole operator less manageable than simply offering maintenance.

On the positive side, many pool service companies prefer to stay away from maintenance and cleaning and simply focus on the repair side. Many pool companies also only build new pools or stick to poolside landscaping projects. A good way into simple maintenance would be to network with pool repairmen by offering repair referrals in exchange for regular maintenance referrals.

Window Cleaning

Estimated startup costs: $750–$1,000

Estimated first-year revenue: $40,000–$60,000

The official definition on thefreedictionary.com of the term *one-armed bandit* describes what is commonly known as a basic slot machine, the one with fruits that roll around, with three-of-a-kind paying off the jackpot. In the window-cleaning industry, this term is used to characterize a one-person window-cleaning operation. Most people who are long timers in this business use an initial sole startup to eventually build up to a small- to medium-size company that has at least two teams of employees. The work is physically demanding, and is definitely not for those who are afraid of heights.

Equipment and Supplies

The biggest factor in determining the cost of startup equipment will be the type of terrain in your region. If you are in the heartland, the flatness of the geography will require much less in the way of ladders and potential safety equipment than a city as hilly as Atlanta, Georgia.

Your investment in startup equipment will vary depending on the ladder heights you need. A 14-foot ladder is a must to get to most interior lighting fixtures and windows; you will need an exterior extension ladder to handle upper story windows, exterior lighting, and gutters. The cleaning solution can vary from industrial-strength supplies purchased in large quantities to everyday dish liquid. Whichever kind of cleaning solution you choose, your supplies will not require a major upfront investment.

Window-Cleaning Equipment Costs

Items Required	Dollars
Interior ladder	$150
Extension ladder	$400
Buckets, squeegees, and rags	$100
Cleaning supplies	$100
Total startup costs	$750

Estimating the Time Commitment

Be prepared for the seasonality of this business. The busy seasons are comparable to interior maintenance services, like carpet cleaning. Spring is always busy. As winter ebbs and the days get longer and sunnier, homeowners are more likely to notice the dust and water marks that have accumulated on their windows and schedule a cleaning. Summer is a much quieter time. This is actually a blessing in hotter climates when the heat makes outdoor work brutal. Your schedule will start to pick back up in September as customers start to focus on getting their homes ready for the holidays.

Success Story

To add revenue during a slow time of the year, one window cleaner set out to land one or two large jobs that he could work on over several days during the summer. He targeted private schools in his area, since they typically do maintenance when school is closed for the summer. He landed one large school with over 1,000 windows. He has always made a point to go beyond the requirements of the work order, and has kept this job for the last 10 years. Not only is it the keystone of his July revenue, but the school superintendent gladly provides several glowing references each year and referrals for a job well done.

As you are starting out, give yourself plenty of time to get the job done well and to arrive on time for every job. Unless you book a very small job, you will want to limit yourself to one job per day, gradually building up to two houses daily as a solo window cleaner. A practical way to budget your time would be one window every 15 minutes, with additional time for travel, unloading and loading equipment, and set-up. Make sure you leave yourself time for scheduling, paperwork, and promptly returning calls.

Pricing and Payments

The window-cleaning market is divided into commercial and residential sectors. Commercial window cleaning is good, recurring work and can be the bread and butter of your operation. If you concentrate on the retail sector, you are unlikely to have to tackle multiple-story buildings before you can afford expensive, very tall ladders. The caveat is that this market is highly competitive; the revenue per job is much lower than residential. You will have to consider how long it will take you to build a steady income stream if you focus on frequent but low-paying regular business.

There is more money in residential window cleaning. Even though the frequency with which a homeowner has windows cleaned is much less than commercial customers, there is a solid repeat nature to this business, although the frequency is more likely to be once or twice a year rather than two to four times per month.

This leaves you with almost half the year of slow time, which is why so many in this business add on other services to complement window cleaning. Most make use of the ladders to generate revenue and include lighting-oriented services like chandelier and ceiling fan cleaning and lightbulb changing both inside and out. In addition, many window-cleaning companies offer gutter cleaning, which is busiest in autumn.

The most common method of pricing is per window, with a separate inside and outside component. Outside is usually higher than inside, which is intended to encourage customers to let you do both. Once you get your ladders off the truck, you will always be more profitable if you build your revenue per job site.

Average price per window is around $9; you might break this down as $5.75 outside and $3.25 inside. Some companies will charge by the surface, with different pricing for larger windows and multipaned windows (like French doors). If you were to add in gutters ($125) and a light fixture ($25) for one out of two jobs, you could easily increase your revenue by another $300 to $500 per week.

Most window-cleaning companies operate with a verbal contract with their customers and handwritten invoices made on the day of service. It is common to present an invoice after the work is completed and to receive payment in full with a personal check from the customer. Consider creating a one-page contract or statement of services that you hand to your customer when your bid is accepted and your first job is scheduled. Clearly outline your payment terms so the customer will be prepared to pay on the day service is rendered.

Special Requirements

Homeowners can be price sensitive, and they are fiercely protective of their largest asset. But they will want a window cleaner who comes with solid referrals and his own insurance. Insurance premiums are the hidden cost of this business, which otherwise has low barriers to entry. You need extensive insurance to protect yourself from future liability and to reassure your potential customers that you are covered in case of damage to their home or glass, or worker injury. If your pricing tends to the higher end of the accepted standard in your area, your marketing information should stress the value you provide by being well insured.

The high costs associated with insuring employees (workers' compensation, bonding, liability, glass breakage) makes a team approach prohibitive for a low-cost startup. The workers' compensation for window-cleaning employees falls into the highest risk. As a sole proprietor, you are not required to carry this type of insurance, but you should make certain you have some kind of coverage, such as individual health or accident insurance.

Add-On Services

To counter the seasonality of outdoor work and boost revenue all year-round, several popular "mini-businesses" are natural complements to lawn care, pool maintenance, and window cleaning. Here are a few of the most popular ones.

Seasonal Flower Installation

Many homeowners add annuals to their flower beds in spring and fall to add color and style to their yards. In the burgeoning days of this industry, specialty companies got into the market early, usually run by graduates of local horticulture programs who knew where to purchase plants in bulk. As the trend proliferated around the country, so did retail sources for seasonal plants. Today it is common for most yard-service professionals to offer seasonal planting of annuals, perennials, and shrubs.

The more popular plants are sold at big-box home improvement stores and neighborhood garden centers. You can learn a good bit about the individual plants from the store salespeople and add to your knowledge with some simple research on the Internet. Pricing for seasonal planting is based on a charge per plant or hour; either way, you will want to add a markup to your cost of the plants to cover your time and expenses. If you are uncomfortable with the concept of designing the layouts and selecting plants, you can have your customers buy the plants and place them in their yards for you to install.

Gutter Cleaning and Leaf Collection

Any outdoor business can add gutter cleaning to its fall schedule. This is a slam-dunk extra for the window cleaners who have extension ladders; you can add this on to window jobs in the late fall and winter. The pricing for gutters is a flat fee and will vary by region depending on the foliage, common architecture, and footprint of the home, and the steepness of the terrain.

Even for homeowners who maintain their own lawns and pools, leaf collection and removal can be a daunting task in certain areas of the country. Many lawn-service customers will expect this as part of their regular weekly or monthly fee. Depending on the time involved, a lawn-care company may want to quote this as a separate fee, especially if it will require a longer service call. Since the only equipment needed for leaf collection is a blower and a good rake, this has the potential to add revenue with very little cost (other than a sore back and calluses).

Pressure Washing and Snow Removal

A pressure washer will be a good investment that allows you to add to your service offerings. Many homeowners need yearly pressure washing of the exterior of their homes. This is more of a necessity in areas where homes are predominantly of wood construction and the climate is humid. Since pressure washing has great results on concrete and cement, a pool service could add this to their pool opening checklist and, for an additional fee, get their customers' cement pool decks spruced up for the summer.

Snow removal is not a viable addition in the southern regions, but for outdoor businesses in the North and the West that already own a truck and have a seasonal customer base, it is a natural to sell regular snow removal in the winter months. You don't have to limit yourself to residential customers, either; you can easily solicit business from small office parks, apartment complexes, and retail shopping areas. You can base pricing for snow removal on square footage and bill it by the snowfall. Larger jobs can be negotiated for a slightly lower price since your travel time and expenses would be lower as well.

> **Bonus Point**
>
> A big factor in running a successful business with once-a-year customers is using reminder calls or postcards to help get work scheduled. Customers will appreciate you considering them for scheduling. This keeps unreasonable expectations in check; if a customer passes on scheduling when called, she will be more understanding if she has to wait a few extra days during a busier time of year.

Chapter 7

Concierge Services

In This Chapter

- ◆ Taking care of "this old house" for others
- ◆ Modern day tour guide
- ◆ Resort house sitting (or *The Shining* revisited)
- ◆ Project "renovation"

Originating in France in the Middle Ages, the term *concierge* referred to the trusted employee who held the keys to various rooms in a castle or estate. "Keeper of the keys" is an excellent visual for today's concierge industry, which has expanded to include servicing every facet of a customer's home, social, and work lives.

Once the domain of the best international hotels and resorts, concierge services are no longer confined to the hospitality industry. Everyday, working people with a more than median household income are seeking help from paid contractors to manage their daily responsibilities. There are endless ways to apply the concierge concept to a money-making venture. You are only limited by your imagination.

In this chapter, we cover business ideas that provide different concierge services to individuals. Rather than focus on serving the very personal needs of the very wealthy, which are typically handled by full-time domestic employees or personal assistants, we have put together ideas that require a high level of professionalism but a much lower level of personal intimacy. This greatly expands the market for concierge services beyond the 1 percent of American households that have an income of over $1,000,000.

Home Property Manager

Estimated startup costs: $250–$500

Estimated first-year revenue: $30,000–$50,000

Traditional home property-management companies specialize in helping people rent out their investment properties or second homes. We have redefined this concept to managing regular home maintenance for homeowners who are too busy to do it for themselves. Home ownership is still the number one American dream, and for many people a home is still the most valuable asset they own. Today's working family is stretched thin when it comes to squeezing in a few hours for their family life, so finding the time to properly take care of a home gets harder all the time.

Any residential maintenance or repair project can be included as a service you provide in your home-management program. Rather than the homeowner dealing with the process of getting a clear diagnosis of a problem situation (water leaking through a window sill, mold in the basement, malfunctioning electrical system)—and the subsequent parade of repairmen and the resulting disruptions—you step in to handle the entire project from start to finish. This is a good business idea for a highly organized and detail-oriented person who understands home systems and their maintenance and who can demand a high level of performance from contractors.

Use survey techniques (see Chapter 3) to determine what type of customer is the best for you to pursue and what home-maintenance services your prospective customers need help with. This will vary based on your geographic location; winterizing a home and snow removal are not concerns in south Florida. Develop a written needs assessment to use for your initial visit to each customer. In the beginning, offer the assessment as a free consultation that allows you entry into the customer's home and an opportunity to convey your competence in person. Once you have a good foundation, you can start to charge a flat fee for the initial consultation.

Equipment and Supplies

There is no tangible equipment needed for starting a home property-management business. What you do need are professional-looking marketing materials, good sources for contractors, and good checklists for managing the work to be done at the homes of your customers. There are many websites (see the Appendix) for finding home-maintenance checklists and recommended schedules for frequency of service.

> ### Success Story
>
> Joe G. spent many years of his career as an on-site house manager for a succession of several well-to-do homeowners. Over time he developed a well-used address book of local contractors and handled almost every problem imaginable (an endlessly leaking edgeless pool, a nonfunctioning but very expensive exterior security gate, poorly installed wiring for a state-of-the-art sound system). All of the homes were always in top condition because Joe made it his mission to keep it that way. Using these skills and his list of reliable contractors, Joe branched out and started his own home-management company. His marketing materials emphasized that his value was not merely the intangible idea of taking good care of a home. Joe's marketing also focused on the cost savings in time and dollars he could provide by building on his relationships with high-quality contractors. Getting the job done right the first time was a great selling point.

Estimating the Time Commitment

Success in this business will depend on good personal referrals and a clear definition of your target market. *Geo-target* your market in order to make site visits to customers on a regular basis and for making emergency visits as prompt as possible.

Plan on dedicating a half day to each needs assessment, to make sure you can take your time with each customer. Make the time pay by learning how to screen potential customers when they call for an appointment. The best way to do this is to give a straightforward understanding of what you do and how you charge for your time. Let the customer know up front how much to expect paying you—whether it's monthly, quarterly, or annually. Most people will not want to waste your time or theirs pursuing services they know they can't afford.

def•i•ni•tion

Geo-target has become the latest buzzword in the world of public relations and marketing. It refers to the strategy of building awareness for your product or service in a very specific area.

Use a simple contract with customers so both parties will have a written reference to understand your agreement. Make sure you review it as part of every assessment meeting. Your goal should be to leave each needs assessment with a signed contract and a retainer check for you to begin services immediately. If that is how you conclude at least half of your "free" consultations, you will be making good use of your time. If your success rate at closing the sale is less than 50 percent, find out the reason that your prospects aren't hiring you. Revise your phone screening process to include questions that address the issues that seem to be deal breakers based on this experience.

Build your network of referrals through other businesses that service the clients you are targeting. For example, you can cultivate relationships with realtors who specialize in helping families relocate to your city within certain high-end neighborhoods. Targeting high-earning customers who are new to an area should be an excellent strategy for building a customer base as quickly as possible.

Pricing and Payments

Structure your pricing schedule for home property management based on an hourly rate. You should price your time between $25 and $40 per hour. A tactic to consider is offering a do-it-yourself approach, especially for homeowners who are new to a city and need help acclimating to their new surroundings, but would prefer to keep their cost lower as they get more comfortable in their new home. For this type of customer, you could create a one-time package that would include the needs assessment, a recommended maintenance schedule, and referrals to your screened vendors. The idea is to avoid doing free assessments for customers who'll drop you after they get to know your vendor network.

Even if your prospects seem financially solvent, you should strive to work on a retainer basis with all new clients. It will always be better for you to maintain this level of control over your business relationships.

Special Requirements

Home property management is not licensed by state authorities, nor will people expect you to have many certifications. There is the National Concierge Association, whose members are almost exclusively hotel and on-site concierges.

This type of customer is much more likely to seek a personal, word-of-mouth referral than to do a search on Google looking for someone like you. You will definitely want to concentrate on person-to-person marketing through networking groups, social gatherings, and high-level charity events that draw lots of well-known, wealthy individuals in support of a cause.

Vacation Concierge

Estimated startup costs: $1,000

Estimated first-year revenue: $32,000–$48,000

In a few major cities and vacation resort areas around the country, there are companies that cater to tourists and visitors to the region. These tourists want to get as much out of their vacation as possible and are willing to pay for guidance that enriches their travel experience. Especially for visitors who are new to an area, there is much to be gained from seeking out locals who are in the business of helping visitors have fun and find those hidden places that make regional vacation spots extra special. Those kinds of experiences keep people coming back time and again and create a favorite destination.

The types of offerings you would include for your potential customers as a vacation concierge are limited only by the region you are in, other business owners you can find to participate, and your imagination. Current cultural trends will help you brainstorm ideas for packages and activities to offer. With today's fervor for all things culinary, an afternoon of food and wine tasting will appeal to locals and visitors alike. For the more active crowd, arranging for afternoons of kayaking, canoeing, or surfing with picnic lunches or a cocktail hour included will appeal.

The only barriers to launching this business idea are from potential partners you approach who say no to your idea—initially. Once you get your business up and running, local businesses will be calling you and asking to be included. You are providing tremendous value to them in bringing customers to their doorstep—it's much more direct than putting an ad in the visitor magazines, and much more cost effective.

This business requires an outgoing person with a big smile, hearty laugh, and genuine desire to help people have fun and get the most out of life. Typically, tourists who look for the edges of entertainment are congenial folks themselves. But you also need to understand that, as good as you are, some people are difficult to entertain no matter what.

Except for a few larger metropolitan areas and already popular vacation hotspots, you will have very little competition from others who are offering activity packages to visitors. Even with competitors, there is plenty of business out there to keep you as busy as you want to be.

Research the statistics about visitors to your area, including how many visit each year, seasonality, and the most popular attractions. The more you educate yourself about the who, what, and when of your potential customers, the better you will understand how to position yourself in offering activity options that people really want.

Bonus Point

You will be able to really expand your customer base by targeting packages to residents of your city as well as tourists who are visiting for a brief period. Ideas here would include targeting corporations and municipalities that entertain many out-of-town guests each year, or hold outdoor activities for families (just for fun or for family events like weddings and other celebrations).

Equipment and Supplies

Although there is no list of equipment required for tourism, a great website is going to be a necessity to help you get the word out about your business. Hire the best professional help you can afford to help you with website design, graphic art, and printed marketing materials. Plan on using much of the $1,000 startup budget on these expenses.

In the beginning, you will be able to use your car to transport your customers from one activity to another. Eventually (hopefully soon) you will need to move up to a van to handle larger groups. At first you can rent vehicles on an as-needed basis, but eventually you may want to own a vehicle to control your transportation costs.

Estimating the Time Commitment

You will need at least 60 to 90 days of planning time before you take in your first dollar. Your initial steps will be identifying affordable marketing support, developing your marketing materials, contacting local businesses, and arranging for interesting tourism partners. You will also need to research the competition in the area to help you identify unique ways to differentiate your company from any other players in the field.

Since you will be working as the sole tour guide, you also need to determine how many full-day options you can handle while you are also running the rest of the business. Once you have even limited success, you will need to hire part-time support to help with answering the phone, scheduling, troubleshooting, and office duties.

Estimating the amount of time for each tour outing will depend on the activities involved, travel time to each destination, and some extra time on either end for organizing arrivals and departures. Make trial runs with family and friends before you finalize your marketing materials, to be sure your advertised time of the trip is sufficient. You don't want to upset your customers by making them late to their next destination.

Pricing and Payments

You need to take both your costs to provide the activities and the going market rates into consideration before you set your pricing. Popular 3-hour food-tasting tours in Manhattan run in the $45 to $65 per person range, including food; these are walking tours, so there are no added transportation costs. Research how much time and how many dollars the average traveler to your area spends to make pricing attractive to the greatest number of people.

Your pricing will have to be based in part on your overall business plan; take the time to crunch the numbers on the front end. Your goal is to generate enough revenue to cover a certain salary for yourself. You will need to work your numbers to calculate how much you need in profit for each customer. (Please refer back to Part 1 to review all the expenses to include in your budgeting and projection process.)

You will definitely need to set up a merchant credit card account that can be accessed via your website. This will require some up-front costs, but is necessary to make sure your customers pay in advance. You won't have time to chase after folks whose check gets returned by the bank, especially if they live on the other side of the country.

Special Requirements

This kind of hospitality business requires no special licensing or education. Most of your education will come from spending time studying websites of competitors in your area and around the country. Look for businesses that have been in existence for five years or more to establish a model for your business plan.

You should investigate your insurance requirements, both for using your vehicle for business, transporting customers on a regular basis, and any possible liabilities that may arise from frequently hosting groups of people.

Snags _____

> Have a lengthy conversation with your insurance agent regarding your personal insurance coverage as it applies to rented vehicles. Many consumer advocates advise individuals to forego the daily coverage offered by rental companies, since your own auto policy often covers you when you are driving a rental vehicle. But beware of the clauses regarding size and tonnage limitations. Make sure your insurance will cover you for a rented vehicle that is larger than your own—say, a 15-passenger van.

Seasonal Caretaking

Estimated startup costs: $200–$500

Estimated first-year revenue: $25,000–$50,000

The growth in the number of vacation and seasonal homes was a major factor in the explosion of home building over the last two decades. Although the U.S. Census Bureau will not release figures for the last nine years until they have tallied the results of the upcoming 2010 census, the estimate is that there are more than 4,000,000 vacation homes in the United States today. Half a dozen states have a higher percentage of those homes, with Florida, Arizona, Maine, and Delaware leading the pack.

If you live in a resort area, like Park City, Utah, or southern Florida, starting a seasonal caretaking business will give you opportunities to profit from this large market. There is already some competition in the market, but it is still quite a new concept that can have a multitude of applications depending on your set of specific skills.

Equipment and Supplies

If you go the route of service coordinator, the only startup costs you will have are setting up your office, marketing, and acquiring your business license. If you perform the home-repair services on your own, you will need a good set of tools. We assume you would already own most of the tools you need.

Common caretaking responsibilities include the following services:

- Opening and closing a home for the season
- First response for security systems
- Regular checks on all house systems and appliances while vacant

- Automobile maintenance

- Monitoring monthly maintenance contractors

- Emergency on-call assistance

- Supervising construction projects during periods of owner absence

- Stocking supplies and refrigerators for returning owners

You definitely want to offer home-repair services, but if handyman chores are not your strong suit, you have the option of hiring other service providers on a contract basis. Seasonal caretaking easily lends itself to the concierge concept because it is just as efficient to be the coordinator of other business services as it is to do the work. Providing services personally will generate a higher per home revenue, however, since you get to keep all the customer's payments.

Estimating the Time Commitment

Building a business that requires you to enter people's homes when they are not present will take time to ramp up; you will need to develop a strong reputation in the community. We have taken this into consideration in estimating first-year revenue. In addition to your early marketing efforts directly to customers, you want to concentrate a lot of time on developing strong relationships with respected members of your immediate community. Start by reviewing the membership lists of your local civic organizations and choosing two or three that have the most appeal to you. Members of clubs like Rotary and Lions are often the movers and shakers in town. They can help introduce you to the people who can most help you with referrals, both of prospective customers and other service providers whom you can work with in your business.

The amount of time you will need to budget for servicing customer needs will depend on the area of the country you are in. A vacation home on the Georgia coast requires much less maintenance and oversight than a similar property on the coast of Maine, simply because of the extreme weather conditions in the northeast. Since you will be the primary go-to person for any problem that arises in the owner's absence, you should anticipate that this can require after-hours time as situations demand your attention. Your customers are counting on you to be on-site to take care of their home, regardless of the day or time the problem occurs. You will need competent backup personnel to cover for you when you schedule off-hours—and your own vacations.

Pricing and Payments

Like other service providers, you should set an hourly rate for pricing your services. The rates for seasonal caretaking vary with the affluence of the regions they are located in. However, you can utilize an hourly range of $25 to $40 per hour. As you establish methods for handling situations and build relationships with reliable home-maintenance companies, you will be able to spend more time dispatching others and less time on each site. This will free up time for you to continue to add new customers.

Establish a goal for the minimum number of hours per customer you would like to bill on a monthly basis. For example, at $25 per hour, if you were able to attract a certain number of customers for 10 hours each month, each one would pay you $250 per month or $3,000 annually. Using this as a base you can project that 10 customers will generate $30,000 of annual revenue and require about 100 hours a month of your time. Use this as a starting point to set benchmarks (see Chapter 3) for yourself in terms of the number of customers you want, how many you will add each month during the startup phase, and how long it will take you to get your revenue to where you want it to be.

Payments should be made monthly based on an invoice of hours you send to each customer. If possible, bill customers on a retainer basis, collecting your cash up front. You should be able to manage collections without the need for a merchant credit card account.

Special Requirements

Having some property-management experience will be helpful, even if it is limited to your experience managing your own home. See the Appendix for links to property-management continuing education courses that provide a formal classroom background to your practical experience. They will also enhance your resumé.

Construction Concierge

Estimated startup costs: $1,000

Estimated first-year revenue: $30,000–$45,000

Many working people who want to make major home improvements often put them off; not because they lack the money but because they don't have the time to manage the project. Even though most homeowners hire a general contractor or GC (see Chapter 9 for a detail description of the GC role) who is responsible for hiring the crew, purchasing all materials and managing the project, your job is to make sure the GC does what he says he is going to do and complies with any special requests made by the homeowner. Good general contractors usually have more than one job going at a time, which means a very busy homeowner is leaving a great deal to luck each day she leaves her home to go to her own job with construction workers on site.

With the proliferation of home-decorating shows flooding the airwaves, home-renovation projects have risen dramatically. This is a perfect time to launch a concierge service targeted at homeowners who want someone they can trust to oversee their home-renovation project. You have the potential to bring a great deal of value to your prospective customers by making sure they get the end result they are paying dearly for. At the very least, you can be on-site supervising and troubleshooting as situations arise that require input from someone with the homeowner's interest at the forefront.

Although there are no barriers to entry in the form of certifications or licensing (you are being engaged as an agent of the homeowner; you are not in the construction business yourself), it will lend credibility to have construction, design, or architectural experience. Learning how to read blueprints and contracts will be extremely useful as you assist the homeowner with navigating the pitfalls of a construction project.

You need to have great attention to detail, the ability to supervise others, and be comfortable in what can be a rugged construction site during the demolition and early reconstruction phases.

Your success in this type of business is going to depend on the amount of home-renovation projects in your area. Many areas of the country, for instance Detroit and environs, have been so negatively impacted by the decline of the automobile industry that it is unlikely that many people are spending on their homes. But in areas that are holding their own in this downturn, you are likely to see homeowners who are postponing the sale of their home until better days and taking this opportunity to make some long-desired improvements and additions.

Your customer is going to expect you to be their eyes and ears, so you will need to spend a good bit of time on the front end getting to know your customer. As each phase of the project begins, take the time to meet with the customer to review the plans and ask lots of questions about what they want the result to be. A happy customer will tell everyone they know about you. (And so will an unhappy one, so be sure to get the job done right.)

Use a checklist as you visit the site to make sure that you've thought of everything your customer is concerned about. Hopefully your contractors will be very competent and require very little supervision. But it's your job to make sure they work efficiently, timely, and leave each day after making sure they have tidied up their space and put tools out of harm's way.

Equipment and Supplies

You should create your own toolkit of sorts to be able to manage your projects. A good system for keeping organized notes is a must-have, both on future to-dos and current issues that need resolution or further action from you or another party. Many people manage this type of information with a good cell phone or PDA. Others rely on a written notebook system. If you prefer to track your tasks digitally, you may need to invest in a new cell phone or the like, to the tune of $300. You will also want on-site access to the Internet, so you may have to add this extra service to your monthly cell phone bill.

Carry a good tape measure and a level to be able to take measurements and check workmanship at any time.

Snags

Unlike a general contractor, you are not responsible for any of the costs that need to be incurred. Therefore you should not be put in the position of advancing funds on the home-owner's behalf.

Another important aspect of your job is keeping in regular communication with your customer. No one will want constant calls during the workday—after all, they've hired you to handle most problems on the site. But at the end of each day you should give your customer a progress report and especially make them aware of any problems that might have arisen that need their attention immediately. Create a regular means of touching base with customers, either by e-mail, phone call, or end-of-day walk-through and meeting on the site.

Estimating the Time Commitment

In most circumstances, the beginning weeks of any construction project will probably require you to visit the site at least once, if not two or three times a day. This may sound excessive, but here is a scenario that is within that realm:

It's Day 6 of your project and the contractor plans to finish up demolition by the end of the day. Accordingly, he has scheduled the delivery of the oak floorboards, which need to remain on site for three weeks to adjust to the climate before they are installed. You have developed a routine where you stop by the site each morning to see who's around and whether the contractors who were supposed to show up actually have. Then you meet the truck delivering the lumber for the floor to make sure they place the wood where the homeowner wants it stored for the next three weeks. You also need to inspect the quality of the wood to make sure it meets the homeowners' expectations as they have described them to you. Finally, you will return at the end of the day to confirm that the general contractor is indeed on schedule and the demolition is complete. You confirm when the dumpster is going to be removed from the site. Before you are done for the day, you will make your report to the homeowner on the day's activities, successes, and problems to be solved.

At first you should only take on one job, to get yourself oriented. Depending on the size of the project, the one job may keep you busy full-time for several weeks or even months. Talk with general contractors and other people in the construction business who have enough experience to have developed rules of the game for gauging time on the job. The workload is always more intense at first, because there are many tasks that can be done. As a project gets underway, the actual work on the job becomes more spaced out and sporadic as the contractors finish up their respective jobs. Gather as much information and advice as you can to help you determine at what point you will be able to start another project as one finishes up.

Pricing and Payments

Set an hourly rate to charge your customer. Most likely you will start at $25 per hour and work your rate up as you get busier. Like other concierge services, the rate will vary with your location, demand, and affluence of your customers. The more expensive the materials being used, the more expensive a potential mistake can be. If you can manage to stave off big errors with your oversight and attention to detail, you will be able to increase your fee in tandem with the additional value you are providing the customer.

Most construction workers get paid at the end of each week, which would be a good schedule for you. If you are supervising the building of a home for an absentee owner (one that hasn't moved in yet), you should consider an advance retainer payment schedule since they may not be around to write you a check each week.

Special Requirements

You should review your state's licensing requirements for construction workers and be sure you do not meet the definition of any workers requiring licensing. Use a written contract with the homeowner to outline your duties and payment terms. Use the language in this document to clarify your role as homeowner's representative and not a general contractor.

Chapter 8

Home Resale Services

In This Chapter

- ◆ Designing for home sales
- ◆ Profiting from selling off other people's stuff
- ◆ Protecting home buyers from potential mistakes
- ◆ Determining the value of homes for sale

We all know the real estate market has taken a huge hit in terms of decreased property values in the last two years. All of us who have been mulling over the idea of selling our homes realize we missed the boat for reaping the best price for our houses. Yet the housing market has been extremely active since the beginning of 2009, with most real estate agents reporting sales in the first quarter greater than all of 2008 combined. In dollars, not just in number of houses sold.

The National Association of Realtors claims that the Existing Home Sales Series is the premier measurement of the residential real estate market. Although the number of home sales has dropped dramatically from its peak in 2006, close to 5,000,000 sales are still expected for 2009. It's obvious from the chart on the next page that the market for home resale services is much greater in the South than the other three regions across the country, with the Northeast sector lagging considerably behind the other areas. This indicates that startups are likely to grow faster in the latter three regions than in the Northeast.

Existing home sales projected by region for 2009.

(Courtesy of the National Association of Realtors)

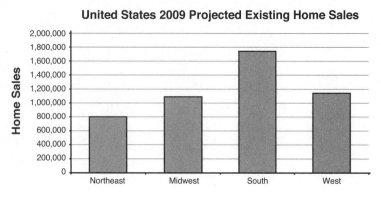

United States 2009 Projected Existing Home Sales

Projected as of May 2009

Business is up not just for real estate agents and brokers. Try getting a home appraisal or inspection for a pending sale, and you will need to wait your turn.

In this chapter we cover four specific opportunities related to residential home sales. Staging homes for resale is the newest concept in supporting sellers in achieving the highest value and faster sales. It also requires the most creativity and more marketing than home appraisals and home inspections, since the latter two are requirements of the lender and everyone who sells a home must have one done. Lastly, we have included the idea of "estate" and "tag" sale facilitators, since many people selling their homes can raise some cash with a well-organized and high-caliber sale of furnishings that are no longer needed.

Home Staging for Resale

Estimated startup costs: $500–$1,000

Estimated first-year revenue: $40,000–$70,000

Home staging means preparing a home for resale. It involves skills that include interior design, color coordination, and a solid understanding of the way to create inviting spaces within a specific room of a house.

The most common approach to home staging, as seen on TV shows such as *Designed to Sell* on HGTV, is to first take an objective inventory of all the items in a homeowner's house. The next steps involve deciding what stays (rearranging furniture and accent pieces), what goes (decluttering, mostly of family photos and cheap tchotchkes), and adding a few new items that accentuate the home's focal points and conceal its flaws.

This type of work requires someone who is objective, confident, and tactful. You are going to have to give people instructions on one of the most personal aspects of their lives: how they keep their home. You also need to be patient, high-energy, and upbeat.

This is not a brand-new field, but the market for home stagers is far from saturated. Your best bet for assessing the competition is a Google search in your area for other professional home stagers. Home Stagers Resource, a company that provides online training and certification, provides an online member directory and encourages newcomers to contact members with questions about the business. This is the best way to get direct input on how others in your area are succeeding with this business.

Your customers are going to expect your work to translate into immediate improved traffic of prospective buyers and a quicker sale of the home. Find out how long it takes an average home to sell and set your benchmarks to beat the average length of time on the market. This will be a quantifiable way to advertise the value you bring to your customers.

Equipment and Supplies

You will need a good website and digital and video cameras for marketing your best asset: your ability to convert an unsold home to one that is under contract in a short period of time. Just like a home organizer, the visual impact of before-and-after photos is going to make the biggest impression on your prospective customers. If you have cameras for personal use, start out using them for your business. Learning how to design and update your own website will be a very worthwhile skill to develop, since it will save you hundreds of dollars in professional fees and result in a site that gets updated frequently.

Some staging companies actually own an inventory of furniture and accessories that they place in customers' homes as needed. This is not a necessary or expected offering when you are dealing directly with the

Bonus Point

Several of the programs for certifying home stagers offer a complete package to get you started in your business—marketing tools, website template, etc. For just under $1,000, you can get certification and the complete business kit. Since it includes the web design, this could be a very cost-effective choice for you.

homeowner. It is part of your job to suggest a few low-cost items for your customer to add to their décor. If you offer to purchase items on behalf of your customers, you should make it understood that you are to be reimbursed.

Estimating the Time Commitment

Although a website will help you attract potential customers, this is a business that will grow based on word-of-mouth referrals. The more homes you stage that sell, the more your business will expand. It may take 60 to 90 days before you have a customer, but you will have plenty of work to keep you busy. In addition to the typical setup tasks (see Chapters 3 and 4), you will also be working on material for your website photo gallery. That means finding people to whom you can offer your talents in exchange for helping you promote your business. Real estate agents are one referral source, but many agents feel they are qualified to offer staging advice after all their years in the business. Home-improvement contractors, like painters and carpenters, handymen, and cleaning companies, are other professionals with residential home customers who will be among the first to know when a homeowner is planning to list their house.

Experienced home stagers package their services into different levels based on the length of time required for the job. Most initial consultations are scheduled for a minimum of two hours to half a day. The goal is to convert a desired hourly rate into a flat fee based on the square footage of the home. Part of the initial challenge you will have is determining how long a certain size home-staging project will take to make sure you get paid well for your time. Your deliverable should be a detailed written recommendation of specific action steps for the homeowner to take in order to accomplish better staging on a do-it-yourself basis. Additional services include actual moving of furniture and physically assisting with the staging, billed at an hourly rate.

Pricing and Payments

Fees are based on hourly rates that range from $65 to more than $100 per hour, depending on location and demand for staging services. In metropolitan areas where there is an existing demand for home staging, fees will naturally be at the higher end. For newcomers, common sense dictates that you start with a fee in the middle to the lower end, and build your reputation before increasing your fees.

The homeowner should pay for an initial consultation at the end of the session. If the customer decides to engage you for a longer duration—say, to redesign several rooms in the house—you should be prepared to quote a payment schedule, such as once a week, or for a room when it is complete, or as certain stages are finished. Since you are not guaranteeing that the home will sell, do not postpone your payment for services rendered until the eventual sale of the home. There are many factors outside of your control that can prolong closing or cause the contract to fall apart entirely.

Special Requirements

Many companies and associations of professional home stagers offer courses, networking, conventions, symposiums, and a listing in an online directory. See the listing in the Appendix for more details. Although anyone who enjoys design will be able to learn this business, it is clearly a natural fit for anyone who has studied interior design and worked in another capacity as a designer.

Estate Sale Facilitator/Liquidator

Estimated startup costs: $200–$1,000

Estimated first-year revenue: $30,000–$60,000

An estate sale facilitator or liquidator assists the heirs of an estate or living individuals with the sale of personal property. Although the term *estate* often refers to the assets of a deceased individual, the definition is really much broader and includes all the assets of a living individual as well. In today's market, it is common to use the term *estate sale* to differentiate from a yard or garage sale and to convey a higher quality of merchandise for sale.

Personal property can include decorative items, antiques, collectibles, art, jewelry, books, and much more. Some high-end assets can require an appraisal, which is usually done by someone certified and highly experienced in this field. Our conception of this business idea is geared toward assisting people who own more easily valued possessions than rare antique jewelry and the like.

The reasons for liquidating assets, such as death of a loved one, bankruptcy, job loss, downsizing, relocating, and so on, often accompany periods of extreme emotion in the lives of the sellers. As such, being successful in this field will require an empathetic person with patience and organization. You will want to be the eye of the storm for your customers, helping them reap some benefit from whatever has caused them to sell their possessions.

You can get a good idea of the competition in your area by searching for similar businesses online. Since most estate sales are open to the public, you should look for the advertisements for ones in your area and go to as many as possible as part of your planning and preparation. This will be an ideal opportunity to learn the trade by observation. You may even want to hire on with another company on a part-time basis to get an insider's view of the business.

Most of the sales will come from aging seniors who are being forced to downsize as they move to retirement communities and much smaller living spaces. Between the current populations of seniors and boomers, over 100 million people in the United States fit the demographic of a prospective estate sale service customer. With families dispersed around the country, even if a relative can make the time to supervise the process, many working people have to use professionals to help them liquidate their parents' estates.

Equipment and Supplies

You can start this business with a basic office setup, marketing materials, and a website. You don't need any special up-front equipment to get started. You will need supplies to organize your sale. Most estate liquidators have their own system for marking items, but generally speaking, you need markers and tags or labels for pricing items in advance, plus a cash box for keeping payments the day(s) of the sale.

Estimating the Time Commitment

You should be able to develop some rules for estimating how long a job will take by doing investigative research at other sales in your area. The smart shoppers always get to the sale before it starts on the first day, or the preview day in some instances. Spend some time walking around to get an idea of the scope of the sale—what kind of things are being sold, how many items, and so on. Go back on the second day to see how much has sold and how much is still left. Use this opportunity to speak with the people in charge and ask them your questions.

The amount of preparation required is going to depend on the size and value of the estate. It can take three to four weeks just to go through everything in the home, sort it by asset type, and price it. It will take some extra time if there are unique items that require in-depth research to determine their value. For example, someone's museum-size stuffed grizzly bear is not the kind of object whose worth you would be expected to know off the top of your head. Don't be afraid to call in a specialty appraiser at the seller's expense to value things that are beyond your knowledge base if the items have the potential to bring a significant profit.

Estate sale liquidation is somewhat a recession-proof business. Down cycles in the economy cause people to have to move and raise cash by selling their belongings. With the right marketing and networking efforts, you should be able to ramp up to profitability fairly quickly.

Pricing and Payments

The standard pricing method for estate sales is for the facilitator to work on a percentage of the total gross basis. The going range is from 25 percent to as high as 40 percent. The fee will vary with the amount of work required to get ready for the sale, and should be determined on a customer-by-customer basis.

You definitely need to use a written contract that outlines your responsibilities and includes clauses for a total buyout (which allows you to buy all unsold merchandise for a percentage of the marked price) or arrangements with a charitable organization for picking up the leftover items. You also want to stipulate exactly who will handle the set-up and clean-up. Most estate sale liquidators prefer to handle all the details so they can do things their way. Many require that no one be living in the home during the process from start to finish.

Special Requirements

Estate liquidators are expected to be bonded and insured, so be sure to contact an insurance agent and get pricing on this coverage. Developing and maintaining a mailing list can be a very valuable selling point to prospects. By adding a newsletter, calendar, and relevant content to your website, you will accelerate your collection of potential buyers for merchandise; many collectors frequent estate sales on a weekly basis to acquire their goods for themselves or for resale. Companies such as Constant Contact (www.constantcontact.com) provide small businesses with an extremely affordable service for tracking e-mails and also do customer surveys for as little as $15 a month for up to 500 contacts.

The American Society of Estate Liquidators offers courses and general guidance to professionals in this industry (www.aselonline.com/index.html).

Home Inspector

Estimated startup costs: $1,000

Estimated first-year revenue: $50,000–$75,000

Home inspection is a great source of revenue and is a business that you can run cost-effectively. Like some of the other startups discussed in this book, it is much simpler to launch a low-cost home-inspection company if you have already taken the certification training and have experience working for someone else before starting your own company. If this is not your situation, you will need good financing to limit your intial cash outlay to $1,000. However, the potential earning power of this startup is so good that we have included it here for you to consider.

The main goal of a residential home inspector is to conduct a visual examination of a single-family home and test the home systems and components. After a physical inspection of the premises, the inspector prepares a detailed report, in a format as specified by either the party ordering the inspection or, in some cases, state regulations.

Often the scope of the work is dictated by the American Society of Home Inspectors (ASHI) standards of practice. Most frequently the inspection is performed in conjunction with a pending sale/purchase of the home, with the real estate contract and the price contingent on the findings by the inspector. It is common for home-sale contracts to have an inspection clause that allows the buyer to rescind the contract if the home receives a negative report. Accordingly, the inspector is expected to deliver the report quickly, since time is of the essence.

In addition to the stress factor of short deadlines, a home inspector has to be physically fit in order to perform many of the duties of this job, such as climbing rickety attic stairs, crawling through damp and cold crawlspaces and foundations, and doing a thorough inspection of the exterior of the dwelling. Your customers are counting on you to protect them from a bad investment, and it is your job to provide them with an accurate assessment of the structural fitness of their potential dream home.

Equipment and Supplies

You will need some tools for testing structures and systems (circuit testers, volt meters, moisture meter, water-pressure gauge, gas-leak detector, carbon-monoxide detector, to name a few) and ladders to access high areas. You can purchase all these items at www.professionalequipment.com for approximately $1,500. Your most important tool is going to be your report-writing program, and there are a variety on the market. Software costs can go as high as $3,000 for state of the art palm technology, but there are also programs available for as low as $450.

Estimating the Time Commitment

Most home inspectors complete two inspections per day and work five to six days per week, depending on the time of year. Home sales are somewhat seasonal and start climbing in March and stay strong through September. Winter holiday time is pretty quiet, so you might want to consider working a heavier schedule in the busier season. By scheduling your first appointment at the start of the day, you will have enough time to travel and conduct an afternoon inspection.

You should definitely spend time networking in the startup phase, with realtors and mortgage brokers being your best referral sources. Small, weekly networking groups (see the Appendix, Chapter 3 link to small business networking groups) that have these professionals as members will be a great place for you to get going on your marketing. Another option is to seek out an experienced home inspector or even small inspection company to join forces with in the first year of your business. Often home inspection "companies" are more like associations of individual inspectors pooling resources to help with overhead and share leads. Since this is a physical business, older inspectors will welcome a "newbie" who can handle more challenging structures and generally share the workload. Revenues are split according to work performed, with common expenses deducted.

Pricing and Payments

While the market determines what a home inspector can charge for an inspection, the American Society of Home Inspectors' 2005 Home Inspection Business Operations Study shows that the average cost of a home inspection is $318. Inspectors can expect to earn gross revenues of more than $75,000. Our Year 1 revenue takes into account that you will not start out with two inspections per day, and that inspection requires time for writing the report, scheduling, administrative duties, etc. Once you have developed a strong network of referrals, you will be on your way to grossing $100,000 or more.

Home inspectors are usually paid by the homeowner with a check after the on-site inspection is completed.

Special Requirements

Most home inspectors pursue certification through a series of courses, although only some states require licensing.

To see if your state requires licensing of home inspectors, go to www.homeinspector. org/stateregulations. Whether or not a license is required, it is a good idea to complete one of the certification courses available. ASHI offers a full series of courses, both on-site in classrooms or online for $3,000 plus membership of $400 annually. Local training and online programs to pass the ASHI exam can cost much less than those by ASHI itself, in the $1,250 range. Whichever training you choose, you will want to use some form of financing to keep your startup costs at the $1,000 maximum. But considering that you should be earning more than $300 per inspection, you will be able to pay back the cost of the certification within the first year.

You may be required to carry Errors and Omissions insurance (E&O) as well as general liability and bonding insurance as a home inspector. For those starting out, your first annual premiums will cost around $1,500, $250, and $300 respectively. Most companies will allow you to finance the premiums over nine months with a down payment of 30 percent when the coverage is activated.

Residential Appraiser

Estimated startup costs: $1,000

Estimated first-year revenue: $50,000–$75,000

Home appraisers have a similar business model to home inspectors, with one major exception. Education and licensing requirements in most states necessitate a college degree or equivalent before working in this field. Many states require a multiyear experience component in addition to the education. In order to make this business conform to our concept of a low-cost startup, we are going to assume that you are already a licensed appraiser who has been employed by an appraisal or real estate company and that you are seeking to set up your own business.

An appraiser calculates a property's market value by comparing it to similar properties that have sold in the area. These previously sold properties used are called comparables, or comps. The appraiser, even though an independent professional, is usually hired by the lending institution that is going to originate the mortgage on the home.

Like a home inspector, an appraiser needs to have good attention to detail, and be thorough and organized. Your appraisal report is going to be needed as soon as you can finish it, so efficiency will play a large role in your success in this business.

The housing market in this country is tremendous. There have definitely been some slow periods in home sales, especially in the latter half of 2008, when very few trans-actions were taking place. However, home sales have come back in volume, and the income of a home appraiser is based on volume since it is priced at a fixed fee.

Even though you will not be paid by the home buyer, the purpose of the appraisal is to get the home sale to the next stage in the transaction process. An appraised value sufficient to satisfy the lender is an important goal of both the buyer and seller. Be prepared to deal with disappointed parties if the appraisal is below the contract price for the home.

Equipment and Supplies

You will need a membership in a realtor association ($400) and a subscription to Metropolitan Regional Information Services (MRIS), $850 per year, payable in monthly installments. (The MRIS is a listing of homes by neighborhood, the homes' selling prices, characteristics of the houses, and days on market.) You also need a laser measuring tape ($550). When added to the cost of classes for certification, startup costs approach $3,000.

Estimating the Time Commitment

You want to be sure to schedule enough time to get your reports written in a timely manner. Visiting the site is critical, but it's the appraisal report that everyone wants. It's going to take time to earn the trust of real estate agents, so plan on a 90-day startup period for marketing to good contacts. Until you become experienced, you should limit your schedule to one appraisal per day, to ensure that you build your reputation for quick turnaround time and responsiveness.

Pricing and Payments

Although the prices vary around different areas of the country, $350 per appraisal is a good comparison number to use in most regions.

If you have been hired directly by the homeowner, you should expect payment in cash or check at the conclusion of your site visit. If you have a contract with a bank or other kind of mortgage broker, you will likely be on a billing cycle with them already from other similar engagements.

Special Requirements

An appraiser will benefit from strong interpersonal skills in dealing with people selling their homes. As mentioned in the beginning of this section, it usually takes education, passing an examination(s), and experience to qualify as a licensed home appraiser. If you are interested in pursuing this business, your first step is to investigate the requirements of your state government.

Part 3

Home Makeovers

This part takes its cue from the overwhelming popularity of home improvement, décor, and design shows on television. Combining the philosophies of following your passion with riding the wave of current trends in pop culture, we explore the various services to homeowners seeking to improve, upgrade, and feather their nests. We not only delve into the design aspect, but also discuss the many professions that implement home renovations.

Chapter 9

Interior Home Renovations

In This Chapter

- ◆ Why the home renovation market is jamming in spite of the economic downturn
- ◆ Putting your own home improvement talents to the test
- ◆ The payoff in painting, tiling, and carpentry
- ◆ Managing the construction process
- ◆ Wired: the neverending business of making technology work

The market for interior home renovations is huge even when housing sales and new housing starts are in a lull. The different renovation and home-improvement businesses covered in this chapter all require small tools, learned skills, and enough business acumen to build a solid customer base. The earnings potential may vary, but all have the potential for generating a good revenue stream with a rapid ramp-up period for anyone who focuses on marketing and follows it up with reliable services.

We have focused this chapter on residential rather than commercial work. Commercial services are more competitive and, even though they can result in good, recurring work (see window cleaning in Chapter 5), the pay for the same work on the residential level is much higher than for commercial customers. Once you get your business past the startup phase, you can analyze the benefits of adding some commercial contracts, but as a startup you will reach your goal of independence much faster by starting out on the residential side of the business.

House Painting

Estimated startup costs: $500–$1,000

Estimated first-year revenue: $30,000–$50,000

Most homeowners understand that painting is the fastest and most cost-effective way to spruce up a house, whether they are updating a current home or moving into a new one. You will make a positive impression if you show up on time to do a bid and actually offer a proposal before you leave. A frequent issue with all home contractors is that they are great about keeping the initial free estimate appointment—but wretched about coming through with an actual estimate. Good general business tactics, including a clean truck and neat appearance will go a long way to winning you jobs. (Dare we repeat the advice from Chapter 3 regarding magnet advertising for the vehicle and a logo shirt for you?) These attributes will also help you secure a higher price because you will look better than your competition.

House painting normally involves interior surfaces (walls and moldings) and house exteriors. Sometimes you might be asked to bid on a small job, maybe one or two rooms, or sometimes the entire interior and possibly exterior work as well. If you do not have exterior painting experience, you may want to limit your bids to interior-only jobs. You could also form a marketing partnership with a painter who prefers exterior work to bring in when the opportunity presents itself.

You can make good money at house painting if you have the confidence to charge enough to make a decent living. Homeowners often work under the assumption that painters are the least skilled of home renovators and should be paid less than carpenters, electricians, and so on. There are many very successful painters, but there are also some who barely make ends meet because they still charge customers day labor rates from 20 years ago.

Equipment and Supplies

You will need several items and a vehicle large enough to transport ladders. In general, you should be able to buy all the startup equipment and supplies for $500 or less. These will include a ladder of versatile height (usually 14-foot ladders will be fine to get you started), drop cloths for protecting floors and furniture, paint brushes, trays and rollers, scrapers, paint stirrers, a drill, masking tape to protect trim and molding, and some rags.

Our recommendation is to have the customer reimburse you directly for paint, or buy it themselves. Since choosing colors is the most important and personal decision in the process, most may already plan to buy it themselves—they may even have brushed a few colors on the wall before making the final decision. This will reduce your earning potential somewhat since you won't be able to mark up the cost of the paint. But the upside is that it will lessen the amount of up-front cash you need to spend out of your own pocket.

Find or create a formal bid/estimate sheet that you use consistently for every customer. Make sure you include all your different expenses to ensure that you don't leave anything significant off your estimate.

Once the customer accepts your bid, present him with a contract for signature, either using the estimate form or creating another document. The contract should also include payment terms. To keep your startup costs low, consider renting any major equipment for your first jobs, such as a pressure washer or extension ladders for painting a home exterior. Once you have some cash flow, you can decide to purchase more equipment as needed.

Estimating the Time Commitment

Before your first job, you need to figure out how long it takes you to paint a given surface in order to calculate your time estimate. Paint some rooms or surfaces in your own home, or offer to do some painting for friends, family, and anyone else who would be a good reference for your new business. You need to be able to translate square footage into time when you bid on jobs. With some practice, you will know exactly how much time to budget for a 10×20 bedroom compared to a bath or kitchen that may be smaller but has lots of cabinets and fixtures. Budget extra time for tall and vaulted ceilings; any painting you do on a ladder will take longer.

Include time in your estimate for proper prep work. This will vary with the type of surface you are painting and the condition of the surface. Old homes with multiple coats of paint that need to be scraped will require much more prep time than a five-year-old house with minimal moldings.

Pricing and Payments

Many painters still quote jobs based on square footage of the surfaces to be painted, correlating square feet with number of hours. You will also need to know your square footage to calculate how much paint you need, regardless of who pays for the paint or goes to the store to buy it. Once you know your square footage, the salesmen at the paint store can help you or your customer determine how much of a certain paint to buy.

Painters charge anywhere from $20 to $50 per hour. Do your homework and investigate the going rates for painting where you live. Again, following good business practices and making the right impression with customers will get you higher rates and more referrals.

It is common in the construction professions to request one fourth to one third of the contract price when the contract is signed, followed by regular subsequent payments. The larger the job, the more payments you will schedule in the contract.

Special Requirements

There are no licensing requirements for painting. You will have to carry insurance, bonding and liability, and workers' compensation if you hire any employees. This business will benefit from website networking referrals from sites like www. servicemaster.com. You will also benefit from your own website.

Carpentry

Estimated startup costs: $500–$1,000

Estimated first-year revenue: $35,000–$70,000

Carpentry has always had a certain appeal to people who love to create things with their hands. Since carpentry encompasses so many different skills and types of jobs, you must narrow your scope to a particular aspect of carpentry and the types of customers you want to attract, and set your prices so you make a good living. Many carpenters earn very good money, but many spend a lifetime providing labor as someone's employee and stay at the bottom of the pay scale. Our goal is to help you put together a business plan that helps you earn top dollar for your time.

Carpenters work in construction, installation, and repair of wooden structures and fixtures. They use a variety of hand and power tools to construct building structures, such as framework, stairways, and floors. They are required to follow local building codes, but are usually not required to be licensed like plumbers and electricians.

More than other construction workers, carpenters are expected to have a keen eye for quality of materials and serious attention to detail. Top-grade work comes close to an art form, and not everyone has the patience to do this for others.

Finish carpenters and those who specialize in constructing high-end structures, such as custom bookshelves, entertainment centers, and cabinetry, will have an easier time selling their services as independent business people. General contractors are more likely to employ rough carpenters and those who can do maintenance, repair, and replacement of existing structures. You will make much more money working for yourself than as an employee in a construction company, where the owner profits from your labor.

Equipment and Supplies

Carpentry is a learned skill, and whether you have on-the-job training or have acquired your skills as a hobby, we assume you already have a basic set of tools and some kind of workshop set up in your home. People who have successful carpentry businesses advise you to avoid the temptation to add much equipment to your workshop as you are launching your business. Use the tools and skills you already have, and postpone any major purchases until you have profits to invest in new equipment. Your supplies will depend on the jobs you land, so you can pay for them with your initial advance on your contract.

You may want to join a website network (see the Appendix for website links) to help with leads in the first year and develop some simple marketing materials.

Estimating the Time Commitment

Each carpentry project is going to be different, so you have to learn how to balance the time to do a job properly and being available to start new projects. Seasoned carpenters advise those new to running their own business to make sure to estimate fees based on how long you think the job will take and then add another 30 percent to cover travel, purchasing, and administration. Even those who have worked in this profession for many years as an employee have a big learning curve when it comes to managing all the details of running your own business.

Your quickest way into the market will be through other construction contractors who have already established themselves in the marketplace. If you do a great job or have a particular specialty needed on many job sites, word will get around. Within a few months you should have more work than you can handle.

Pricing and Payments

There are way too many variables in building something beautiful out of wood to price your work by the job. You definitely want to figure out how much you need to pay your bills and arrive at an hourly rate that will get you to a higher level of income than working for someone else. The low end for carpentry is $25 an hour, with $50 and $60 being fairly common for top-grade finish carpenters. You will want to assess rates in your particular area of the country. The overall economy and the state of the commercial and residential construction market for new structures will impact your pricing to some degree.

Special Requirements

Carpenters need to be familiar with the building codes that affect the types of structures you will be creating. If you are going to work independently, you will have to depend on yourself to stay within code, so take the time to get educated in this area. The codes that have been adopted in all or part in over 40 states are the International Building Code (IBC) and International Residential Code (IRC) for residential structures. Visit the website of the International Code Council (iccsafe.org) for details. Since the code is adopted on a state-by-state basis, check with your state department of community affairs (or a comparable government division) to make sure you know exactly which codes apply in your area.

You will also need to carry liability and bonding insurance. These are included in our $500 startup cost budget.

Ceramic Tile Installation

Estimated startup costs: $500–$1,000

Estimated first-year revenue: $29,000–$58,000

Ceramic tile is a decorative material used to cover floors, walls, and countertops in both residential and commercial construction. As a professional tile installer, you will be expected to understand everything about flooring and subflooring and be able to identify structures that will need bracing and reinforcement to bear the load of the tile. Tile installation can be straightforward and requires minimal tools, but talent and attention to detail is extremely important. If you make a mistake in your layout calculation, or have problems installing a type of tile you are unfamiliar with, there is no covering it up. Your customers have to live with the surface every day, and they'll want their investment to last in good condition up to the day they sell.

You will be expected to assist with layouts, patterns, and placement of special decorative tiles in a solid background. There are different shapes of tile for different types of uses. You need competency in both floor and wall installations, although tile is much more popular as a floor covering. If you have some do-it-yourself background in setting tile (and enjoyed the projects), there are resources for reasonably priced training programs, which we'll discuss shortly.

Equipment and Supplies

You can go to http://www.tiletool.net/tool_kits.asp to purchase a complete kit of the tools needed to start your installation business, which can be purchased online for a total price of less than $250. You will also need supplies (grout, coloring) which can be either added on to your customers' invoices or priced into your hourly rate or rate per square foot.

Learn to estimate the amount of tile and supplies for each job before you take on a paying customer. Practice on at least two spaces in your home or that of someone you know, and take the job from start to finish. Create checklists and formulas for calculating your material requirements. (See also the Appendix; the Ask the Tool Man website has an estimator tool free of charge.) Your customer will supply the tiles, but will rely on you to determine how much of what color and shape they will need for the square footage to be covered.

Estimating the Time Commitment

Just like with painting and carpentry, you will need to use your "practice" jobs to measure how much time to allow for each job. You will get faster as you get more experience. In the beginning you want to err on the side of estimating too much time and do the best job you can. As you progress you will learn the difference between being marginally and extremely successful.

Bonus Point _____

One of the basic tenets of estimating your time is that installations of diagonal patterns are at least 30 percent more time consuming than straight tile installations. If this is news to you, check out the "Special Requirements" section and sign up for a professionally taught class to enhance your installation skills.

Pricing and Payments

Pricing for ceramic tile installation is all over the place, from $15 to $75 an hour and $3.75 to $15 per square foot. This makes sense, since there are all different kinds of jobs: commercial restrooms with simple one-color tiles, and high-end residential homes with intricate patterns and more challenging architectural details to tile around. Find out what others in your area are charging and how you can price your services for profitability and marketability. If you can't charge at least $25 per hour for this work, choose another business where you can.

See the preceding sections on painting and carpentry for typical construction payment terms.

Special Requirements

Tile installers do not require professional licensing. There are some good, economical courses offered by several tile associations. Check out www.tilecareer.com for two-day classes starting at $295 for the new Certified Tile Installer program. This certificate has been offered since 2008 by the Tile Council of North America, Inc. (TCNA).

General Contracting

Estimated startup costs: $500–$1,000

Estimated first-year revenue: $40,000–$60,000

A general contractor (GC) is the project manager of a residential or commercial construction project, taking the customer's vision and the architect's drawings and turning them into the reality of a finished structure. An experienced GC will have an array of subcontractors to call on to perform the actual construction tasks—masons, tile installers, carpenters, and the like. He or she may have construction experience, but use their brains and organizational skills, not their hands. It is the GC's responsibility to get the job done well, on time, and in budget. Some specific duties are …

- Scheduling subcontractors in the right order—you can't put up walls until the wiring is complete.

- Coordinating, meeting, and supervising the subcontractors to ensure an on-time overall project.

- Paying the subcontractors as required.

- Arranging for all necessary permits with local governments and meet all inspectors to make sure the inspection goes without any hitches.

- Make the customer's life much easier so they deal only with you and not the myriad of people needed to complete the project.

In the last decade it has become much more common for states to require the licensing of general contractors. You will need to check with your secretary of state's office to determine what your professional licensing requirements are.

A successful GC must first and foremost be extremely organized and detail-oriented, as well as a good manager of people. Another important quality is learning from previous experiences and improving your customer's end result with helpful and creative suggestions on design as well as construction. Especially when a customer is his or her own architect, using your experience and eye for detail can make a very positive impression. For instance, things like convincing the homeowner that a double-sink vanity is not all that helpful in a small bathroom, or suggesting the addition of something as simple as an "insty hot" dispenser in a new kitchen, will be appreciated for years to come.

You don't necessarily need to have worked in the construction industry to start a GC business; homeowners who have experienced one or more major renovation projects are potential candidates for this profession. Having excellent contacts in both the marketing of prospects (good neighborhood connections, real estate developers, architects, and so on) and hiring good-quality subcontractors are critical in launching this startup.

Equipment and Supplies

You will need a good software package to compile your bids in an organized fashion. There are many software products on the market priced between $100 and $200. Since you are managing the job, you can rely on your subs to provide their own tools.

You will need to invest in liability insurance and bonding as the overall responsible party for the construction team. Using subs who carry their own insurance will greatly reduce your coverage requirements and associated costs.

Estimating the Time Commitment

With the decline in the housing market in general, there are many more construction workers chasing much less work than two to three years ago. That doesn't mean there isn't room for another highly professional general contractor. This profession has traditionally carried a bad reputation, mostly because of the challenge of taking a highly skilled technician, like a carpenter, and turning that person into a manager and businessperson. If you can approach this work with a project-management skill set and deliver quality service on each job, you will be way ahead of the people who got into this field in its heyday.

A profitable GC will need to manage more than one job at a time. As discussed in the construction concierge section of Chapter 7 (see "Estimating the Time Commitment"), there is much more cash flow in the first half of the job when things are happening every hour of each day. As the project moves toward completion, the work and cash flow slow down. You will need to coordinate your job scheduling with your cash flow needs.

Pricing and Payments

General contractors sometimes get a flat fee, or weekly payment, over the course of the job. But by far, the more common pricing method is based on a percentage of the overall costs of construction, both materials and labor. The norm is 15 to 20 percent depending upon the location and size of the project.

The payment schedule is also very important to maintaining good cash flow and being able to pay subcontractors on time. Payments are often scheduled for the end of each week or as certain phases of the project are completed, such as carpentry work, electrical, plumbing, and so on. This makes staying on schedule important to your pocketbook as well as your reputation.

Special Requirements

Be sure to follow up on licensing and insurance requirements. Many state licensees must pass a statewide examination. In Georgia, for example, the exam can be taken online at any time by the applicant and costs $72.

Audio/Visual System Installations

Estimated startup costs: $500–$1,000

Estimated first-year revenue: $30,000–$60,000

It is commonly understood that "our lives are made simpler by advances in technology," is a statement of both truth and irony. Yes, having information at our fingertips via the Internet makes life immensely easier. Getting your TV remote control to work as it should is another issue entirely. Anyone who has set up his own equipment knows this to be the case. In the early days of television, the picture might not have come close to the clarity of today's models, but operating that old TV was child's play; all you needed was the dexterity to turn a knob from left to right and back again. And you had to know the difference between two controls, volume and the channel changer.

Today's world of electronics is far more complex, with many of us having to phone a friend just to get our cable working properly. As the cost of high-definition plasma-screen televisions continues to fall, they have become more affordable to a great number of people. And those people need help getting them installed, wired, and hooked up to the cable or satellite provider. As wireless equipment comes of age, understanding how the audio and visual (AV) components work is becoming more important than knowing how to pull the wires through the house.

The work expected of an AV professional is the installation, maintenance, repair, and upgrades for new products for visual and sound electronics. Components you will be called upon to install include:

- Home entertainment centers
- TV/video
- Sound systems/audio
- Home security/protection
- Intercom/baby monitors
- Telecommunications/phone, Internet, cable

Technology geeks who love reading about the latest in electronics and audio systems are good candidates for working in this business. Especially important are problem-solving abilities and being able to figure things out independently.

Part of your competition will come from companies that retail products to consumers and utilities that provide the monthly connectivity like Comcast, AT&T, Dish Network, and ADT. These companies have direct access to the customers at the point of sale of the equipment or connection. Geek Squad, with its partnership with and presence in all Best Buy locations, has successfully added audio/visual installation and repairs to their core computer troubleshooting services. Geek Squad has done an excellent job of promoting its brand; it is also a great business model for an independent sole proprietor.

All of their pricing is clearly identified at www.geeksquad.com.

Equipment and Supplies

Hand tools with a few specialized items are all you need to get started in the AV installation business, plus a basic knowledge of wiring techniques and simple carpentry ($150). If you want to augment your skill set you can take classes at your local community college or technical school.

A laptop computer ($450 and up) is a must-have for use at customer sites. So much information on electronics is available via the Internet. You will want to have access to various sites for repair and installation information as you are doing the work.

Bonus Point

Most of your customers will be one-time installations, which will require you to schedule jobs at new customer locations every day. Consider getting a GPS devise—it will reduce the amount of time you spend hunting for directions and pulling off to the side of the road to look at a map on your way to a new customer. The investment, starting at $200 for an intro-level Garmin GPS, will have a rapid payback by making your travel time direct and efficient.

Estimating the Time Commitment

You can handle many simple, one-component installations in a site visit of one to two hours. Jobs that involve several different items, such as a home-entertainment center, will require an additional planning visit, usually an hour long, to evaluate the type of home construction, room acoustics, access for wire routing, and locating the sources of electrical power and cable and telephone outlets. Most companies in the higher end of this industry charge a minimum of $100 for the planning site visit. In the early stage of your business, you could consider waiving an evaluation fee for jobs over a certain dollar amount ($1,000 or more).

Pricing and Payments

You will find pricing based on a per-job, per-component installed basis (a la Geek Squad) but most AV equipment installers use an hourly rate including a flat fee for travel time (we call this the showing-up fee, anywhere from $35 to $100). Rates run the gamut from $25 to $100 per hour. Originally a service for the high-income home-owner, in more recent years the market has expanded greatly so that any consumer of a large, flat-screen TV with surround sound is a potential customer. The more competitive your rates, the broader your market appeal, and the more quickly you will build up a customer base. (See Chapter 3 for tips on researching your competition and pricing techniques.)

This business is a good candidate for taking credit card payments. As your schedule books up you can require online payments in order to make an appointment. This prevents you from having unbillable gaps in your day from no-shows and cancellations. You should be paid for your services before you leave the customer's home.

Special Requirements

You should have a solid understanding of the building codes of your local jurisdiction in order to stay in compliance and apply for any permits that may be required. Most states do not require a professional license to do audio or cable wiring, but you should check with your secretary of state. Any work that involves the electrical box may require you to work with a licensed electrician.

This business is a perfect fit for a servicemaster.com affiliation for getting a web presence and lead source established for a fair price. Infocomm International is the leading nonprofit association serving the professional AV communications industry worldwide. The organization offers three AV certification programs to its members (see www. infocomm.org).

10

Interior Design Services

In This Chapter

- How incorporating feng shui into your design services can help attract abundance to your life

- Focusing on the most popular rooms for home improvements

- Taking your interior design talents to a professional level

- Selling window coverings with pizzazz and energy efficiency combined

The housing market has cooled from its peak in 2006, but you would never know it from the proliferation of home design shows on cable TV. In some ways, people's need to improve the house they have (rather than sell it at a loss) has even fed into this trend. With some natural talent for design, a well-conceived business plan, and possibly some online courses taken in your spare time, you can be on your way to a successful interior design business.

There are many variations on the theme of interior designer, and we represent a broad spectrum in this chapter. The interest in feng shui and its influence on interior home design and décor continues to grow in this country. Kitchen and bath renovations are still considered the best investment a homeowner can make—and the ones for which homeowners are most likely to call in a professional designer. With more Americans choosing to remain in their houses, and an active market of first-time homeowners thanks to the lowest home prices in decades, businesses like interior decorating, reupholstery, custom draperies, window shades, and closet upgrades will be great ways to tap into the homeowner dollars.

"Americans in general are still embracing the idea of completing home-improvement projects despite this difficult economic period," says Scott Marden, director of marketing research for Vertis Communications, a Baltimore-based provider of marketing and related services to leading retail and consumer services companies.

Feng Shui Consultant

Estimated startup costs: $1,000

Estimated first-year revenue: $30,000–$50,000

Feng shui, in a design application, is about creating positive (healing) energy and reaping the benefits right in one's home or work environment. The words *feng shui* literally mean "wind" and "water." The design is based on ancient Chinese concepts centered on the Five Elements: water, wood, fire, Earth, and metal.

A feng shui design approach has applications in a variety of settings in addition to a prospective customer's residence. It also is used in office organization (see Chapter 12) and home staging (see Chapter 7). Since a great deal of emphasis is placed on feng shui as it relates to financial well-being, office space design and redesign is a large part of this market. Many well-known individuals, such as Paula Abdul, have publicized the feng shui-ing of their work places and the resulting benefits to their good fortunes.

Feng shui design is a good fit for a creative, design-oriented individual with a strong belief in directing one's own energy and life choices. Feng shui can be the basis for a standalone business once you are established as an expert in the field. Initially, most feng shui consultants add this as an extra to their existing work in office organization, home staging, interior design, or even yoga practice. It is not merely a mystical approach to furniture arrangement, but a style choice that fits in nicely with the concepts of decluttering and other disciplines where simplification and minimalism are employed.

Equipment and Supplies

If you haven't already studied feng shui philosophy and techniques, plan on taking an online course. This will give you the education and understanding you need to start your business, as well as a certificate of training from one of several centers around the country. Several websites boast that they are the premier feng shui school in North America. Since your customers are not likely to know the difference in the various schools or programs, do your research to find a program that best suits your interest and cost and travel constraints. You can choose between online and on-site courses. Certification programs cost anywhere from $500 to $1,000 depending on the school, institute, or individual offering the program. You will have to limit your certification choices to the lower end of the cost spectrum to keep your startup low cost.

Estimating the Time Commitment

Many feng shui experts offer free consultations to attract prospective customers, ranging from a 15-minute phone call to 1-hour on-site sessions. Review the office organization section in Chapter 12 for in-depth suggestions on how to kick off your marketing efforts, utilizing practice sessions with friends and family, a website photo gallery of before and after shots, and regular blog postings. It could take anywhere from 6 to 12 months for this startup to get to a positive cash flow because of the unique nature of the service. Those experts who make it beyond the startup phase are thrilled to be doing something they love for a living, so hang in there if this appeals to you.

Work sessions with customers range from two-hour meetings, resulting in a written or verbal report of recommendations, to a group of sessions when an entire home or office suite is being redesigned.

Pricing and Payments

Like any designer fee range, feng shui experts have hourly rates that start at $50 per hour all the way to $195 per hour or $1,000 per day. Much depends on the reputation of the person performing the services and the geographic location. With time and good marketing, this fee range would provide a very respectable income even if you only managed to bill customers 20 hours a week.

You should expect payment at the end of the first consultation, with a written agreement for timing of payments for any further work you do.

Special Requirements

Prospects who are interested in feng shui consulting will be drawn to reading a blog and an expert's virtual community of like-minded users. To broaden your reach in the marketplace, having your own website with relevant content and links to related websites will help bring you attention and subsequent business from readers who seek out your services.

Kitchen and Bath Designer

Estimated startup costs: $500–$1,000

Estimated first-year revenue: $40,000–$60,000

All homeowners aspire to have a beautiful designer kitchen and bath, but few have the confidence or talent to manage a design on their own. Years ago, access to high-end fixtures and construction materials was limited to the trade or designer community. This has changed over the last 20 years, and now almost anything is available to today's consumer. You don't need to have credentials from the American Institute of Architecture (AIA) or the American Society of Interior Designers (ASID) on your business card to have access to distributors of fixtures and appliances at all price levels.

With some natural talent for design, a well-conceived business plan, and possibly some online courses taken in your spare time, you can be on your way to a successful kitchen and bath design business. A designer is responsible for taking customers' ideas, refining and adding to them with suggestions, and drawing out a design plan to follow during the renovation phase. Typically, designers stick to the planning stage of the project and avoid getting involved with managing the installation. Once the plans are delivered, you move on to your next assignment.

A kitchen and bath designer will have to be well-schooled in current design fashions, have a good eye for form and color, and be knowledgeable about the fixtures available and their price ranges. Even though you may love your concepts for a customer's space, you also have to deal with balancing your design sensibilities with the needs, desires, and budget of the customer. This takes a special kind of creative person, one able to compromise esthetics with good business sense.

Equipment and Supplies

A huge boost to new designers is the advent of affordable design software. Check out a free product by Google called SketchUp, available for free download at www.google.com/sketchup. You will also need a good printer to generate copies of your design for your customers. Although you can buy one for just under $1,000, you can also consider an alternative approach—using a company that you can send your files to via e-mail and pick the prints up on your way to meet with your client. (See the Appendix for print shop links.)

If you are not inclined to create your own drawings, or don't have the time to learn a new software program, you can use a service that provides finished plans in digital format, such as CadKitchenPlans.com. According to Gerry Snapke, Cad Kitchen Plans president, "… designers can play up the 'wow' factor during presentations by unrolling large, architectural-style renderings for clients. When these uniquely stylized renderings hit the table, they will serve as further validation to clients that they have chosen the right kitchen and bath specialist."

Estimating the Time Commitment

Kitchen and bath design is a competitive market, with much of the competition coming from bigger companies like Home Depot, Lowe's, and large kitchen and bath cabinet distributors who offer design services for a fee. These companies will entice customers with an offer to apply the design-fee payment to the future purchase of the cabinets and fixtures from their showroom. That said, you still have an opportunity to make a place for yourself in the market. This is not a business you can quickly ramp up. You will spend several months concentrating on intense marketing efforts through networking groups, speaking engagements, involvement in your community, and an effective Internet site.

If you position yourself as a local blogger who has information and guidance to offer, you will bring a lot of traffic to your site, and win business early on from customers who appreciate your online presence. Entering local design contests, building an e-mail distribution list for sending newsletters, and even free consultations to influential individuals can help you get your name better known and bring you some business.

Pricing and Payments

Fees for design services run from $50 to $150 per hour. If you're just starting out, especially if you don't have any of the usual credentials, definitely start at the lower fee. You will need to budget time for two to three visits to the client site. The first one to take measurements, talk about the intended use for the space, what kind of cooking they do, how much time they spend in the bath and/or kitchen, and what amount of storage space will make them happy. For the best results, create something for the client that accommodates all the items important to them in an easily accessible way. This is the most life-changing part of kitchen and bath redesign for the customer.

During the initial client meeting, review your client's options for working with you. If you have some lower and higher cost options that involve more or less of your time, let the client decide how much to spend. You want to give yourself plenty of time to create the space and the drawings, so be sure to add an extra cushion to your fee estimate. Bring an adequate document to use for a contract, with blanks you can fill in with the client. Leave with a signed contract, retainer, and clients who are excited to be working with you.

Special Requirements

The National Kitchen and Bath Association offers certification programs for novice designers and membership at various levels for affordable annual dues ($150 per year for an associate member).

The American Society of Interior Design (ASID) is a well-known entity in the interior design world. You need at least a technical school education to qualify as a professional member, but they do have other membership options available. ASID are worthwhile letters to have on your business card and marketing materials.

Investigate your options for a networking website referral service. This will be your best bet for generating leads early on. If you lack formal training, you can consider one of dozens of designer certification programs available for online study. Sheffield Design School offers a "go at your own pace" interior design program for $1,200, with a monthly payment plan over the first year.

Faux Painting

Estimated startup costs: $1,000

Estimated first-year revenue: $35,000–$60,000

Faux painting generally refers to a decorative style of painting that simulates other materials, such as wallpaper, plaster, wood, and marble. There are many different styles of faux painting, which has grown in popularity in the last two decades since it is easier and cheaper to apply than wallpaper and far more versatile. Whereas wallpaper requires hours for removal, faux-painted surfaces can be changed with minimal wall preparation and priming.

Faux painters earn significantly more per hour than a regular house painter, since their work is more time consuming and specialized. Skill levels range from the beginner (usually a homeowner taking on a project in a smaller room or hallway), to the highly skilled artisan trained in the Italian styles of *trompe l'oeil* (painting that "fools the eye") and wood graining.

Anyone can learn faux painting if they have a reasonably steady hand and enough patience to rework any areas that don't turn out right the first time. There are far fewer faux finishing painters than regular house painters, and it's rare to find a professional who does both. This makes for a great potential pairing of businesses that can refer work to one another, making established house-painting companies a great referral source for new faux finishing businesses. With home décor trends focusing on going bolder with colors (watch any home-staging show to see how "out" the all-white walls of a home for sale has become), this is an excellent time to start a faux finishing business.

Equipment and Supplies

Starter kits are available including paints, brushes, sponges, and sample boards for $600 and up (www.fauxpaintingproducts.com). To build confidence in your skills, consider taking a course; you can take classes from basic to advanced at home-improvement centers and community art centers. More advanced classes are offered at specialty studios around the country, such as the Faux Finishing School in Louisville, Kentucky (www.fauxfinish.com). Ralph Lauren in New York (www.ralphlaurenhome.com) offers a one week program for $1,000 that provides you with an RL certification on completion.

You will also need a ladder and dropcloths, as discussed in Chapter 9. Plan on including your paint supplies in your bids to your customers, and getting enough money when the contract is signed to cover the purchase of the specific colors and glazes you will need for each job.

Estimating the Time Commitment

Your requests for bids will come from people who have seen a certain technique somewhere else and want you to duplicate it exactly. A few customers will want to work with you to create a unique finish for their home or office. Custom work is always billed at a *much* higher fee than a standard finish. You want to give yourself enough time and money in your estimate to cover the extra work and aggravation that is much more likely with a custom assignment. You will need to include time in your bid for working on sample boards for your customer's approval before you begin the job.

Faux finishes are classified from basic (sponging and ragging) to the complex (hand-painted murals); it is common to find pricing escalating accordingly. A professional who will do sponging for $5 per square foot will charge $25 or more per square foot for a Venetian plaster effect.

During your startup phase, decide which types of finishing you are going to offer, and practice timing yourself on walls in your home. Do some painting for friends and associates who will help you get the word out about your business. Whether you price by the square foot or by the hour, you need to develop a method for estimating how much time to budget for each job. At first, give yourself two to three days for all the paperwork, purchasing, and preparation for even a small job.

> **Snags**
>
> Keep in mind that the work you are doing is quite physical; six hours including set-up and clean-up should be as much as you try to accomplish.

The pace of your initial growth will depend on word of mouth from the jobs you complete. Have a clause in your bid or contract that includes your right to photograph the completed project for your portfolio. If possible, put one or more of your practice pieces in commercial spaces like a popular coffeehouse or restaurant—this is a great way to advertise your business with sweat equity instead of startup dollars.

Pricing and Payments

As mentioned above, pricing is quoted by the hour, by the job, or by the square foot. You will have to research the most common pricing method in your area. Experienced faux painters target their earnings to be between $350 and $400 for a six-hour work day. An excellent resource for starting a faux painting business is Rebecca Pittmen's *How to Start a Faux Painting or Mural Business: A Guide to Earning Money in the Decorative Arts.*

Special Requirements

Founded in 1984, the International Decorative Artisans League (IDAL) is an international nonprofit organization dedicated to the promotion and preservation of the art of stenciling and related decorative painting. Membership provides opportunities for artistic and professional growth through education, certification, public awareness, and networking. Membership for a home-based business runs $75 annually.

Reupholstering, Slipcover, and Drapery Construction

Estimated startup costs: $700–$1,000

Estimated first-year revenue: $35,000–$50,000

Sewing on a professional level requires a great deal of experience. Starting a reupholstery, slipcover, or drapery business is a solid money-making idea if you have made any of these a hobby in your past. The reupholstery and furniture-repair industry has experienced a strong uptick in the last two decades and has been growing significantly. Specializing in reupholstery services for autos, RVs, and boats can generate additional income (at higher hourly or per-project rates) for a furniture reupholstery business.

There are many sources for custom draperies, but window treatments will always be an interior design item that homeowners spend money on. It is important to know a great deal about fabrics. You want to be able to assist your customers with selecting fabrics that will enhance the beauty of their rooms or furniture. You want fabric that will make your workmanship look its very best. Trying to do a good job with a delicate or difficult fabric can have unhappy results: a poor end product with ruined fabric that needs to be replaced. A customer will expect the finished product to make the room look like new.

Equipment and Supplies

We assume that you already own a special heavy-duty sewing machine that you can use in your startup phase, along with a fabric steamer. If you are reupholstering furniture, you are going to need a truck or van large enough to pick up and deliver pieces to your customers. To save the expense of acquiring a vehicle, you can consider making arrangements with a third-party delivery service and adding it to the cost of the project. Either way, you should be charging for your traveling expenses.

Your startup budget will not be large enough to afford sample books of fabrics or any quantity of fabric in stock. Inventory is simply too costly to acquire and maintain. Your business plan should require that materials be supplied by the customer. In the interior design profession, it is quite common for furniture to be ordered COM— customer's own material.

Additional items needed in a professional workroom include:

♦ Large cutting table ($150)

♦ Sawhorses for holding the furniture up where it'll be easier to work with (2 for $60)

- Small tools such as good scissors, staple guns, rubber mallet and hammer, and button-maker ($150)

- Reasonable supplies of cloth welt, foam, cotton, dacron (pillow-stuffing), zippers, needles, and threads ($250)

- Stains for touching up scratched wooden furniture frames ($50)

Several online businesses sell the items you need to get started and have lots of helpful information for newcomers to the reupholstery business. See links included in the Appendix for resources.

> **Bonus Point** _____
>
> Take the extra time to clean up the frame of the furniture and apply scratch remover and polish to the wood surfaces. You want the whole piece to look beautiful and garner compliments to give your customers the chance to rave about your work to their friends.

Estimating the Time Commitment

Although it will take some time to build up a clientele, there are many different avenues for networking your services. Homeowners hire upholsterers or drapery makers directly. Restaurants, offices, furniture showrooms, antique dealers, interior designers, and don't forget home-staging specialists are all great referral sources for potential business. Most of your competition will price by the project. You can still compute your project pricing based on an hourly rate. Draperies are often priced based on the yardage of the fabric and window sizes. Upholsterers use charts of basic furniture shapes (sofas, wingback chairs, loveseats, and so on) to convey basic pricing to customers. Consider fabric selection and the condition of the frame in the pricing equation as well.

Snags _____

Be enough of a perfectionist that your work has a professional look, but don't be overly obsessive to the point of being unable to let a project go. The only way to make money as a sewing professional is to combine quality with time management.

Pricing and Payments

Pricing is quoted by the piece or the project (for example, $900 for a sofa, $500 for a basic set of drapes) but it is based on an hourly rate. Determine the number of hours on a project-by-project basis. Your time investment will be affected by variables such as length and number of cushions for a sofa and type of fabric and number of panels for draperies. You will have to research the most common pricing method in your area. Hourly rates are between $35 and $75 per hour, with the higher range charged by larger, high-end design workshops.

Most upholsterers and custom drapery workrooms require the customer to leave a deposit when the project is begun. The balance is paid upon the completion and delivery of the work.

Special Requirements

Certified Workroom Professional and Certified Window Treatment Consultant are two of the professional designations that are available through the Window Coverings Association of America (WCAA).

The Custom Home Furnishings Academy (CHFA) is for individuals looking to begin a home-based career in custom décor furnishings as well as established professionals seeking a higher level of sewing instruction to increase their skill-set. They offer on-site and online classes. Go to www.chfschool.com for more information.

Having a dedicated website with a great-looking photo gallery will go a long way to attracting business. Upholstery and draperies are visual crafts. Prospects will see items you have done for other customers and start imagining your work in their homes.

Window Blind Sales and Installation

Estimated startup costs: $500–$1,000

Estimated first-year revenue: $40,000–$60,000

Selling window treatments encompasses several popular trends all at once. Foremost is home décor and design. All those large homes with tons of windows built during the housing boom of the last 20 years have created an enormous market of windows that need covering and recovering. The growing focus on energy efficiency gives window blind and shutter sellers a one-two punch in their sales presentations to customers. With some moderate math skills you can calculate how the energy savings over time will pay for beautification now. The U.S. Department of Energy recommends closing window coverings during hot summer days to minimize solar heat gain and to keep a house warm in winter months (www.energysavers.gov/seasonal/tips_summer.html).

Variety in window shades has exploded since the early years of white vinyl roller models or wooden-slat Venetian blinds. Today's versions include multitasking cellular (honeycomb) shades that filter light, improve energy efficiency, and eliminate computer screen glare. Motorized shades are the latest rage, not only because they appeal to our remote control–crazed society, but also because they have an energy savings benefit. With timers and sun-activation controls on your shades, you can put them to work lowering your utility bills even when you are away from home!

Your first decision is whether to do both sales and installations or to delegate the physical task of installing the blinds to another independent service provider. As your sales grow, this decision will be made for you—you will want to do more selling and hand over the installation to someone else. But starting out, if you are handy with tools and have basic skills, you will want to learn as much about installation as you can, to make sure when you delegate the task it is done to your standards and specifications. Even though a sale is already complete by the time the installation takes place, you always want this final contact with your customer to seal their loyalty. The most profitable customers are the ones who tell their friends and keep coming back for more.

You will need to develop relationships with window blind wholesalers and manufacturers to supply you with quality products. If you have significant competition locally, it may be difficult to acquire agreements with the top-line window blind manufacturers, which would not make this the best choice for a startup for you.

Equipment and Supplies

You will need tools for measuring and a toolbox and ladder for installations. Your primary startup costs will be your marketing and website, your best ways of penetrating the market.

The advantage to this business model is that, even though you are selling a product, you are not expected to carry an inventory of items. You will be dealing strictly with custom-ordered window blinds, individually measured and made by the manufacturer for each of your customers, and each of your customers' windows. When you take an order, you will ask for a deposit of at least 50 percent of the total sale. This will more than cover the deposit your vendor will require to place your order.

Estimating the Time Commitment

This is essentially a sales business. You are selling a product by finding interested buyers, making appointments, and taking sample books of photos and materials to prospective customers' homes. If you have great sales skills already developed from selling products for another company, you have the ability to do this. If sales are not your cup of tea, this business is probably not a good choice for you.

Good salespeople develop their own benchmarks for activities that will keep them on track for hitting their sales goals. For example, say you get five leads a day from people who fill out the form on your website asking for more information. If you track the percentage of those inquiries that turn into appointments, you can figure out how many leads you need each week to get 10 in-home appointments. If you sell to 30 percent of the customers to whom you make presentations, and you average $1,000 in *gross margin* for each sale, you can meet a goal of $3,000 a week in your share of the total revenue.

def•i•ni•tion

Gross margin is your share of the money from sales after you pay for the product you sell. The formula to keep in mind is:

revenue − cost of goods sold = gross margin

The term **gross profit** is frequently used interchangeably with gross margin.

Pricing and Payments

As an independent reseller of window blinds and shades, expect to negotiate separate contracts with each manufacturer or line distributor. In general, you will base your pricing on a 100 percent markup—this means taking the cost you pay for the product and multiplying it by two. So if an order costs you $250, you charge $500 to the customers.

You will need to accept credit cards to be competitive with online window treatment companies.

Special Requirements

There are no professional organizations dedicated to window blind and shade businesses. However, there is opportunity for window treatment business owners to participate as members of the Window Coverings Association of America. See the section on draperies for more information.

Interior Decorating

Estimated startup costs: $500–$1,000

Estimated first-year revenue: $35,000–$60,000

Even as home-design shows and magazines inspire more people to beautify their homes, the trend in do-it-yourself projects is on the decline. This leaves the field wide open for new interior decorators.

Customers expect that you will come to their home, define the scope of the project (the whole house, or perhaps just the family room), and come up with an evaluation. At this point you would present a contract for agreed-upon services for them to sign, with you receiving a retainer to start. Your next step would be to generate some drawings that would outline the furniture to be purchased for a recommended room layout. After approval from the customer, you would start ordering the items to complete the decorating plan.

You will be expected to have a business license and a sales tax resale number. In order to purchase items as a designer, you must prove to the vendor that you are buying on behalf of a customer with the intent to resell the merchandise to them. It then becomes your responsibility to bill, collect, and remit sales tax on the goods to your state department of revenue.

Interior decorating is highly competitive, but if you have a passion for decorating and have a home that has won you compliments from your friends and family, this is definitely a business idea within your reach.

Equipment and Supplies

You need the same small tools that are required of other professionals in the design industry. In addition, a color wheel and a digital camera will be very useful tools. Taking pictures of "finds" to e-mail to your clients will allow you to fulfill your primary responsibility—doing the legwork and finding the items they need to create the perfect décor for their homes.

You need a business card for entry into exclusive showrooms and a sales tax reseller's certificate. If you want to use your own drawings, you can use a free program like Google SketchUp. (See the earlier section on kitchen and bath design for more details.) For about $99, you can purchase a design program specifically for home decorating.

Estimating the Time Commitment

Spend your startup time reaching out to wholesale and "trade only" distributors to develop a pool of easily accessible and reliable suppliers. You don't want to reinvent the wheel with every new client. Certainly you'll have ongoing opportunities to explore new suppliers and furniture lines, but in order to deliver a finished project to your customer, you need a roadmap to follow when you begin soliciting business.

Dedicate serious efforts to networking with other home-improvement service providers with whom you can exchange referrals, such as painters, general contractors, professional home organizers, and so on. Decorators often build very successful businesses working their way through the homes of neighbors, church acquaintances, volunteer organizations, and one or two other contractors. Using your decorating talents to do a model home, a clubhouse in a residential complex, or your spouse's office are great ways to get samples of your work into high-traffic environments.

Estimating time for each customer's project is going to vary dramatically based on many factors, such as scope of the project (one room vs. an entire house) and personality of the client (some will okay everything you suggest, others will want lots of options). You will have to play this by ear in deciding how many projects you can take on at one time. The upside is that you can always shop for more than one customer at any particular vendor, so there will be some built-in efficiencies to working multiple jobs at the same time.

Pricing and Payments

The traditional method for billing customers is on a cost-plus basis. Traditionally, decorators invoice the customer for the actual cost of the item, say an ottoman, and add a fixed percentage to cover their fee. Typical fee percentage is 20 percent. Here's an example of how you would bill for your time and knowledge:

You buy an ottoman:	$500
You add sales tax at 7 percent:	$35
You add 20 percent of pretax cost for your fee:	$100
Total invoice to customer:	$635

You will remit the $35 sales tax when you send in your monthly or quarterly sales tax return, pay the $500 to the vendor, and deposit the $100 fee into your business bank account.

To work on the revenue portion of your business plan, use your experience decorating your own home to estimate a range of cost for different rooms in a home, office, or clubhouse. Don't let the perfect be the enemy of the good. We don't expect you to hit any exact numbers. We just want you to get an idea of how many projects you have to complete in order to make a certain income for yourself. If you are aiming for $50,000 in annual income for yourself, you will need to have annual projects in excess of $250,000 to generate enough fees to cover your expenses (which won't be very much) and pay yourself what you need to meet your personal obligations.

Special Requirements

Having a photo portfolio of your projects, whether in a book or on a website, is an excellent marketing tool. Similar to the recommendations in the kitchen and bath design section, ASID membership will add a great deal of clout to your business card. You can take one of many online design and decorator courses (such as Sheffield Design) that will give you a certificate of completion. They are good confidence builders, but only necessary if you feel the need to add to your skill set.

Closet Design and Installation

Estimated startup costs: $350–$650

Estimated first-year revenue: $35,000–$50,000

Closet design services have taken a hit along with the decline of new construction, since many of the newer homes were being built with designer closet accessories. However, according to a May 2009 article in *Closet* magazine, "the bulk of the market-place continues to be smaller firms." In 2008 "three-quarters of [closet design] companies had sales below $1 million."

Many closet design companies have expanded their offerings to include makeovers for home or commercial offices, laundry rooms, home entertainment units, and garages. While the larger companies, like California Closets, are franchise operations that install products manufactured by the parent company, many small closet design and installation companies purchase the components they need from manufacturers. Therefore there is no need for inventory on hand. They simply order what they need by the job.

You will need a calm, patient demeanor and the ability to be a creative designer, good salesman, effective customer service representative, and skilled installer. Many closet design companies have one owner/employee, and this can be a difficult challenge for someone who is used to doing one specific type of job all day long. The upside is that as a solo owner, you can make a good living in this business with fewer than one job per week. See the pricing section for more on the numbers.

Equipment and Supplies

You will need a basic carpenter's toolbox to be able to competently install a closet system. The beauty of this industry is that the ease of installation has improved greatly over the last several years, since so many products have been created for the DIY market. Since you need to already have basic skills in order to install, we assume that you own most of the tools you will need to get started. An alternative choice for this business is the same as with window blind installation: you can focus on sales and hire out the installation work or partner with a carpenter looking to expand his recurring projects.

To get started you will need contacts with vendors who will sell you closet components at below retail cost. There are many companies in the marketplace, so don't get discouraged if you have to knock on a few doors. ClosetMaid and EasyClosets.com are manufacturers that have open territory dealers without a royalty requirement. These companies sell direct to installers who use the manufacturer's name in their advertising. To get more information, go to www.closetmaid.com or see the Appendix for more source suggestions.

Estimating the Time Commitment

Anticipate a few months to build up this business. If you are running the entire operation by yourself, you will have many responsibilities to handle—set aside one or two days for installations, two days for sales, and a day in the office for purchasing and paperwork. You will have to make free consultation meetings a part of your sales process, since you can't bid a job without seeing it. You also need to be mindful of any prep work to be done before the closet components are installed. All painting, repairs to walls, new carpeting, and so on needs to be completed before the new closet is assembled and attached to the closet surfaces. This will give you a great opportunity to partner with painting and carpentry contractors who can refer business to you.

Pricing and Payments

Generally speaking, the markup on closet components, including installation, is a minimum of 100 percent. You will need to set benchmarks for the number of systems you install per month to project your revenue stream. Keep in mind that, for every $1,000 in charges to your customers, your share is $500, with the remainder going to the system manufacturer. You have to allocate a portion of the $500, or your gross margin, to pay other business expenses before you cover your own salary.

Like any custom design project, ask for a deposit of 50 percent up front when the order is placed. It is common to run the charge for the second and final payment when delivery is scheduled.

Special Requirements

Having your own company website will help draw a lot of prospects to your door. A smart way to market your services is by comparing your pricing to a do-it-yourself system. In many instances, you can offer a prospective customer a professionally installed and designed closet system for only 25 percent more than it would cost to do it themselves. This is probably the best motive for hiring a closet installation specialty company: why do it yourself if the marginal difference is under $1,000?

Chapter 11

Exterior Design Services

In This Chapter

- ◆ The home design fad spills over to the outdoors
- ◆ Constructing the hot items for America's backyards
- ◆ Profiting from building good fences and party-sized decks

The growing obsession with all things designer is spreading rapidly to the outdoor areas of American homes. Homeowners are staying home more in the down economy (the word *staycation* has just been officially added to Webster's Dictionary). They are investing in improvements, both interior and exterior, in place of buying second homes and larger primary residences. The American Institute of Architects reports an increase in structural design and construction of outdoor projects.

This trend bodes well for those interested in working in exterior design and installation businesses. Landscape design is still very much in demand, as people seek guidance for creating or improving their gardens. Hardscape construction is wildly popular as Americans choose to participate in building a more eco-friendly world. People are moving away from the easy do-it-yourself projects to ones that include things like recirculating fountains, outdoor lighting, and plans that help with low maintenance and low water usage. There are large and small opportunities, especially for those with some experience and talent in the landscape and hardscape industries.

Landscape and Garden Design

Estimated startup costs: $500–$750

Estimated first-year revenue: $30,000–$60,000

If you are a passionate gardener with a strong working knowledge of planting and maintaining a wide variety of trees, shrubs, and flowers, you have an opportunity to develop your hobby into your profession. There are many highly trained and formally educated landscape architects in this field, but their focus is on large commercial projects like office complexes and public parks. The average homeowner looking for someone to help them create a welcoming outdoor environment is not prepared to pay the fees of a landscape architect. Rather, they want to find someone who has the knowledge they lack to get them started with a plan, and guide them through the process of implementing a design.

A landscape plan includes the conceptual rendering of planting recommendations and designs for a specific area of a property. It can be for a small garden area or an entire front and back yard. It should be detailed to the point that a contractor or the homeowner can use it in the implantation phase. It should specify the types and positioning of plants along with any hardscape materials and focal points (such as a fountain or birdbath). Although you don't need a degree in horticulture to be successful as a professional landscape designer, you do need an understanding of the sun and shade tolerance of the plants you select, drainage, soil conditions, and the amount of maintenance that will be necessary to sustain the design.

Equipment and Supplies

You will need tools for measuring (e.g., a set square, tape measure, string and chalk lines) and sketching out the area to be included in your landscaping plan. Your most important startup investment will be in a software program to create the actual plan drawing. Fortunately, there are many choices for inexpensive landscape design packages. Review your options before selecting the software that seems best for your needs. Plan on spending $80 to $100 to purchase one that will accommodate you in your startup phase. The Better Homes and Gardens website offers a variety of landscape design choices.

Estimating the Time Commitment

Our concept for this business is for design only, although if you love playing in the dirt you can certainly add installation to your contract. You can even develop a complete design-to-garden package. Our focus here, however, is on the design aspect only.

Some designers sell packages of their time for a set fee. This makes it possible to control the amount of time spent for a particular phase of a project. Small gardens for a typical city backyard may be designed in a three-hour session. Other larger projects may take several days of design time. Do your homework and gather input from other, more experienced, professionals on how they budget their time. This is another opportunity for practicing on your own and others' gardens to get your process honed, methodical, and profitable.

This work is very seasonal. Nothing prohibits you from creating a design in the winter months, but people tend to retreat to the interiors of their homes. In the southern states, summers are so brutally hot that it is not possible to plant anything and expect it to live in the heat. Plants need to be installed in the spring and fall if they are to survive. You will need to be able to adapt to an uneven work flow during the year, and be a creative marketer to come up with ways to increase your outreach to potential customers during the slower seasons.

Pricing and Payments

The hourly rate varies by experience and locale, but is usually in the $50 to $100 range. As mentioned above, many landscape designers offer packages or sessions, say $400 for a four-hour design session. For a smaller garden and a homeowner on a budget, this is a chance to get professional input and a hand-drawn plan as a starting point.

You should be paid at the end of any initial consultation session, even if the customer indicates a desire for more work. Use a contract to outline future services to be provided, a time frame for delivery of the project, and the date payment is due.

Special Requirements

A website will be a very helpful marketing tool, especially with new and younger homeowners who do all their shopping and research online.

You can give yourself the chance to network with other professionals and add more credentials by joining one of several professional organizations for landscape designers. The Association of Professional Landscape Design has an associate membership for $200 a year.

Bonus Point _____

> To help promote your business, offer to plant some beautiful flower containers for local interior décor retailers with your business card attached. This is a great way to build rapport and get your work seen in your neighborhood.

Hardscape and Landscape Installation

Estimated startup costs: $500–$750

Estimated first-year revenue: $40,000–$50,000

Objects and materials in a landscape design made from rock, gravel, concrete, brick, or metal are referred to as hardscape. This term also encompasses fencing and decking, which we cover in the upcoming section. Anything from a wooden structure like a gazebo to a slate patio or walkway are included in the hardscape portion of a landscape plan. This business requires some basic knowledge in landscaping and an understanding of all that is involved with moving and stabilizing large amounts of Earth, drainage, and materials construction.

If you have enjoyed doing your own hardscaping projects at home, you can start out marketing yourself for smaller projects. You will need to check with the state professional licensing requirements for outdoor construction. You should refer work to experienced contractors when it involves heavy machinery.

As "zero-scaping" gains popularity, the landscape industry has responded with greener installations, those requiring less water and chemicals that still serve the purpose of creating an outdoor living space. This trend is evident in the growth of decorative stamped and stained concrete structures; backyard kitchens; and great rooms, patios, and terraces.

Equipment and Supplies

You will need the same measurement tools included in the landscape design section, along with some basic installation items like a wheelbarrow, lumber for creating clean edges (2×4's), gloves, safety glasses, pick, shovel, rake, broom, and a sledge hammer or mallet for removing existing materials. In the beginning, plan on renting the bigger equipment on an as-needed basis, such as a roto-tiller, gas-powered plate compactor, and guillotine-type stone cutter or masonry saw with diamond tip blade for more precise stone cuts. Your basic startup costs for small tools should be around $250.

Since you are installing permanent structures, you want to make sure you have complete agreement from your customer and use a detailed contract to outline, in writing, the understanding for the project design (backed up with a detailed drawing), materials to be used (included in a bid sheet), and timing of the project and payment schedule. This is not like softscaping with plants; you cannot easily satisfy an unhappy customer with a simple change. Any changes will cost you money and probably mean a job with zero profit, or even a loss.

Pricing and Payments

Many hardscaping companies use the same pricing structure as a general contractor. They compile the bid including materials and labor and add an overall percentage for their participation in the process. The industry wide percentage is 15 percent of total costs.

Also, like a general contractor, you will want to get paid based on percentage of completion of the project. You will need payments from the customer in order to pay for your labor and materials without having to use your own cash.

Special Requirements

Hardscape contractors can earn professional certification from a variety of technical schools and other programs. If you are not already trained in outdoor construction, pursuing a two-year degree or certification from an online or technical school is the best way to advance in this industry. In the meantime, supplementing your hardscape income with landscape maintenance is a common approach for other professionals. This is not only to support them through the learning process, but because this business is so seasonal, especially in the northern United States. Most hardscapers push snow or develop another part-time business to help them through the slow winter months.

Fencing, Decks, and Play Structures

Estimated startup costs: $700–$950

Estimated first-year revenue: $40,000–$50,000

With the growing interest in outdoor living spaces, the fencing and decking business has become a great way to get involved in exterior designing. If you have basic carpentry skills, a good eye, and a decent toolbox, you can get this business going in time for the next busy summer season.

As a large number of Americans have moved out of the city to suburban subdivisions over the last 30 years, "good fences make good neighbors" has become a more important credo. Many homeowners use custom-built wooden privacy fences to separate themselves from their next-door neighbors. Depending on your skill level, you can start out doing fences and work up to the more complicated decking. Several other outdoor wood structures are a natural addition to the portfolio of a deck and fencing contractor. These include gazebos, hot-tub surrounds, arbors, and pergolas.

Wood is not the only material used for fencing—wrought iron, including security gates, has returned to popularity.

Pressure washing, staining, and sealing decks and fences are good maintenance services to offer to complement your building projects. Once you complete a fence or deck, you have automatically added a future stain or sealing customer to your database.

Equipment and Supplies

To get started in fence and deck design and construction, you will need the same tools as a landscape designer for measurement and planning, along with a good set of basic carpenter's tools. You will also need a posthole digger ($75), pneumatic nail gun and compressor ($200), and a circular saw ($125). Materials for each job can be purchased with your initial payment from your customer.

Estimating the Time Commitment

One factor that will be a major influence on your time commitment to each job is how much authorized permitting you will be required to get; this will depend entirely on where you live. Be aware of any homeowner association restrictions and covenants if your customer lives in an area governed by one. Even though it is the homeowner's responsibility to honor the guidelines in their homeowners' bylaws, building something that is not in compliance can have negative consequences for you and the reputation of your company.

Success Story

Billy S. has been installing fences and decks since 1984. These days he runs one or two crews, but he started out building every project with his own hands. He charges customers $2,000 for a typical fencing job, which represents one day's work for a two-man team. The $2,000 covers his material and labor costs and leaves him with a healthy profit at the end of the day.

Many construction companies build decks and fences; this work is one of the more straightforward construction jobs that can be completed by a sole contractor. You will have to spend time marketing your services and connecting with people who can help you get the word out about your new business. Even though it doesn't pay as well as working directly for a homeowner, contracting out to another general contractor is a good way to grow your reputation in the beginning.

This business can be highly seasonal in certain climates. It is impossible to dig a hole in the ground or work outside in many states during the winter months. People will wait until the first thaw to start planning their upcoming outdoor projects. The best time to start your business would be right after New Year's with a big marketing effort. You want to be ready by spring to actually go out and give bids.

Bonus Point

In warmer climates, the post-holiday season can bring some business activity. One southeastern contractor refers to it as "Christmas puppy season." Apparently, getting a dog for Christmas creates a terrific need for privacy fencing by late January into February.

Pricing and Payments

Many contractors will price by the linear foot for fencing or square feet for decks. Other outdoor structures, like pergolas and gazebos don't readily lend themselves to these formulas. A simple pricing method that is preferred for all types of projects is simply based on the standard general contractor formula:

(Cost of materials + Cost of labor) × +(20 percent of materials and labor costs) = Price to customer

The caveat here is that if you provide the labor, you get paid for that, too. So taking Billy D. as our example, when he works a job he may charge the customer $35 to $50 an hour for his time, with a slightly lower cost for any helper. When he calculates his profit formula, he adds 20 percent to his labor cost to arrive at a final price for his customer. Here's a more detailed calculation:

Labor Costs

Billy D.	$35 × 6 hours = $210
Helper	$25 × 6 hours = $150
Total labor costs	$360
Materials	$840
Total labor and materials	**$1,200**
Profit @ 20 percent	$240
Total price to customer	**$1,440**
Total to Billy D., owner	**$450**

In addition, sales tax and permit fees would be added as required.

There is nothing to keep you from marking up the cost of lumber and labor, especially if you are getting particularly good pricing on the lumber. If you do your own installation, you get to keep both the labor charge and the 20 percent markup.

Special Requirements

Having your own website will help win you leads, but you can also be listed as a professional by geographic location if you join one of the professional organizations for the fence and deck industry. The American Fence Association (AFA) has an annual conference for its members. They are a resource for training classes as well. Membership dues are $500 a year. The North American Deck and Rail Association is another professional organization with annual dues of $350.

Part 4

Personal Touch

Just when you think there can't possibly be any new self-help concepts left to discover, a new book or personality hits the marketplace like a firestorm. Today, we not only have coaches for almost every aspect of our own daily living, we have caretakers for our children from birth through young adulthood, elder care for our parents, and now, overtaking both these areas as the industry of greatest expansion, pet care. Each of these categories has unlimited opportunities for creating rewarding and lucrative startups while making a contribution to the well-being of others.

We are also taking better care of ourselves and spending more than ever on professionals who help us achieve our life goals. Whether with physical fitness, nutrition, beauty, or wardrobes, we cover a variety of business ideas for getting in on this trend of personal care.

Chapter 12

Personal Services

In This Chapter

- ◆ Booming market for organizational and efficiency experts
- ◆ Shopping that pays
- ◆ Home-based administrative services
- ◆ Tailored for you: custom alterations

Selling personal services can take a variety of forms. We are focusing on four types of work that have common characteristics: they are services that people will always need and do not require a formal education, professional licensing, or certification. With the growing trend of home-based businesses, helping business owners organize their home-based offices has become a big business. With the job market growing more competitive all the time and people being less and less inclined to spend an entire afternoon at the mall, personal shopping is a great way to put your love of shopping and fashion to work for you.

Many small business owners working from home would love the help of an efficient assistant but cannot afford a full-time employee. Besides, one goal most people working from home have is to increase their flexibility. This is exceedingly difficult if you commit to keeping someone else busy full-time. What better opportunity for someone with keen secretarial skills to increase their own flexibility than to freelance for several business owners, with none being so dependent that you can't take the two-week vacation you've been dreaming of?

For a taste of something out of the ordinary, we help you put that fancy sewing machine to work. As home-based businesses become more common, there is no longer the requirement that every alteration shop have its own storefront. By eliminating the need for expensive retail space, you can put your creative talents to work making and altering clothes right in your own family room.

Organization and Efficiency Expert

Estimated startup costs: $200–$1,000

Estimated first-year revenue: $50,000–$100,000

At one time relegated to the realm of amusing movie plots (*Cheaper by the Dozen*, *Desk Set*) the role of the office organizer and efficiency expert has become very well accepted in today's business world. There are several very popular cable TV shows about decluttering. Everyone from Oprah to Katie Couric has had their before-and-after office pictures featured on their TV programs. This cache has elevated the level of respect, earning power, and demand for this service.

An organizer's services can range from designing an efficient home office to organizing a cross-town move. Some organizers work on a room-by-room basis for space planning and reorganization. Other specialties include estate organization, improved management of paperwork and computer files, systems for managing personal finances and other records, and/or coaching in time-management and goal-setting. This profession has gotten so popular that it helps to start out with a concept of a particular niche you might want to fill.

In addition to needing the gift of organizing other people's stuff, you need to bring a lot of empathy and patience. This is a relationship-based business. It is important before you enter someone's home that you know where your boundaries are, what work you will do, and what you won't take on.

Equipment and Supplies

Since you will be working on rearranging other people's offices, you don't need much in the way of equipment. You will want to arrive prepared with a methodology to use as you work with your customer. If you need some support, you can consult the numerous books, blogs, videos, and websites that are available on the subject. If you recommend favorite office supplies like Post-It's, multicolored folders, or a labeling device as part of your process, bring these things with you as a convenience to your customer. Plan on adding the cost of these supplies to your customer's invoice.

Estimating the Time Commitment

When starting out with a new customer, you will want to dedicate an entire day to your first session. Eventually you will develop a questionnaire you can use when you set up your new customers' appointments to estimate the number of hours you will need for a specific assignment. Set a minimum session of, say, three hours in length, in order to make your travel and planning time worthwhile. Frequently, the first day will continue into the afternoon. Your customer will get very excited over the results of your work together and want you to keep going. It is common for one assignment to last over a period of a few weeks or even months.

Pricing and Payments

Organizing professionals charge by the hour. The fee can range from $50 to $100 per hour depending upon the credentials, experience, and reputation of the individual consultant. Avoid pricing by the job, especially with new customers, since the length of the project will depend more on the personality of the customer than on the amount of clutter you have been hired to transform. Once you complete a session with a new customer and decide you would enjoy a long-term relationship, you can offer a slight discount on bundled sessions that are purchased with an up-front payment.

Since you will continually be working with many new customers, you will need to have a pay-as-you-go policy. This is best discussed when you set up the appointment. You can set up a merchant account so you can process credit card payments. In the beginning, let your customers know that payment for your services are due in full at the end of each session. This will prevent you from having to spend any time or energy on collections.

Snags

Getting customers to pay up front for a bundle of sessions is great for cash flow. Unfortunately, it requires much more detailed accounting since it is your responsibility to track the hours paid versus the hours used. The last thing you want is a misunderstanding about how much of a balance your customer has for future work to be performed.

Special Requirements

This is an excellent opportunity to use your startup funds for a dedicated website and blog as part of your business launch. The most likely source of initial business will be people seeking organizational help using Internet searches. With the demand for organizational professionals growing each year, a website can start to bring you customers almost immediately. You can use your startup period to create an online portfolio of before-and-after pictures. Offer your services to friends and relatives at a reduced rate or for free. The photos of the makeover will speak volumes for your talents.

You should also consider membership in the National Association of Professional Organizers (NAPO). At a cost of $150 per year, NAPO provides networking opportunities, access to classes, and certification and other benefits. You will get a listing in the NAPO directory, which is made available to the public and can be sorted by zip code. This will give you a searchable web presence in addition to contact with other professionals.

Personal Shopper and Wardrobe Consultant

Estimated startup costs: $200–$1,000

Estimated first-year revenue: $50,000–$100,000

This service seems like the most enjoyable (especially to those who love to shop), but to be successful and make good money you really have to have an eye for fashion, thorough knowledge of your area's better retail clothing stores, and good people skills (lots of patience and a desire to help others look their best). There are dozens of self-study courses that offer information on becoming a personal shopper and/or wardrobe consultant. But there is enough free information available on the Internet that paying for course materials isn't really necessary.

You have many options for packaging yourself as a personal shopper and wardrobe consultant. You can focus on helping people add good-quality items to their wardrobe. Many consultants model their process on extreme makeover shows on TV; their first tactic is visiting the customer's home and doing a complete closet review, which includes bagging a good deal of stuff for Goodwill. There are many opportunities for virtual wardrobe consulting, seminar presentations, and group outings to other cities for intense shopping at hidden boutiques. The first challenge is deciding what your strengths are and how to best package them to maximize your revenue.

Equipment and Supplies

If you include closet and existing wardrobe inventory in your service, you will want to accumulate some simple accessories, like good-quality hangers and dividers for separating colors or clustering outfits. Otherwise, you should plan on investing your startup dollars in marketing materials, including a good web presence. Many wardrobe consultants use blogs to present themselves as experts in their field. This can be done for little out-of-pocket cost but will go a long way to getting your name to the top of the search engine listings.

Like other professionals who help customers present themselves more attractively and confidently, you will want to invest in anything you are lacking in your *own* wardrobe. You can't convince others that you are a shopping expert without looking great yourself.

Estimating the Time Commitment

If you already have an expansive Rolodex and network, you will be ahead of the pack in terms of getting started in your new role as wardrobe consultant. This is a luxury service for many people, and before they commit their hard-earned dollars to paying for your services, they will want to be absolutely sure that you have the skills to help them with their image. It is so much easier to win business with a personal referral in this type of work, since you want your customers to trust your taste and judgment.

Be creative in your marketing to get the word out about your services. Offering free consulting to well-connected friends and influential members of your community is a great way to build references for future paying customers. It will also help you develop your process, identify which aspects of wardrobe consulting and personal shopping you enjoy the most, and determine how much time you need for different kinds of consultations.

Many wardrobe consultants and shoppers sell their services in packages, bundling an initial consult, closet analysis, and reorganization with a timed shopping trip. In the beginning, you might want to consider a free, 30-minute phone consultation for explaining your services to prospective customers.

Pricing and Payments

Wardrobe consultants consistently charge by the hour, with the rate varying depending on geographic location. The range of hourly rates starts from $50 and can go as high as $165 per hour for areas like Manhattan and San Francisco. Consider the amount of time you are going to spend on marketing and client relations in setting your rate. Still, considering the almost nonexistent costs to maintain this business, you should be able to do extremely well once you get started.

There is also a good potential for getting commission payments from the businesses you bring your customers to. Arrange to meet with the boutique owners and retail managers of your favorite shopping establishments to discuss possible commission arrangements before you set your pricing schedule for customers. If you can generate revenue from the clothing stores, you can start out with more reasonable pricing to individuals and build your business up. Once you have a comfortable customer base, you can raise your prices accordingly.

Special Requirements

To avoid false starts and less profitable strategies, take advantage of the numerous websites of your competitors and contact several of them to ask about their success stories. (You'll get the "what not to do" without having to ask.) There is so much variety in this field, you will want some guidance in getting your pricing and service offerings established.

Business-Support Services

Estimated startup costs: $200–$500

Estimated first-year revenue: $30,000–$80,000

One of the best-kept secrets of the business world is that it is not really run by the overpaid team in the C-suite. The people who truly keep this nation's economy going are the administrative workers who actually get things done. If you have always wanted a chance to demonstrate your ability to run the show, now is the time to start your own business-support company and run it right from your very own home office.

Although you can do a good bit of this work at your own desk, this is not exclusively virtual-assistant work (see Chapter 15). Many former corporate executives now working on their own as independent consultants and small businesses need on-site support. Being open to working on-site will differentiate you from a remote virtual assistant. The importance in this distinction is that you will be targeting a different market: a higher level of customer service for what are likely to be more demanding individuals with different needs. The benefit to those with the experience to fill these needs is the higher hourly rate they can earn by physically working in someone else's office. There is also much less competition in this market.

The following is a list of skills that are commonly considered in the category of business-support services:

- Word processing
- Tape transcription
- Phone-in dictation
- Desktop publishing
- Spreadsheet design
- Mail receiving and forwarding
- Packing and shipping
- Database/mailing list management
- Bookkeeping, check preparation, and billing
- Proofreading
- Notary
- Appointment scheduling

One way to think of these services is as a long-term office organizer. If you have worked in support services before, you're familiar with the characteristics of your prospective customer. They will depend on you to keep them on task. This expands your opportunities to provide unlimited services well beyond the traditional secretarial role. You also have the benefit of a potential market that includes the sole proprietor to the largest corporation.

The recent economic downturn has eliminated many jobs, but there is still work that needs to be done by someone, and businesses have figured out that they can successfully outsource many administrative roles at a tremendous cost savings to the company. So if you've lost an administrative office job in the last year, take heart. You have all the skills required to turn your period of unemployment into a successful startup focused on business-support services. You are in a position to have a great income, lots of work, and the flexibility and autonomy you deserve.

Equipment and Supplies

As a startup, you will want to use the computer equipment you already have, perhaps adding one or two new items to enhance your service offering. Postpone any major investment in equipment until you have your first customers. Remember, you will be spending most of your time at client sites; you will be providing services and using the client's equipment.

We assume you already own a computer, printer/copier/scanner, and the basic software you may need to perform some of your duties from your home office. You can look into web-based alternatives to fax machines if you don't already own a fax machine at home.

Estimating the Time Commitment

Your customers may have a hard time estimating their needs and you will have to develop a process for evaluating the time commitment required on a customer-by-customer basis. You will want to set a minimum of at least two hours per visit, since you want to control your travel time. Your goal is to establish a regular client base that will keep you busy as many hours a week as you care to work. Some opportunities will have a clear schedule from the start; for example, two mornings per week to correspond to your customer's office hours. Others will be more interested in matching the time spent with the tasks that need to be accomplished.

Be firm about charging your full rate even on days the customer might not have a full slate of work for you. As you build your customer list, you may easily be able to fill in with short project work when a regular customer's needs are light, but in the beginning it is best to have an agreement with customers that you will be paid based on the time you have committed to them, even if they have not been able to organize a full workload for you.

Pricing and Payments

There will be some market pressure to set different fees based on the type of work you are doing. Increasing your rate with the complexity of work is not to your advantage. You should set an hourly rate commensurate with your experience and skill level. Even the simplest jobs can be done more quickly and efficiently by a more skilled person. There will be a wide pricing range depending on your area of the country and the type of customer, but nationwide the overall range is $15 to $50 per hour. If you are especially good at spreadsheet design or PowerPoint presentations, you can get a higher rate for those kinds of projects.

Use a weekly payment schedule for new customers; present an invoice for hours worked before you leave and wait while the client writes you a check. Eventually you can negotiate this depending upon the length of the commitment and the amount of time you are working each week. You want to consider your weekly cash flow to meet your obligations as well as protecting yourself from potential nonpaying customers.

Bonus Point

If possible, you should arrange to get paid in advance and work on a retainer basis, re-invoicing the customer when they have used all the hours paid for. This keeps you in control of the relationship.

Special Requirements

Develop a specialty—determine the type of customer you want to target (small businesses, out-placed executives, retired executives, sales reps, and so on). If you have worked in a specific industry for years and know it well, you can market to customers who will benefit from your expertise. Office and executive suites are thriving in the current economic climate. You can find these types of offices through an Internet directory. They will have customers who will need additional support. Some of these office suites offer these support services themselves, so a direct mailing to the tenants may yield better results than trying to get a flyer posted. You could also rent a conference room in the office suite (frequently available to the public for a modest fee), sponsor a lunch, and learn about an administrative topic or train on software. Invite the tenants in the building and use the opportunity to talk about the services you offer.

Custom Tailoring and Alterations

Estimated startup costs: $500–$1,000

Estimated first-year revenue: $30,000–$80,000

According to the Association of Sewing and Design Professionals (formerly Professional Association of Custom Clothiers or PACC), the majority of their 500 members across the United States and Canada run home-based businesses. This industry has seen a real spike in revenue over the last decade as a result of the media focus on fashion, home décor, and, above all, weddings. Custom tailoring and altering bridal gowns has become a big business. With clothing being made around the world for people of all shapes and sizes, alterations businesses have seen growth as more people shop in discount retail stores that no longer offer their own free alterations.

Equipment and Supplies

Most home-based alteration and tailoring businesses are started by people who have been sewing for themselves and their loved ones for years. A common pattern is for sewers to develop a local reputation among family and friends for their sewing talents and use that as a springboard to starting their own business.

If you already have a home sewing machine, you can begin with that and, as you build your clientele and revenue, you can invest in some fancier equipment. If you need to purchase a basic machine to get going, plan on spending $250 to $500 for an inexpensive sewing machine. With stores like Wal-Mart and Target located in every town across the nation, you do not have to inventory every color thread in the universe. Use common sense and limit your supply budget to $100 before you open for business.

Estimating the Time Commitment

You will need to create a changing room or space in your home office/workspace so your customers can try on their clothes for you. This can be as simple as having a sewing room/office with a door; you can step out while your customers change. Establish a schedule of days for appointments. This can be Wednesdays and Fridays, 9 A.M. to 5 P.M., and noon to 4 P.M. on Saturdays. By setting aside specific days and times for customer appointments and fittings, you are creating days available for you to just sew and get the work done without a flow of traffic interrupting you.

If you decide to specialize in basic alterations, you can anticipate that each customer appointment will last 30 minutes. Moving into custom clothing design and tailoring will require you to spend more time scheduling appointments and meeting with customers for fittings. The time for each customer will vary depending upon the type of garment you are creating.

Pricing and Payments

The recommended method of pricing alterations and tailoring is to estimate the time it will take you to accomplish the task, including the drop-off appointment time of 30 minutes, and multiply that by an hourly rate. Rates will vary by location, reputation, and complexity of the project, but range from $20 to $75 per hour.

There are many opportunities for specialization in this field. The wedding and bridal market offers both custom creation and alterations. You should consider different specialty options as you study the market and work on your business plan. You can start by offering more basic alterations and work on a self-study plan to improve your skills. You can draw upon a wealth of publications, videos, and DVDs to improve your skills and increase your revenue potential.

Typically alterations are paid for when the customer picks them up from you. You will want to schedule your pick-ups for the same days you have drop-off appointments. Payment will be due on the date of delivery. Many customers are busy and may forget that they have left work with you. If you want to improve your cash flow, make it a habit to call the customer when the work is done, especially if it is a big project. It doesn't do your cash flow any good to have completed work hanging in your fitting room.

Bonus Point

As part of your startup planning, devise a professional approach to keeping track of your customers' garments and your delivery date commitments. The more professional you are with your business, the better your customers' perceptions of your services.

For custom tailoring, your payment requirements should depend on the customer. For new customers, it is a good idea to get an initial payment when the order is placed, with payments scheduled at the end of each fitting. As you develop a relationship with customers, you can modify this to a point. Some custom work can be seasonal: heavy in the spring and summer for prom, graduations, and weddings. If you allow people credit as their garment is being made, you will have a lot of work with not much money coming in during your busiest times. This can be discouraging, especially to a new business owner.

Special Requirements

For newcomers, membership in the Association of Professional Sewers and Designers can be a great way to get a lot of information and guidance in your startup phase. Membership for individuals in the development stages or the first two years of a sewing-related business is $100 annually.

Having your own website can go a long way to accelerating the growth of your business. In fact, a website in today's business world can rival the exposure that you would get in a storefront in a neighborhood shopping center. Include a simple website as part of your startup costs and work on developing content for it over time. The more knowledgeable a web presence you create, the more confidence your prospective customers will have in your abilities. This will not only bring you more business, but also a better caliber of customer relationships.

Chapter 13

Personal Health

In This Chapter

- Helping others look and feel great
- Great ideas for succeeding as a personal trainer without your own gym
- Relaxing customers with massages at the right price
- Creating the perfect at-home spa for your esthetics business

Even as the economy has spiraled downward in the last two years, reports from business people in personal health services indicate that one of the last things people give up are services that help them look and feel good. Apparently even those who are out of work feel that maintaining their personal appearance is essential to getting back into the workplace.

As our society has matured and become ever more a melting pot of various cultures and belief systems, feeling great has become equally important to looking great. This is an open-ended market, since most working people can afford to allocate some of their budget to taking care of themselves, whether that includes a gym membership, taking yoga classes, learning about nutrition, regular skin care, or even indulging in (or believing in the necessity of) regular massage therapy.

This is a strong favorable indicator for focusing on an aspect of personal well-being as your startup idea. Personal trainers and yoga teachers do not require licensing in most states; individuals interested in these fields can obtain certification from a variety of sources and begin business rapidly. Dieticians, massage therapists, and estheticians all require licensing in most states. Accordingly, the ideas presented for launching a home-based business in these three fields will be directed to people who have already trained and are licensed but have worked for others as employees.

Personal Trainer

Estimated startup costs: $500–$750

Estimated first-year revenue: $50,000–$90,000

It seems that every personal-training professional loves what they do. Once perhaps regarded as a passing fad, Americans have grown more devoted to their workouts since the early 1970s, when small gyms started proliferating in all neighborhoods. We have seen many changes to the brick-and-mortar fitness establishment. The local businesses have all but faded, having been chased out of the market by the likes of LA Fitness, Crunch, and Gold's Gym. But this is still a great opportunity for the niche businesses of individual trainers, who specialize in working one-on-one.

Success in this field requires the 4 Ps:

1. Physique

2. People skills

3. Personality

4. Passion for fitness

You need to be in excellent shape (and we mean obvious to the casual observer). People want to work out with a trainer who exudes strength and fitness. This is a people business and to be successful you need to have a warm and genuine personality and great communication and social skills. Your passion for what you do should be apparent and contagious.

Equipment and Supplies

The great part about launching a successful career as a personal trainer is that you don't have to invest in all the training equipment yourself. You can start a vibrant business using someone else's gym! We have a business plan based on the recommendations of people in the top of this field that allows you to get started with very few startup costs and ramp up to a great income almost immediately.

The consensus among professional trainers is that liability insurance is a must, so be sure to check out rates and secure coverage before you start training.

Estimating the Time Commitment

You will need a few weeks to get your certification and to put together your work-out programs for individual customers and your classes. Armed with your business card and a nicely designed flyer, you will start calling on the leasing managers of apartment and condominium complexes in your area. Both real estate developers and property-management companies have a keen interest in providing value-added benefits to new and current tenants. That's where you come in. You offer to hold regularly scheduled fitness "boot camps" (a.k.a. exercise classes) at the apartment or condo fitness center. These have become an expected amenity at all middle- and high-end living communities.

You could start out with a schedule of three to six classes per week. The best times for classes will depend on the demographic of the community; before and after work on weekdays and one weekend class would be appropriate for the young adult to baby boomer crowd. If you have adult communities of retirees, you can offer midday classes. Your value proposition to the property manager is not only on-site classes, but a discounted pricing structure for residents. You can charge residents $15 per class and $20 for nonresidents. You can also offer a discount for payments by the month or multiple sessions or classes.

In addition to boot camps, you negotiate access to the gym for any personal-training client you work with as long as you are on-site with the customer. This gives you a facility for individual and group training during low-usage periods at the fitness center.

Following is a snapshot of the revenue potential from six weekly boot camps. Keep in mind that you have the choice of setting up this arrangement with more than one complex to expand your marketing efforts beyond one location.

Weekly Calendar

	Sun	Mon	Tues	Wed	Thurs	Fri	Sat
Morning	X	6 A.M.	X	6 A.M.	X	6 A.M.	
Evening	X	X	6 P.M.	X	6 P.M.	X	Noon

At $15 per person with 15 participants per class, you're making $225 per class, or $1,350 a week, just from your 6 classes. This gives you plenty of room to make introductory offers such as "first class free," "buy 10 classes get 1 free," "bring a friend for free"—you get the picture. While many people view personal trainers as working at a hobby, that is far from the reality.

By offering your boot camps, you are also giving yourself the time to build a one-on-one training clientele.

Pricing and Payments

We have already covered standard pricing for boot camps and classes. For one-on-one training sessions, the cost per person is much higher than a class, usually in the range of $50 to $100 per hour depending on your location. It is common to offer half-hour sessions at slightly more than the hourly rate. If your hour session is $50, a half-hour would be $30. It is also customary to have two or more people share a session. This appeals to many people who do much better with a buddy than on their own. It does require more work on the trainer's part, since you often have to run two or more routines concurrently for groups that are not all at the same fitness level. Where normally you might charge $30 for a half-hour for one person, you can charge $45 for the same time slot for two people.

Special Requirements

You will have much more credibility from the beginning if you obtain certification from one of several national organizations that offer it. The gold standard in this industry is the National Strength and Conditioning Association (NSCA). Membership in the NSCA precertification is $120; you will save more than this on the members' benefit of reduced certification exam rates. You can purchase test-preparation guides for under $100 and take the exam online for $285. For $505 in certification costs plus another $200 for general marketing and your business license, you are ready to get started.

Bonus Point

Help establish your reputation with a website and well-developed Internet presence. You can start out with a blog on a free site, like Google blogger. You can build your blog with content, short instructional videos, and success stories. This can bring you a side business in virtual clients, fitness buffs who want to train with the latest techniques and equipment but are motivated enough to work out on their own. If you can attract this kind of business, you can bring in additional revenue by writing training programs that you update at the beginning of each month for a regular monthly fee.

Dietitian and Nutritionist

Estimated startup costs: $500–$750

Estimated first-year revenue: $50,000–$75,000

More nutritionists and dietitians are setting up shop to serve people interested in improving their diet and overall well-being. In most states, a license is required to practice as a nutritionist or dietician. In fact, a majority of states with laws governing the field of dietetics require a license, the main criteria for which is having an academic degree from a four-year college with a major in nutrition sciences or similar course of study. The Commission on Dietetic Registration of the American Dietetic Association (ADA) awards the registered dietitian credential to those who pass a certification exam after completing their academic coursework and supervised experience.

This is not a hobby that can easily, quickly, or inexpensively be turned into a home-based business. If, however, you happen to be a licensed registered dietitian (RD), a great deal of statistical evidence does encourage launching a startup in this field. According to the Bureau of Labor Statistics, jobs in nutrition and dietary consulting are expected to grow by 9 percent by 2016, from 57,000 currently to around 62,000. Many of those "jobs" will be dieticians working on a freelance basis.

Equipment and Supplies

To start your own practice as a dietitian, you will need a good scale for weighing your clients and a tape measure for taking beginning and interim measurements. You may want a body fat calculator as well. Purchasing software programs to help you create meal plans, calculate caloric intake, and break down daily menus into protein, carbohydrate, and fat grams will enable you to design a comprehensive program for clients. A budget of $500 for startup costs will cover the purchase of all of the above.

Estimating the Time Commitment

Perhaps more than with the other personal health services, it is more difficult to build a practice based on repeat clientele. We all know the statistics for weight-loss programs and those who continually start them. It's hard to get people to stick with a program. That includes clients who seek out private diet coaches. You are going to have to spend a great deal of time marketing and networking to spread the word about your services. Creating and maintaining an informative website with regular postings to a blog will be an important tool to bring in a continuing flow of new clients.

Plan on setting up standard appointment times so you can control your pricing, which you will want to set by the hour. New clients will need a minimum of a 90-minute appointment with regular follow up appointments on a weekly, semimonthly, or monthly basis for 30 to 45 minutes. A good way to keep in contact with clients is to have them fax or e-mail their weekly food diaries to you. You can use your software programs to analyze their consumption, encourage certain behaviors, and discourage others. Keeping people accountable is an excellent motivation to successful weight loss and good health.

Pricing and Payments

Rates for registered dietitians in private practice range from $60 to $150 per hour. Any additional products provided to clients, such as a food diary, calorie counter books, and so on, should be charged in addition to the hourly rate. You can also set a new client rate that includes both consultation and products to simplify matters and eliminate the client's ability to choose not to purchase tools they really need to be successful because of the cost.

Special Requirements

You will have to create a home office that is conducive to receiving clients. Alternatively, you can choose to partner with other fitness centers or professionals and see clients on their site. For example, many health clubs have a need for a nutritional professional but don't have enough business to add a full-time employee. You can create a win/win situation by providing services to the club's clients and arrange to use the consultation space to see your own private clients as well.

Yoga Teacher

Estimated startup costs: $200–$500

Estimated first-year revenue: $35,000–$60,000

The popularity of yoga has exploded in this country over the last two decades. Once viewed as a special type of exercise for the highly cerebral, yoga has become a part of the physical fitness landscape. Although more popular in metropolitan areas than rural ones and western states more than the South, there are yoga studios and practitioners in every state in the country.

While the costs associated with teaching yoga are not tremendous, the business concept of a yoga studio is, with the investment in décor, wood floors, and the lease for studio space being prohibitively high for a startup. As a result, as the economy has declined, so too have the number of viable yoga studios in many areas. But the number of potential customers for yoga is still strong enough to support a home-based yoga business that uses other people's real estate for teaching classes.

Equipment and Supplies

The simplicity of the practice of yoga extends to the required equipment. All you need is the space, a yoga mat, and possibly some music, incense, and a small gong or bell. An equipment budget of $200 is more than adequate to buy everything you would need for your portable yoga studio.

Estimating the Time Commitment

The business model recommended for personal trainers in the first section of this chapter would also work well for building up a solo yoga business. Rather than using a gym full of equipment, you would approach apartment and condo property managers with the idea of teaching classes in their clubhouse. You would want to scope out properties that have clubhouses with some privacy and avoid those that share open space with leasing offices and restrooms in order to ensure a quiet atmosphere where you can hold a class without interruptions. Other potential spaces that could be available for free or little rent are public libraries and recreation centers. But focusing on the complexes with a concentration of residents will help you get your classes booked and your business ramped up more quickly.

Typical yoga classes will be anywhere from 45 minutes for a before-work class to an hour and a half for more intense workouts. You will have to determine how long you need for travel time between classes depending on location, and how many classes you can hold at each location every week will depend on the level of interest among the residents of the complex. An early goal for your startup could be to get 10 classes per week scheduled with 10 students per class on average. This would create a great foundation of income to build on, again with very low recurring expenses.

Pricing and Payments

Most yoga classes are priced at $15 to $20 for drop-in students with the option of saving a small amount of money on purchasing a group of 10 lessons. Studios offer a monthly rate to regular students who can then come by to any class they want during the month. Students expect to pay in advance, either in cash or by check, for both individual classes and a monthly card. This is great for your cash flow since you will get paid before you ever teach a class.

Many yoga teachers also take on private clients and go to their homes to teach. This could appeal to certain individuals who either have time constraints or want the personal attention of the instructor. You could also market your classes for corporate retreats, wellness programs for recovering patients, and neighborhood clubhouses run by homeowner associations. These will be good filler programs you can branch out to once you establish your regular multistudent classes.

Special Requirements

Yoga teachers are expected to be certified. The certification process is an intense education that includes numerous hours (usually at least 200 hours) of class participation. Certification is often offered by certain larger yoga studios and can cost upwards of $2,000. As such, a startup yoga business can truly be low-cost only if the instructor is already certified. For the newly certified yoga instructor, the startup model outlined here is a very viable way to build your own business and make much more money on your own that you would teaching in someone else's studio.

Massage Therapist

Estimated startup costs: $200–$1,000

Estimated first-year revenue: $50,000–$80,000

If you have your massage license but have always worked in a spa or other type of facility, this could be the right time to make the move to a home-based massage business. In the past, spa owners could create a much more sophisticated environment for massage patrons. Special lighting, soft terrycloth robes and slippers, and cascading fountains come to mind. In today's world, the average consumer is much more focused on price than extra luxury, and a competent massage therapist with a comfortable and attractive home massage room can offer just what customers are looking for.

While customers are willing to sacrifice the extras, there are some basic aspects of creating the right atmosphere for a proper massage. In addition to the visual aspects that should be pleasing, it is important to retain the feel of serenity that a good spa conveys to its customers. If you have small children, pets, or any other constraints that will prevent you from maintaining a quiet and peaceful atmosphere, you will want to establish hours or arrange for offsite daycare (either for children or pets).

Equipment and Supplies

It is now possible to buy a good massage table for under $200. If you have particular requirements (and the cash), you can make a larger investment in this one essential item for a massage therapist, but it is by no means necessary. Other startup equipment includes small items such as something for playing background music and appropriate relaxation CDs. Of course this can be anything you already own to play music, like a CD or MP3 player.

Common massage-therapy supplies include a few sets of linens and blankets, pillows, and face covers, along with your preferred brand of massage oil or lotion. A budget of $250 will more than cover these expenses.

Estimating the Time Commitment

Since you will be required to be your own receptionist and schedule all your own appointments, you will need to calculate the number of hours you actually need to be working on massages based on your revenue requirements.

Pricing and Payments

Most home-based massage therapists charge a lower rate than spas. In regions where a spa massage goes for $85 for a 45-minute session, a home-based massage therapist can charge anywhere from $60 to $75 per massage. If you have a solid base of customers that will follow you to your home, you will be more likely to get the higher rate. For those therapists who need to grow their customer base, you can make your home-based massage very attractive to prospective customers by offering a lower price, special packages, and deals for new customers.

Payment is expected when service is rendered. Initially you will want to avoid the extra cost of a merchant credit card account, but eventually this can become a great way to improve cash flow. Since many people view massage as a luxury, they are more likely to charge the service, especially if paying up front for packages and gift certificates (which you definitely want to offer).

Special Requirements

You will absolutely need to have a separate room in your home with adequate privacy to set the proper tone for relaxation. A set-up with a separate exterior entrance is ideal but not necessary. The room does not have to be lavish, but cleanliness and neatness are a must.

There is no reason why, with some effort and creativity, you cannot set up an inviting space at home that makes clients want to come back often. You may even consider trading services with an interior designer or feng shui consultant who can help you create just the right energy and feeling in your home spa.

Esthetician

Estimated startup costs: $1,000

Estimated first-year revenue: $40,000–$60,000

Most states require estheticians to be licensed, which requires at least a year at an accredited school. To meet the criteria of a low-cost startup, this section is for those who already have their license and have found themselves out of work with the closing or downsizing of an employer's spa or salon. If you have some loyal customers who will gladly continue to come to you for facials, the idea of creating your own facial salon will work even better since you will have an existing stream of revenue from loyal customers.

An esthetician provides a whole range of services for enhancing the physical beauty of a person. A typical service list includes hair removal by electrolysis or waxing, skin care, and the proper use and application of beauty aids such as makeup. Aroma therapy and various versions of hand, foot, and cranial massage have become popular add-ons for enhancing the customers' experiences.

You will need to dedicate a room in your home that has privacy, similar to the advice provided in the previous massage therapy section. If that is workable for you, here's how to get yourself set up and opened for business.

Equipment and Supplies

All of your $1,000 in startup expenses will be spent on setting up your facial room, with a minimum equipment list of a facial table, steamer, and good-quality lamp. Lots of websites (see the Appendix) offer equipment, some with financing packages available. Financing may be your best option, since you will also need to invest in tools, linens, and products in order to start operating. If you are careful, and especially if you have steady customers from the start, you should have no problem making a reasonable monthly payment.

You will eventually want to add a line of skin care products for sales to customers. The markup to the retailer on products is usually around 40 percent and many spa owners report about a 10 percent revenue stream from product sales. If you don't feel ready to get involved with all the extra paperwork and accounting for product sales, you can base your services on a well-known product, such as Aveda or Jurlique, that are available locally at hair salons and retail outlets. For a low-cost startup, it will not be feasible for you to carry much inventory because of the initial cash investment necessary.

Estimating the Time Commitment

It will take time to build your business beyond any existing clientele you may have at the beginning, so you should have a plan for covering your personal expenses for the first six months of your startup. You will need to allocate a portion of your working hours to networking and marketing your business. The more successful you are at identifying people who will be good referral sources, the faster you will achieve a sustainable cash flow.

Good targets for your marketing efforts will include service providers to your type of customer. Hair salons are excellent referral sources because they have a client base that already spends money and time on looking good. Salons also tend to set regular appointments with customers, which gives them frequent access (or, in marketing lingo, touches) to your potential customers. You could create a special offering to salon personnel to allow them to try your services, and extend a special price schedule to clients they refer to you.

Pricing and Payments

Your market research and past experience should give you an idea of pricing for various levels of services in your geographic location. The prices of facial treatments tend to run from $20 for simple waxing procedures to over $100 for extended facial treatments. It is common practice in this industry to bundle visits at a discount, say 5 facials for $300 if the individual price is $85 per facial.

You may want to offer special clients a prepayment package deal. If you know from experience that January is a slow month, you can offer special packages to preferred clients based on their prepayment before the end of the year. You will need to budget time for these services during the year and plan on delivering service having already received the payment. But getting an extra influx of revenue in advance of a slow period will go a long way to keeping you in business during leaner times.

Special Requirements

Each state has its own licensing requirements, so you will need to review the licensing section of your secretary of state's website. In particular, research whether there are special requirements of running this type of business in your home, for example, certain sanitation regulations that must be observed.

Another requirement for license renewal is continuing education. Online courses provide easy and inexpensive access to classes that qualify for many states' continuing education requirements.

Chapter 14

Child Care

In This Chapter

- ◆ Infant to pre-K daycare in your home
- ◆ On-site newborn nursing and new mother assistance
- ◆ Babysitting
- ◆ After-school care
- ◆ Summer programs for children
- ◆ Special-needs child care

The child-care industry has always had tremendous upside with regard to market size. The trends toward two-income families and single households with children put pressure on the child-care industry to keep expanding its facilities to meet the needs of the marketplace. According to the Bureau of Labor Statistics, the number of jobs in child care will increase by a whopping minimum of 33 percent, or more than 300,000 jobs, by 2016. Self-employed individuals represent 37 percent of child-care workers. That translates into 100,000 more home daycare centers.

Snags

All of the child-care businesses in this chapter require serious research into the types and levels of insurance coverage necessary to protect you from all potential liability involved in working with children, whether in your home or another setting. Be sure you are well protected before you take in your first student.

The downside, which has not changed in spite of the enormous demand, is that certain child-care services are among the lowest paying professions with the fewest benefits to employees, regardless of the size of the center where they work. In this chapter, we cover basic in-home child care and also include some unique ideas for child care that can be more financially rewarding.

Home Child Care—Infant to Pre-K

Estimated startup costs: $1,000

Estimated first-year revenue: $30,000–$40,000

In-home child care is providing for the care and well-being of small children, from infancy through the pre-kindergarten stage. Daycare hours are Monday through Friday, usually 7 A.M. to 6 P.M., with most children spending 10 hours each day. Since there is only some regulation for home facilities that have five or less children in most states (your own child counts in this equation), the programs offered by an in-home provider will vary. Some people provide a safe and clean environment, with meals, snacks, and diaper-changing included. Other daycare owners, especially the numerous ones founded by former educators, will offer an age-appropriate curriculum for the children.

Those who are attracted to this industry, often working mothers who prefer to stay home with their young children, can certainly launch a successful in-home child-care business. The question is whether it will pay you enough to meet your obligations.

Bonus Point

Many working parents, especially single mothers or fathers, have a greater level of difficulty finding child care for hours when they are scheduled for shift work. If you are leaving a shift work environment and are already used to working other than a 9-to-5 schedule, an excellent opportunity for you might be to run a home-based child-care program for your former co-workers who work a 3 P.M. to 11 P.M. shift.

Each state has its own licensing requirements depending upon the number of children cared for in the home. It is critical to review your state's requirements and make sure you are in compliance. You will need a huge amount of patience and love to spend every day with several small children who are not your own—and their parents are frequently even more challenging to handle.

Equipment and Supplies

The startup costs for this business will depend on the amount of educational activities you plan to provide to your children. In-home daycare centers make the effort to create kid-friendly spaces in their homes that have tables and chairs, room for play areas, hooks for hanging coats, cubbies for backpacks and sleeping pads, and lots of toys and supplies for activities. You can market this business with a website, but you will more likely fill your slots by word of mouth from people you tell about your new business. With enrollment limited to five or six children (unless you hire staff), you can outfit your daycare center for $1,000 and expect to create an attractive environment for the children.

You can add extra fees for meals and snacks or simply include these costs in your monthly tuition. Either way, parents will expect you to feed their children two to three times during the 10 or more hours a day they are in your charge.

Estimating the Time Commitment

Daycare workers tend to work a long day, Monday through Friday each week. One of the reasons for the low hourly pay for child care is the length of the day the child-care provider is expected to work. Since your customers are depending on you to be there for them, you will need to sacrifice extended vacations. This goes for summer vacations, too; parents need child care 52 weeks a year, unless you can organize your customers to all take off the same weeks each year.

Pricing and Payments

Payment for daycare centers tends to be by the week or month. Rates are all over the map, depending on the geographic location (rural or urban) and the extent of demand for good care. Cities like New York and Chicago have daycare prices that seem outrageous compared to the rest of the country. Expect to charge from $125 a week or $500 a month for pre-K children, to $750 to $1,000 a month for infants. Toddler rates tend to fall somewhere in between, with lower rates for toilet-trained toddlers.

Estimating that you will have between three and six children as a sole child-care provider (depending on your state's regulations), you can expect to earn between $6,000 to $12,000 per year per child. For the hours you are working, the pay is not the most you could make from a home business. You have to love working with children to make this business work for you.

It is extremely important to get paid in advance, whether it's weekly or monthly. Many child-care providers have the policy that after a day or two of nonpayment, the child cannot be left for the day. This is difficult to enforce once you have built a relationship with a family, but unfortunately quite necessary unless you want to end up working for free. Another industry standard is for parents to pay a full month's fee even if you are closed for a holiday.

Special Requirements

Many people who start home child-care businesses are former educators who have an obvious advantage in attracting customers. Some states require a minimum of formal training; Georgia has a 10-hour requirement in order to be licensed for three or more children. Most parents, especially before the pre-K year, are looking first and foremost for a safe and loving environment for their children. It is not necessary to have an education background. Several websites offer monthly preschool for as little as $15 a month to help you plan activities for the day. And don't forget, there's always naptime!

On-Site Baby Nurse and New Mother Assistant

Estimated startup costs: $500–$700

Estimated first-year revenue: $40,000–$50,000

The market of potential customers for baby nurses is much more limited than general child care because of the cost to new parents. A baby nurse can earn between $300 and $500 per 24-hour day, or $20 to $35 per hour for an overnight shift. The most popular schedule for a baby nurse tends to be the 8- to 12-hour night shift, as getting the baby on a sleep schedule continues to be the most important goal for new parents. The good news is that to be a fully employed baby nurse, you don't need many customers to fill your schedule because an average assignment is usually three months long. Once you start in this profession you will likely stay as busy as you want.

In spite of the terminology, baby nurses are not usually registered nurses (RNs) or even licensed practical nurses (LPNs). They are people with experience with babies, their own children, babysitting, nannying, or daycare center employees with specific training and/or certification as a baby nurse. On-site and online training programs are available (see the Appendix). The basic responsibilities of a baby nurse are:

- Breast- and bottle-feeding support

- Sterilizing, cleaning, and preparation of bottles

- Nursery set-up and restocking of baby products

- Emptying of diaper containers

- Creating and initiating a sleeping and eating schedule

- Waking up at night with baby

- Monitoring baby's nutritional intake

- Burping techniques

- Bathing of infant

- Infant laundry

- Umbilical care

- Circumcision care

- Infant massage

- Accompanying baby and parents to appointments

Equipment and Supplies

Your startup expenses will be comprised primarily of the cost of obtaining the certifications you need in order to increase your ability to attract business. Classes are offered locally in major cities at a cost of $350 to $500 for a complete range of certifications, including pediatric CPR and first aid, labor assistant, lactation specialist, and lactation educator. Distance learning courses can cost somewhat more but still under $1,000. Since this work involves a very intimate level of contact with your customers, staying and sleeping in their home and caring for their infant, you will want to use personal contacts as your primary source of referrals.

Estimating the Time Commitment

It will take some time to establish yourself in this market, and you will have to be aggressive at first about your marketing efforts. Contacting other baby nurses in your area who may have full schedules is a great way to seek referrals of business they cannot take on. You can also get your start working for an agency that places baby nurses until you start to get your own referrals. After an initial ramping-up period, be prepared to be very busy. You need to be able to live with spending a great deal of time away from home. This is not a great or even feasible business for someone with her own small children. It is possible to get assignments for partial days or nights, but you will have to adjust your rate of pay accordingly.

You should have a process for meeting the prospective couple well in advance of the baby's due date, submitting to a background check and supplying several references. Since babies do not always come when they are expected, you will need to come up with protocols for how you handle premature babies. You will want to build some sort of flexibility into your schedule so you can accommodate your customers' needs.

Pricing and Payments

The pay for baby nurses is often a daily rate, anywhere from $300 to $500 for a 24-hour day, depending on where you are located. The pricing for multiple births is higher. You should be able to find out what others in your area are charging and you may not want to take on multiples in the beginning, or ever. That is certainly a decision to be made once you have some first-hand experience.

Require a significant deposit when you are hired in advance of the baby's arrival, with weekly payments to be made on a regular basis for the duration of your engagement.

Special Requirements

Classes required to become a baby nurse include child development, health and nutrition, child safety and accident prevention, universal precautions, breast and bottle feeding, car seat safety, crying and colic, homemaking skills, and infant CPR and first aid.

Success Story

Vonda is a very successful baby nurse in Los Angeles, California. After a few years of working solely as a nurse herself, she has expanded to running an agency that not only places baby nurses but also trains every baby nurse they hire. Her certification program is offered over a two-day weekend and covers everything needed to be hired by Vonda's agency (www.thestorkstopshere.com). She recently added nanny-placement services for special-needs children, which got so much traffic on its website that she had to shut it down and regroup for a much bigger business plan.

Vonda strongly advises baby nurses to only work with a contract for their prospective customers. She says that one piece of advice is crucial to making a good living at this profession. You depend on customers scheduling your time in good faith, but sometimes things come up that make them change their mind. Having a significant deposit policy is another necessary tool to ensure that expecting parents live up to their promise to hire you at a certain time.

Babysitting

Estimated startup costs: $100–$250

Estimated first-year revenue: $17,000–$30,000

We define babysitting as an experienced adult looking after someone else's minor child (or children), providing care and supervision on a scheduled basis (meaning you have a time commitment) as frequently as you are asked to by the customer. This includes part-time nanny work as well as hourly babysitting on a Saturday night. Many parents require the help of other adults to supplement their child-care arrangements. Some parents don't work full time, or at all, but are in need of babysitting for several blocks of time during the week.

An adult babysitter can expect the hourly rates to be a good bit more than those paid to a teenager. Typically, an adult can provide transportation on a regular or as-needed basis and is able to handle more challenging situations than a typical teen sitter. Some parents, especially when infants are involved, feel more comfortable relying on an adult than a teen.

A babysitter has to love children and be able to respond to their needs and activity levels. Next to the safety of their children, dependability is the second most important characteristic your customer will demand of you. There is a huge market for babysitting; for some parents this is their sole form of child care. Accordingly, you should be able to stay booked and make a fair hourly wage in the process.

Equipment and Supplies

Even though the Red Cross Babysitter's Training Program is geared to teenage sitters, there is much to be learned from this program. Creating checklists of emergency phone numbers, permission slips to seek medical care if necessary, and other good suggestions will be helpful to you. The more organized and professional you are, the more business you will get. You can start this business with virtually no cash outlay. You can do flyers instead of a business card and leave them anywhere families with children go: daycare centers, pediatrician offices, grocery stores, pharmacies, and so on. Many virtual babysitting service websites, such as www.myjambi.com give service providers and seekers an Internet-based referral network free of charge. Many subdivisions and communities have a web page of service providers where babysitters can be listed.

Estimating the Time Commitment

Success won't happen overnight, but in a matter of weeks you should have some regular jobs established and calls with more opportunities. You will need to schedule travel time to be sure you are prompt. It will take some discipline to disengage from one home or workplace and move on to the next. You may want to establish minimum lengths of service—say, at least 3 hours—before you accept a job, especially from a new customer.

Pricing and Payments

Even as an adult, it is common to be paid by the hour and at the end of a babysitting job, unless you have a recurring commitment of more than one day per week. The longest you should expect to go without pay is until the end of the week (or possibly every two weeks if a customer gets paid biweekly). Your minimum hourly rate should be $15 with additions for more than one child ($1 more per hour), with a high end of $25 per hour to be expected for this kind of work.

One clever idea for extra money is to sit for a group of families, say two or three couples going out together or to one of the families' homes. This kind of arrangement can yield a higher hourly rate, while offering a savings to each individual family.

Special Requirements

Red Cross training is helpful; CPR and first aid are a must. Many well-paid adult babysitters are education majors supporting themselves through college or graduate school. Although seemingly an easy profession, it demands a great deal of level head-edness and the ability to react quickly and decisively in certain situations.

After-School Programs

Estimated startup costs: $500–$750

Estimated first-year revenue: $20,000–$30,000

Working parents are still on the hook for child care even once their children start kindergarten. Since most full-time working parents work until 5:00 P.M., after-school programs are a must in order to have supervision for the child until a parent can get to a place to pick them up. There are institutional forms of after-care; many pre-schools have buses that pick up kids when the elementary schools let out in the mid-afternoon. Most parents prefer to have after-care in close proximity to their home, not to mention the desire to have their children cared for in a home setting after an already long day at school.

An after-school caregiver is expected to provide safe transportation from the school to her home; this may require a large station wagon or van depending on the number of children you take in each day. Your state may have some regulations specific to after-care that you will need to review as you prepare your business plan.

Children who attend an after-school program are older than the typical daycare students; usually the ages will range from 5 to 10 years old. The challenge is to provide snacks and activities for the up to three hours you will have responsibility for the children, given the potential age range.

Equipment and Supplies

In addition to the daily snacks you can purchase on a weekly basis, you will also need art supplies and an appropriate setup for keeping the children out of trouble while they are in your care. These children will be old enough to watch a movie or educational TV show at least once a week, so you will want to be able to create movie time with a TV and DVD player.

Since older children will have homework to do, you can definitely use part of the afternoon to supervise homework time.

Estimating the Time Commitment

Most elementary schools dismiss their students around 2:30 P.M. each day. You will need to plan on heading out for your daily pick up by 2:00 P.M. If you require parents to pick up by 6:00 P.M., that will give you a 4-hour day, 5 days a week. You will want to accommodate your customers on school holidays that don't necessarily correspond with business days off. This will give you the opportunity to earn some extra money for those parents who need your help with occasional full-day coverage.

With a decent marketing effort and some advance notice of your availability before the school year, you should have no problem filling all your slots by the time school starts in the fall.

Pricing and Payments

After-school programs are usually priced by the day with a requirement for full weekly payment regardless of whether the child comes every day of the week. Pricing runs from $10 per day to $25 per day and up, depending on the area you will be serving. If you are looking for a business that earns as much as full-time employment, you will need to run a minimum of an eight-week summer program to supplement your after-school earnings. Since you are only working part time during the school year, you could consider another part-time job or business venture to augment your earnings even more.

The preceding estimated first-year revenue includes the addition of income from a summer program of at least eight weeks in length.

Special Requirements

After-school programs should be run by responsible adults who enjoy being with children. Home-based after-care is frequently provided by the mother of a child who attends the same school as the paying students. If you have an education background, that is certainly a plus but not a requirement. A creative and artistic background often makes for a beloved after-care provider.

Summer Programs for School Children

Estimated startup costs: $1,000

Estimated first-year revenue: $25,000–$30,000

Running a summer camp from home is not going to earn enough to replace a full-time income, but it will give you a chance to pursue your passion, whether it's preserving the planet or teaching youth to cook great food. Depending on the demographics of your neighborhood, you should be able to charge enough for each camper to make this effort worth your while, whether you are supplementing other income from a teaching position or a spouse.

Children might get the summers off from school, but the majority of working parents have to work most of the summer. It has always been even more challenging for working parents to find good all-day programs for their children during summer months. And children can get so bored and worn down by institutional programs that too closely resemble their school day. This creates a huge market for good neighborhood home-based programs, run by people with children of their own to entertain during the summer.

All you need to put together a summer camp program is creativity and a love of spending time with children. Having enough space in your home to accommodate a crowd will be helpful, but kids are content to be in a cool space (that's temperature and vibe) with someone who's interested in them. Your ability to entertain them with hands-on crafts or projects will make the time pass more quickly and leave you with children who want to come back for more.

Equipment and Supplies

Your equipment and supplies list is going to depend on exactly the activities you plan for the week. You can either prepare an agenda that repeats each week for a different set of children, or one that changes each week for the same children. Most camps for older children take the former shape, so you will have to face the challenge of recruiting all the students you need to be at capacity for the summer, or those weeks that you want to work.

Plan out your itineraries and activities well in advance to make sure you have a success on your hands. Be sure you use a daily schedule and realistically plan how you are going to fill each hour with a fun activity. You want to budget for your supplies to make sure you don't spend more money on entertaining your campers than you planned.

Estimating the Time Commitment

Spend time during the school year on both planning and scheduling activities and marketing your camp to potential customers. The most popular camps with parents are the ones that start the week after school ends and run all the way to the first day of school in the late summer or fall. Some regions will have a 10-week summer; others will have summer vacation for 12 to 13 weeks. This will affect your earning potential.

Pricing and Payments

Summer programs are usually priced by the week, with no discounts offered to those who cannot attend all five days, whether due to travel or illness. If you are interested in making as much as possible for these weeks, set a minimum rate of $175 to $200 per week. Expect parents to pay at the time they reserve the space for their child. Most programs do not take partial deposits unless it is for a summer-long program.

Special Requirements

Just like with regular daycare, an education background is going to be a plus, but it is not a requirement. You will need to carefully review the state's licensing requirements for keeping school-age children in your home. Good insurance coverage, especially if you are going to be driving students on field trips, will be a must.

Special-Needs Child Care

Estimated startup costs: $500–$1,000

Estimated first-year revenue: $27,500-$40,000

Parenting a special-needs child takes an enormous amount of love and effort each and every day. Although public schools have been required to accommodate special-needs children, private facilities, especially daycare centers and home providers, are not required by law to accept these children. These facilities simply do not have the personnel and facilities to deal with meeting these children's needs. The result is an extremely under-met need for working parents of special-needs children, and an opportunity for someone with the skills and experience to quickly ramp up a business in this arena.

Many special-needs children will require one-on-one attention. Others will be more than ready to socialize and their parents would prefer to have them in a setting where they can be with other children around their age. You will have to be focused in terms of what type of program you want to offer, whether you have space in your home to accommodate a small group, or you would prefer to go on-site to the child's home. This decision will have a major impact on your startup costs as well.

This is a great business concept for someone who has a special education degree and experience, but it can be done by anyone who has helped raise a special-needs child as a parent or sibling. Some situations are also right for those willing to take on the responsibilities of taking care of a special child for the part of the day the parents are working, and merely playing with them, driving them to therapy sessions, or just an afternoon at the pool in the summertime.

Equipment and Supplies

If you are going to set up a space in your home in order to have several children at a time, you will need to spend time to create the appropriate environment. What you need will depend on the age of the children you accept and the amount of time each day or week you will spend with them. You should have ample money in the $1,000 startup budget to cover all the necessary equipment to get you started.

Estimating the Time Commitment

With the right networking, you should not have a problem finding all the children you can handle, because the demand is much greater than the available supply. Marketing to your local school's special education department, counselors, and even PTA will help you get the word out. Leave brochures or your card at local daycare centers that are forced to turn away certain applicants; people always are grateful to refer business that they themselves cannot handle.

Parents work out so many different arrangements for their special-needs children that you will be able to set hours that suit your schedule. After-school care is a huge need, but you are not limited to this option. Since many special-needs children require supervision even in the tween and teen years, you have the potential to care for a child for a much longer duration than a regular daycare provider. Often an older child with special needs will make a wonderful helper with the younger children.

Pricing and Payments

The pay rate for caring for special-needs children is significantly higher than a regular daycare or after-care program. The rates will vary depending on the actual services you will be rendering. Typically you can expect to charge at least 30 percent more than the going child-care rate. A potential range of fees could look something like this:

Special-Needs Child Care Sample Rates

Child's age and program	Average rate	Special-needs rate
Daycare Infant	$1,000/month	$1,300/month
Grade school after school	$25 per day	$33 per day
Babysitting	$20 an hour	$26 an hour

Special Requirements

Consistency and dependability are especially important to both the parents and child in a special-needs situation. Make sure you have the qualities to meet these basic expectations. See the Appendix for resources for training classes and materials for learning more about working with special-needs children. You will need to check with your state authorities about the licensing requirements for an in-home daycare program.

Chapter 15

Elder Care

In This Chapter

- ◆ Concierge services for the elderly
- ◆ Companion and aide
- ◆ Transportation for appointments
- ◆ Moving and transition management
- ◆ Hospital or hospice sitter

It's common knowledge that our population is living longer, and that with the aging of the baby boomer generation there will be approximately 75 million people over the age of 70 by 2022. Although that creates a large demographic on which to base a business concept, it also challenges those starting elder-care–focused businesses to define exactly what services they are going to offer this market. In the last 10 years, various elder-care franchises have literally flooded the market with agencies that offer caretaking services to seniors. These services primarily offer in-home care, with low-skilled, marginally paid workers being hired as the front-line care providers.

The majority of seniors who need assistance do not require intense medical treatments at home. Most of the franchise services directed at the elderly involve assistance with transportation to doctor's appointments and shopping, companionship, meal preparation, and general hygiene. An independent businessperson looking to venture into this marketplace needs to carve out a slightly unique niche to avoid competing head-to-head with national companies. You will have the benefit of being a smaller company or sole service provider who can offer a much more personal touch in delivering these caretaking services.

In this chapter we offer some suggestions for doing something with a more unique angle for senior services. All of these ideas are scalable to allow you to grow beyond just yourself as a service provider, to improve your revenue potential, and help more people in the process.

Although there are elderly everywhere in the United States, many warmer regions have concentrations of older populations, such as south Florida, and the southwestern states. These areas will have more opportunities for elder-care businesses.

Elder care has a low barrier to entry since you are not required to have a medical or social-work degree. You need to be extremely patient, caring, and sensitive, with a strong desire to help people cope with difficult life situations.

Elder-Care Concierge Services

Estimated startup costs: $500–$1,000

Estimated first-year revenue: $23,000–$35,000

Nonfamily members have an increasing opportunity to step in and assist the adult children who usually have the responsibility for caring for their elder parents. These family caretakers often work full-time jobs and have children at home of their own. The main goal of an elder-care concierge is to delay transitioning elderly customers to an assisted living facility. Prolonging their ability to live independently will have tremendous value to them and their loved ones.

Concierge services include but are not limited to the following tasks:

- Check-in visits, which can include daily visits
- Bring in and sort mail, pay bills, go to post office
- Home security check
- Medication reminder service
- Grocery shopping and delivery
- Appointment setting

- Basic pet care

- Prescription pick-up and delivery

Essentially you can offer to help with the everyday errands and tasks that become more difficult for elderly people to handle by themselves. You might be asked to stop by a customer's house for 30 minutes every day, or come by once a week for two hours to handle mail and errands.

Equipment and Supplies

You will need a car to run errands and some marketing materials, but otherwise no special equipment is necessary. Seniors with mobility issues will have their own canes, walkers, and wheelchairs.

Estimating the Time Commitment

Each customer will start out with a unique list of needs. As he or she ages, your concierge opportunities for that customer will expand. Like other types of concierges, it is good practice to have a minimum fee per visit, at least for the first few visits. A 2-hour minimum fee is a good idea, to avoid making trips only to be paid for 15 minutes of your time.

Most senior citizens rise early and go to bed early, and take naps at different times of the day. You will have to work on a case-by-case basis to map out a schedule for yourself. Although you want to be as helpful as possible, you also want to focus on getting in as many billable hours as possible. Marketing to prospective customers who live in the same or nearby retirement villages will allow you to maximize billable time with reduced travel time.

Snags

It is important to remember that, in addition to the senior who is your primary customer, you will likely be paid and managed by one of their adult children. You need to anticipate phone conversations and meetings with the entire customer "team" and make sure you bill for your time accordingly.

Pricing and Payments

Your pricing will be based on an hourly rate that can follow a sliding scale based on income if that suits your situation. For example, a concierge might commonly charge

$20 to $30 per hour in your area. Since most seniors live on a fixed income, they might resist a high hourly rate. In some cases it might be preferable to charge in 30- to 60-minute increments. If you are hired to drop by daily for 30 minutes of medication check and reminders, mail handling, and bill paying, it might be more advantageous to quote a per visit fee of $15 per half hour than $30 per hour.

Special Requirements

Having a website is a great way to be found by the seniors' family members and sometimes by the seniors themselves. Word of mouth is an invaluable marketing tool in this business. Networking with other professionals in the geriatric field and introducing yourself to the managers of large adult living complexes is a great way to get your business known.

Elder Companion and Aide

Estimated startup costs: $250–$500

Estimated first-year revenue: $17,000–$30,000

According to the U.S. Bureau of Labor Statistics, "Employment of personal and home care aides is projected to grow by 51 percent between 2006 and 2016, which is much faster than the average for all occupations. This occupation will be amongst the occupations adding the most new jobs, growing by about 389,000 jobs. The expected growth is due, in large part, to the projected rise in the number of elderly people, an age group that often has mounting health problems and that needs some assistance with daily activities."

In order to continue living independently, many seniors need the help of a part-time or full-time companion or aide. Sometimes these are live-in caretakers; frequently they are hourly or daytime jobs. A companion's duties can overlap with those of an elder-care concierge service, but typically involve more direct caretaking tasks as a primary responsibility. Some of these duties are:

- Assistance with morning routines of bathing, dressing, and meal preparation

- Providing company throughout the day

- Accompanying and driving senior to doctor's appointments, errands, and meals out

◆ Help with medication schedules

◆ Assistance with daily hygiene

Often, people in this line of work become virtual members of the senior's family. You will need to be able to handle dealing with family members as an extension of the customer you are servicing. Once you find your way into an elder-care community, you will probably never lack work again, since you will be recommended to neighbors and friends.

Equipment and Supplies

Unless you are in a large metropolitan area like New York City with a multitude of transportation options, you will need to have a vehicle. Under certain circumstances, the senior will have a car that you can use to drive them as needed. Other than basic marketing materials to launch your business, no special equipment or supplies are required to get started.

Estimating the Time Commitment

You can create a business model that suits your needs. There are opportunities for living with seniors; others will need nursing care and you will be able to pick up hours relieving the nurse in charge. There is also the possibility of working different days for different seniors; even older folks crave their own space and privacy. Often your customer's spouse may be the primary caretaker in need of respite on a regular basis, or help with certain tasks he or she cannot handle alone.

Many elder companions and aides will stay with the same person for many years. This line of work demands some flexibility on your part. It is difficult to predict how long your assignments will last. There is also the likelihood that as time goes by, your senior will need more and more of your time.

This business has the potential for you to expand into agency services. This would involve hiring or contracting with other independent aides and placing them into home care positions. You would charge your customer the $20 to $30 rate and pay the contractor or employee between $8 and $12 per hour. This is the business model that the national elder-care franchises use around the country. Most home care workers find their jobs through agencies.

Pricing and Payments

Most assignments that do not require a live-in commitment are priced on an hourly rate of $15 to $25 per hour (depending on your location). Daily rates of $150 and up are the norm for 24-hour, live-in work.

Special Requirements

It is not necessary to be an RN or LPN, although many people who gravitate to in-home elder care have worked in assisted-living facilities. Having a nurse's aide designation will be extremely beneficial in attracting work in the beginning. At a minimum, you should have training in CPR and first aid.

The National Association of Home Care and Hospice offers an online Certification for Homemaker/Home Care Aides program. It is composed of three competency-based elements: training, skills demonstration, and a written examination. Go to www.nahc.org/education/home.htm#ol for details.

Transportation for Appointments

Estimated startup costs: $250–$500

Estimated first-year revenue: $25,000–$30,000

Many single and widowed seniors live independently but can no longer drive their own vehicle. These people need someone not only to drive them from point to point, but also to assist them in getting from the car to the point of service (whether physician's office, pharmacy, and so on).

Seniors need transportation for a wide variety of reasons. Some of these are doctor's appointments, treatment centers, therapy appointments, going shopping, visiting friends and relatives, rides to airports, movies, libraries, restaurants, and regular bridge or Mah Jong games.

Retirees who spend part of the year in a second location also have transportation needs. (In Florida these people even have a special name—Snowbirds. These are people who come for the winter months from up North. You also have a summer migration to cooler climates for the Florida residents.) Some companies provide a special set of services for helping elders move to a winter location and back again. These services may include help with packing for the trip, closing up a house, driving the senior to the second location, unpacking, opening the second house, arranging for mail forwarding, managing utilities to be lowered or shut off, and many other details.

Equipment and Supplies

You will need a car in order to provide transportation services on a regular basis. Sometimes you will be asked to drive your customer's vehicle. Other than good organizational skills and a lot of care and patience, no other tangible items are required to start this business.

Estimating the Time Commitment

Similar to companion services, each time commitment is going to vary greatly depending on the specific need of the customer. Some older ladies will need to be taken to their regular Friday-morning hair appointment or their Wednesday-evening canasta game. Others will need intermittent rides to doctor's appointments or ongoing medical treatments, like chemotherapy or radiation.

This is clearly a business that you can mold to your preferences, in terms of hours worked. Many seniors who can drive fine during the day lose their ability to drive once it gets dark because of vision problems. This would provide an opportunity for transportation services as a business you could operate from noon to 9 or 10 P.M., leaving your mornings free for attending college classes.

Pricing and Payments

Your pricing for your services should be based on the hourly rate you need to earn plus an amount to cover your auto expenses. You can use a mileage rate for expenses and base your rates on a calculated per mile charge, similar to a taxi. When quoting fees to your prospective customers, you can use a per-trip fee to keep things simple.

Say you want to earn at least $20 per hour. Spend some time in your neighborhood clocking your trips to the places your customers are most likely to go—the local drugstore and grocery, library, hospital complex, and so on. This will give you some insight on how much you need to charge for each trip. Use this information to create a fee schedule that fits the majority of the requests for transportation you receive.

Bonus Point _____

With a reputation for being extremely cost-conscious, seniors will be open to ride sharing as a way to keep their transportation costs to a minimum. If you have two seniors headed to the same destination, offer to take them together for a reduced fee to both, say $12 each, for a trip you would charge $20 for a single rider. This arrangement would save your customers money and earn you 20 percent more for the trip, a win/win for everyone.

Special Requirements

In many states it may be necessary to obtain a special chauffeur's license if you are going to be driving a number of people around in your vehicle. You should check with your state's Department of Motor Vehicles in order to ensure you are in compliance with the licensing requirements. (See website links in the Appendix.)

Moving and Senior Transition Management

Estimated startup costs: $500–$1,000

Estimated first-year revenue: $40,000–$60,000

Part organizer, part moving company and logistics coordinator, a senior moving or transition manager goes on location to a home of a senior about to move to a smaller residence or assisted living facility. They help their customers decide what to take and what to give away. They contact local charities to pick up donation items.

While many adult children often handle this responsibility, it is trying and time con-suming. Furthermore, a neutral, professional moving manager is less likely to ruffle emotional feathers and be seen as having ulterior motives. Sorting household goods among keepers, donations, and trash is usually the first step in the move preparation. You will want to have ready suggestions and resources for helping your customer dispose of items that will be left behind. Other responsibilities include making arrangements with movers, boxing items for the move, and unpacking and helping the customer settle into the new residence.

If possible, visit the new space in the early stage of the process, in order to see first-hand the end destination of your planning. Having a detailed drawing of the new home with specific dimensions will help with decisions on which furniture to keep and what to give away or sell. You may even suggest hiring an estate sale facilitator (see

Chapter 7) if the items being left behind are not wanted by family or friends and have enough value.

You need to have a firm but caring demeanor as you help people come to terms with letting go of keepsakes and heirlooms that have been treasured for a lifetime. It is a good idea to have a methodology to rely on to help you through the process. Firm guidelines with standard recommendations will help you handle difficult customers and situations with confidence and grace.

Equipment and Supplies

There are no equipment requirements for this business. Everything from packing supplies to transportation can be purchased and contracted by the customer directly, with your assistance.

Estimating the Time Commitment

Several variables will affect the length of time each job takes: size of the house being vacated and length of time the family has owned it, distance from old home to new one, health condition of your customer, and number of relatives involved in the process. You will want to price your services based on a full- or half-day of work. Expediency in accomplishing each move will increase your value; the faster you can accomplish each project the less anxiety and stress for everyone involved.

This is a budding business idea that will need some good marketing and time to get off the ground. You may need to add some more basic services, like elder transportation and concierge services, to help bring in revenue while you are building up a customer base. This business would also dovetail nicely with estate sale facilitating and home staging and organizing.

Keep in mind that marketing your services to the adult children of the seniors is another important avenue for getting customers. Networking with the staff at senior retirement facilities is a good opportunity to get the word out to people who can recommend your services to incoming residents.

Pricing and Payments

It is difficult to find competitor pricing on the web. Most FAQ sections address pricing as something to be given as part of a free estimate process. Experienced senior relocation specialists basically charge by the hour, with a scale of hourly rates that correspond with the level of the particular company personnel. Here's a sample of pricing for a typical downsize move from a three- or four-bedroom home to a one- or two-bedroom condo:

Senior Relocation and Transition Pricing

Level of Service	Hourly Rate
On-site consultation	$125
Continued planning	$75–$90
Packing and unpacking	$40–$50

A typical total cost for this type of move would range from $2,000 to $5,000, depending upon all the variables. This business will require you to hire employees once you reach a level of more than one job per week. You'll probably want to bring in some contract help for packing early on.

Special Requirements

The National Association of Senior Move Managers (NASMM) is a professional association of organizations dedicated to assisting older adults and families with the physical and emotional demands of downsizing, relocating, or modifying their homes.

The Senior Transition Society Council was established in 2004 to advance the quality of home transition services through administrating a standardized exam. Those who pass the exam are designated Certified Relocation and Transition Specialists (CRTS). The program and training is extensive and offers several levels of certification. Initial training is offered as a three-day, self-study, podcast course for $895, with the required exam priced at $295. (See the Appendix for website link.)

Hospital or Hospice On-Site Caregiver

Estimated startup costs: $150

Estimated first-year revenue: $15,000–$30,000

When elderly patients are hospitalized or transferred to a hospice facility, family members frequently request referrals to individual "sitters" to be with the patient in the evening hours. The idea is to relieve the immediate family so they can go home, get dinner and some rest, but to ensure that the patient is not left alone.

The level of service required will depend on the status of the patient and the quality of care provided by the health-care professionals. If your patient is awake and lucid, you might be asked to help with feeding, assist in taking walks or using the restroom, reading aloud, answering the phone, and even writing notes to distant friends and family. You will not be expected or allowed to administer medication. There may be times when the patient asks you to fetch the nurse on her behalf. You may be asked by the attending nurse or nurse's aide to assist with turning the patient.

This type of work is similar to that of an elder companion or aide, but located on-site at a hospital or hospice. A hospice facility is a final destination for terminal patients, and the work will take a special kind of person to handle it.

Equipment and Supplies

There are no equipment requirements for this business. We estimate $150 in startup costs for business cards and other basic printed marketing materials and home office incidentals.

Estimating the Time Commitment

Hospice and hospital caregivers work an hourly-based shift, ranging from 8 to 12 hours. There are people who do this work as a full-time occupation, and others who pick up weekend shifts to supplement other job earnings. The best way to market your services is by contacting the hospital or hospice facility and asking to be placed on the caregiver (or sitter) list. You will want to have references from other employers. You can prepare yourself for this career by attending one of many training programs offered through the National Association for Home Care and Hospice. This training is free of charge and can provide you with hands-on experiences through on-site training opportunities.

Pricing and Payments

This type of work has the least beneficial pay scale of all the elder-care services presented in this chapter. The hourly rate ranges from $10 to $20 per hour depending on the location. If there is relatively little competition and on-site caregivers are hard to find in your area, you will be able to charge at a higher rate. That is also true if you live in a high cost-of-living region, like Los Angeles or New York City. The benefits of this business are definitely more in the nonexistent startup costs and self-satisfaction for those who want to work in health care. The flexibility alone lends itself to a good job to have while working your way through a college or technical program.

Expect to be paid as an independent contractor on a daily or weekly basis.

Special Requirements

The National Association of Home Care and Hospice (NAHC) is the nation's largest trade association representing the interests and concerns of home care agencies, hospices, and home care aide organizations. According to its website, NAHC is the one organization dedicated to making home care and hospice provider's lives easier. The organization's website offers information and links to articles on what is current in the home care and hospice world. There are several continuing education options to choose from.

Chapter 16

Pet Care

In This Chapter

- ◆ Pet sitting trend more popular than ever
- ◆ Daily dog walking services on the rise
- ◆ A well cared for pet is a well groomed one
- ◆ Learning how to be the Alpha dog in your castle
- ◆ Creating underwater animal worlds

> "More pet owners will pay for these services as it is becoming socially unacceptable in most cities, to leave your dog alone during the day or your cat alone for the weekend. In addition, very stable growth will be seen in pet services such as grooming, boarding, pet photography, dog walking, and pet sitting."
>
> —*Small Business Trends*, Jan. 2007

In the last five years, Americans have spent over $1 billion each year on pet-care services, such as pet sitting, dog walking, doggie daycare, boarding at kennels, grooming, and much more. Pet spending continues to climb, exceeding $45 billion including products, food, and veterinary services in 2009. Pet care has exactly the kind of demographics that beg for more independent businesses. Customers want to indulge a beloved member of the family, and the big spenders have high paying, demanding jobs and they're prepared to pay for the services they can't or won't do themselves. Pet popularity is at an all-time high, with celebrity pet owners setting the fashion and high standards of care for the rest of us to follow.

U.S. Pet Industry Expenditures 2001–2009 (Est.)

(Courtesy of the American Pet Products Association)

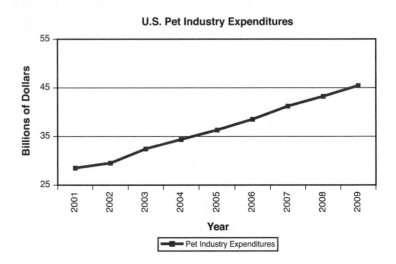

In terms of just pure size, the market for pet services is greater than that of senior citizens. Starting a pet-care business that is service- rather than product-oriented has extremely low startup costs. The going rates for pet services in today's marketplace are more than sufficient to create a profitable business. The icing on the cake for animal lovers is working at something that you love—taking care of animals.

Dog and Cat Sitting for Vacationing Customers

Estimated startup costs: $250

Estimated first-year revenue: $35,000–$40,000

Pet-sitting services were virtually unheard of 30 years ago. Today it is more common to know people who would loathe to board their pet in a kennel, even if it means paying more for someone to come to their home. For people who travel for business or vacation, there is an incredible peace of mind to know that someone they trust and who knows their pets will be coming by while they are away from home.

A pet sitter's responsibilities vary depending on the needs of each customer. Typical service offerings include going to the customer's home at a specific time each day, feeding the animals, cleaning litter boxes for cats, walking dogs, and possibly spending a few minutes interacting with the animals before leaving for the next appointment. Frequently, pet sitters include simple home maintenance chores such as bringing in the mail, turning lights on and off, and watering house plants.

It will be difficult to do this type of work and not be an animal lover. Most of your customers will be very attached to their pets and expect you to feel the same. Otherwise, there are no other barriers to entry to this type of business.

Equipment and Supplies

No specific equipment is needed for this business. The most important startup costs will be marketing your services effectively. Some good sources of referrals include veterinarians without boarding facilities, pet breeders, groomers, and pet product retailers. A website will be helpful, but since there is a good bit of competition on the Internet, you will need to create an especially alluring website to differentiate yourself from other pet sitters in your area. Word of mouth is going to be more effective thanks to the precious nature of your potential animal clientele.

Estimating the Time Commitment

A reliable scheduling software program will be essential to be sure you don't overbook yourself, especially at busy times of the year. Speaking of busy seasons, you will need to consider the fact that in order to develop loyal customers, you will have to forego vacationing during peak holiday times. Most kennels require advance deposits and reservations at least 30 days out during peak travel periods, like Thanksgiving and Christmas. As part of your startup planning, develop policies in advance to make sure you don't wind up sacrificing your holidays for less than top dollar.

Spend some time analyzing your competition and selecting a geographic area you can service without spending too much time traveling between customers. Most pet sitters require their customers to hire them for no less than two visits per day for a dog. As a sole-proprietor pet sitter, you won't need too many bookings each week to pull together a full calendar.

Pricing and Payments

Many professional pet sitters offer a menu of services for different price points. For example, a quick 15-minute visit twice a day would cover dropping by, letting dogs out into a fenced yard, bringing in mail, replenishing food and water. A half-hour visit might have a 15-minute dog walk included. Some pet sitters will take dogs to a park for social hour for an additional fee. Here is a sample service menu:

Pet Sitting Pricing Menu

Service	Time allotment	Daily Fee
Drop by	15 minutes 2× day	$30
Drop by + dog walk	30 minutes 2× day	$50
Trip to the park	Includes second visit	$75

It is common to add a minimal amount for an additional pet, say $2 per visit for another dog, or a cat plus a dog. This is where a pet sitter can offer the most economical solution to someone away from home, since a kennel does not usually discount for a second animal to be boarded.

Special Requirements

The National Association of Professional Pet Sitters (NAPPS) offers tools and networking support to help its members succeed in business. The annual membership is only $95. The association has manuals and information for those getting started in the pet-sitting business.

Consult the NAPPS site and a commercial insurance agent for recommendations for liability and bonding insurance coverage.

Everyday Doggie Daycare

Estimated startup costs: $250

Estimated first-year revenue: $35,000–$40,000

Doggie daycare facilities have sprung up as the most current trend in pet care over the last decade. This form of business is neither low-cost or home-based; however, it does offer a great concept on which to design something similar that does work as a home-based business with low startup costs. Let's look at the basic concepts and how they might be recreated in a simpler fashion.

Some dog owners would be content for their dogs to remain at home during the day but want someone who can come by and give them a walk. Others might be happy with a daily trip to a local park with a designated dog play area. There is also the possibility for providing transportation to a doggie daycare facility or groomer, or taking a pet to the vet for regular or special care.

Daily caretaking services can offer a great complement to other pet-oriented businesses, such as obedience training and pet sitting. Just like in other service businesses, these regular customers keep cash flowing in throughout the year.

Equipment and Supplies

See the previous pet-sitting section for a discussion on startup costs.

Estimating the Time Commitment

The time commitment will vary with the nature of the services your customer signs up for. Many professional pet-care providers make a free evaluation visit to a prospective customer's home. This time is used to assess services needed, take notes about the pets involved and routines preferred, and introduce yourself to the pet and owner. It's always a good idea to have some prescreening criteria in order to avoid spending time with prospects who are unlikely to buy your services. Most fees range from $12 to $20 per visit, so there is little room to negotiate on price. Avoid taking on more of a pet challenge than you are equipped to handle. For example, you may not want to work with breeds that tend to be aggressive, especially when their owner is not around.

Snags

Matthew R. tried using a pet sitter for his male chow years ago when he was only going to be away overnight. Even though the sitter worked at the dog's veterinary clinic and was experienced in dog sitting, she had a time getting inside the front door when the owner wasn't present. She ended up using a chair to fend off a rather upset chow dog. Not a situation any of the parties cared to repeat in the future.

Pricing and Payments

A menu of services and corresponding fees would be similar to the previous one for pet sitting. You might charge slightly more than the competition but include complementary brushing after every visit. Be sure your prices cover transportation costs when appropriate.

Special Requirements

Pet Sitters International (PSI) offers new membership for $150, which includes a certificate. They sponsor conferences throughout the year that provide members with opportunities for further education and networking. In order to become a member, a minimum of 51 percent of revenues must come from pet-sitting services.

Dog Grooming

Estimated startup costs: $600–$900

Estimated first-year revenue: $43,000–$55,000

Dog grooming can be quite a lucrative home business, with this caveat: you need to check the zoning regulations for your neighborhood. Since dogs are typically dropped off in the mornings on their owner's way to work, you will need to create a proper space for a holding area. An important thing to keep in mind is lowering the noise factor so as not to create angry neighbors or violate any noise ordinances.

Once you determine that setting up a grooming salon in your home will not cross any social or legal boundaries, you can move into the startup phase. If you are an experienced groomer moving into the home-business arena, you already have the experience and training you will need to be successful. Although grooming does not require a long period of study, if you are a novice you will need to create a training program for yourself. Fortunately for you, there are several choices in distance learning programs that offer accreditation (see "Special Requirements").

There are many ways to approach structuring a grooming business. One option is to limit potential pooches to no more than 50 pounds or to develop a specialty in certain smaller breeds. This will keep your startup costs lower and give you a chance to hone your skills before deciding to add larger dogs to the mix.

Equipment and Supplies

You will need a grooming table ($150), tub for bathing ($180), a basic grooming kit ($200) that will come with clipping and shaving tools (for nails and claws, too), and a dryer ($110). You will also need some shampoos and soaps before you take on your first customer.

A strong grassroots marketing campaign will quicken the ramp-up period. Your referral sources should be the same as for pet sitting.

Estimating the Time Commitment

If you are new to grooming, you should practice on as many dogs as possible before taking on your first paying customer. Start out slowly to get the pace of the work down pat. You will need to know how many dogs you can handle in order to properly schedule your work. You do have the benefit of a long day for working pet owners who will want to drop off their pet before work and pick up after work. Once you get some experience, you should have no problem grooming at least one dog every hour. In the beginning, however, you will be wise to limit yourself to a maximum of four per day, to allow extra time for doing a great job. This is your best selling point and will bring you all the business you need.

Bonus Point

Just like a salon that services people, the perception of cleanliness is going to make an impact on your customers (the ones paying the bill, especially). Make a habit of sweeping and vacuuming after each pet is handled. You want your first impression to be positive.

You may want to consider being open on both weekend days for the convenience of your customers, and taking off two days midweek. This could allow you to charge more for your services and will certainly appeal to customers as an added convenience factor.

Pricing and Payments

Pricing in the dog grooming world varies based on breed, weight, size, and customer preferences. Shaving a large dog can be a much quicker proposition than getting mats out of a long-haired breed. Rather than a time-based fee, you will want to explore the competition's pricing before setting your own fees.

The following price ranges are typical for most dogs:

- Small dogs: $30–$50

- Medium dogs: $50–$70

- Large dogs: $70–$90 and up

Some groomers add special services, such as teeth and gland cleaning in order to build their average fee per dog by an extra $10 to $35 per visit.

Special Requirements

The National Dog Groomers Association of America provides a variety of on-site classroom training and a certification program to its members. The annual membership fee is $90. Private training programs are offered by JKL Grooming ($850) and Basics and Beyond ($325).

Obedience Training

Estimated startup costs: $250–$1,000

Estimated first-year revenue: $35,000–$45,000

Most professional dog obedience trainers working in the United States today are self-taught and self-employed. The standard entrée into a career as a dog trainer is through teaching a pet of one's own. Often someone will find that they enjoy working with their own dog and continue through various levels of certification in training with the American Kennel Club. Many books on the market give step-by-step guidance. Other training programs are relatively cost effective and condensed in length.

You can establish levels of training as a basis for setting a pricing structure. Different options include housebreaking for first-time puppy owners all the way to teaching a dog to respond to hand signals. You will need to be thorough in your research to determine what bundle of training results will work best for your customers. You will definitely have some trial and error in the beginning.

Even though your focus appears to be on your animal charges, you need great people skills to be a successful obedience trainer. Often the pet owner needs the most coaching and encouragement to be consistent in his responses to his pet. Obedience training is a lot like teaching. It requires passion, patience, and fortitude.

Equipment and Supplies

The startup costs for an obedience training business vary depending upon whether you plan to hold classes in your home or to teach at another location, such as a school or park. Many obedience trainers set up classes through veterinarians and use space on their premises for training. In these cases, the most you might need is an open tentlike covering for rain and sun protection ($150). If you have the space and zoning approval, you can use a garage or basement with minimal build out.

If you are going to take classes for certification, check out the websites in "Special Requirements." Prices for training programs range from $325 to $7,000, with many choices in between. Most of these certification schools or organizations offer directory listings for pet trainers by zip code, so their programs offer marketing support as well as education.

Estimating the Time Commitment

Teaching animals and their owners will require preparation both on your part and the customers'. Since many pet owners hold full-time jobs and must sometimes be present during the training (remember you are training them as well as their pets), you may find that your schedule is limited to evenings and weekends. Similar to our personal training business model (see Chapter 12), holding classes with multiple participants will probably have more revenue potential than one-on-one training. Many professional trainers recommend incorporating other pet-care services, like pet sitting, walking, or grooming into your service offerings as you build your reputation as an obedience trainer.

Pricing and Payments

Most trainers charge by the hour, with hourly rates from $50 to $150 depending on their background, experience, and the level of complexity of the animal's behavior. If you use your residence as a training center, try offering neighborhood training at a discount, or even host a free clinic to your immediate pet-owning neighbors. This will help you stay on their good side—always a good idea, even when you have the proper zoning. It's another way of getting the word out about your business.

> **Bonus Point** _____
>
> It's important to have a written agreement with the pet owner prior to starting a series of sessions. You need their commitment in order to be successful. The contract should detail a start and end date, number and length of sessions, and how much the training will cost. Be sure to specify payment dates and the consequences of interrupted training (sudden trip or illness of pet or owner) or cancelled sessions.

Taking credit cards is certainly not necessary, but it will come in very handy for charging for cancelled sessions.

Special Requirements

There are several associations for obedience trainers, all with certification options. One example is the Association of Pet Dog Trainers (APDT), which has annual membership dues of $100 and a locator directory for its members. Since it has criteria for membership that include having a certain number of training hours, a pet owner can garner extra confidence when contacting someone listed here. The National Association of Dog Obedience Instructors (NADOI) also offers certification and directory listings.

There are many obedience trainer schools that are private with affordable programs (less than $1,000). Their website links are included in the Appendix.

Aquarium Set-Up and Maintenance

Estimated startup costs: $500–$1,000

Estimated first-year revenue: $40,000–$50,000

Anyone who has ever kept as much as a small goldfish in a fishbowl can tell you that there is nothing intuitive or easy about maintaining a healthy environment for fish to thrive in. It takes a huge amount of experience and learning to tackle aquarium design, installation, and maintenance as a vocation. These are not skills acquired on the fly. On the other hand, if you have made a hobby of keeping fish alive and well in a home or office aquarium, you have a skill set that is definitely marketable. If this is the case for you, read on about how you can turn your hobby into a full-time business.

"Industry research from the Marine Aquarium Council (MAC) and other aquarium trade organizations and publications show that more than 600,000 homes and offices in the United States have a marine aquarium. From 1997 to 2002, more than 3 million marine ornamental fish were imported to the United States, making America the number one consumer in the marine ornamental industry ... and, as a result, there has never been a better time to start a saltwater tank in your home or office."—Ret Talbot, author of *The Complete Idiot's Guide to Saltwater Aquariums* (September 2009)

Many aquarium-related businesses offer design and installation in addition to maintenance services, but this is not a requirement for a viable startup. You can certainly begin with maintenance services, which requires no inventory and just a couple hundred dollars in basic equipment, which you might already have on hand for your own aquarium maintenance. Aquarium maintenance encompasses regular cleaning, water conditioning, and the following regular services:

- Water change

- Gravel vacuum

- Water quality tests

- Cleaning aquarium glass inside and out

- Adding needed chemicals

- Servicing all pumps and filters

- Inspecting of livestock for disease, or any complications

- Arranging décor to customers' tastes and creating a comfortable habitat

Equipment and Supplies

Most of the equipment needed for aquarium maintenance can be purchased for around $200. Necessary items include portable diatom and canister filters, testing kits, algae scrapers, hoses, brushes, buckets, and towels. You will need some kind of organizing system or container for transporting your equipment between customer sites in a professional manner.

Estimating the Time Commitment

Clearly there will be a great difference in the time commitment of designing and installing a new aquarium and ongoing maintenance. The cost of the materials, especially in a commercial setting, is going to be well over $1,000 depending on the dimensions of the fish tank and whether the customer is opting for a freshwater or marine environment. As a new, low-cost startup, you will have to exercise discipline and caution in constructing your contract for new installations. You will definitely want to craft your agreements such that your customer pays for all materials in advance of your purchase on their behalf. Since we are working under the assumption that you have some experience creating your own or some other aquariums, you should have some idea of the time commitment required to get through a design and installation project.

A good business plan should include an allocation of time to new projects with time allocated to building a bread-and-butter recurring maintenance income stream as well.

Pricing and Payments

Aquarium professionals advise using an hourly rate or a price per gallon when quoting fees for maintenance work. The going rate for maintenance is $1 per gallon. You will want to have a minimum visit charge based on your rate for a 30-minute visit. Since it is commonly understood that marine, or saltwater, environments are more time consuming and costly than their freshwater counterparts, you should structure your rates accordingly. Your customers are relying on you to protect what will inevitably remain an expensive investment; your services should be priced comparably to the value of the tank you are maintaining.

You will have to measure your fee schedule against the competition, but given the cost of the materials you are taking care of, your fees should be in the $50 to $100 per hour range, with a healthier profit margin on design and installation services.

You can also offer a discounted pricing schedule for weekly or biweekly customers.

Special Requirements

No professional licensing requirements are required to turn your hobby into a full-fledged business. Most of the organizations that have formed around this industry are state societies for the amateur hobbyist as well as the professional.

The need for good insurance is a recurring theme in many of the resources on starting an aquarium installation and maintenance business. The biggest concern is potential liability from water damage to the premises. There is concern among professionals that when a problem occurs, especially if there is damage to property, they will be held responsible regardless of the actual cause. This is one business where you will want to have coverage from the beginning.

17

Teaching and Tutoring

In This Chapter

- ◆ The growing business of tutoring
- ◆ Helping parents and students with college selection
- ◆ Teaching foreign and English languages
- ◆ Turning others' homeschooling into your startup
- ◆ Sharing your artistic talents as a teacher of your craft

After-School Academic Tutoring

Estimated startup costs: $1,000

Estimated first-year revenue: $43,000–$69,000

The focus on academic achievement is not only for those with college aspirations. In today's school environments, with nationwide programs like No Child Left Behind propelling school systems to be ever more test oriented, the academic tutoring business is better than ever. The caveat is that tutors are expected to be either certified teachers or possess similar credentials, so this business does have prerequisites for entry. Teachers tend to be creative types and are not always successful when dealing with finances, scheduling, business requirements, and fee collection. There is enough market demand and money in tutoring to allow for a partnership or small company approach where the skills of a businessperson and experience of a teacher are brought together for positive results.

Tutors are hired to assist students from kindergarten through grade 12 with specific subjects, standardized test preparation, homework skills, and so on. There is also a great need for special education professionals to work with special-needs children outside the classroom environment. An experienced teacher will understand that a child with autism may be a visual learner and not respond well to verbal instruction. Similarly, students with attention deficit hyperactivity disorder can require more in the way of auditory instruction than their peers.

Equipment and Supplies

Most tutors use a combination of the classroom textbooks their students are currently using and their own materials, either purchased from instructional curriculum companies or self-created. The investment in these can vary greatly, so your startup costs will vary depending on the type of tutoring you decide to offer. There are also hundreds of free online programs for use by the general public—everything from science experiment ideas to standardized testing pre-exams.

Estimating the Time Commitment

Since many tutors come from academic professions, they are often able to rapidly fill up their schedule through referrals from previous co-workers. Former public school–teachers frequently have an entire e-mail system at their disposal for spreading the word about their new tutoring service. The same is true for private school–teachers, whose relationships with staff and families involved in the school can be all they need to develop referrals.

Success Story
After 20 years as a special education teacher, Renee K. decided to start her own tutoring business with an emphasis on special-needs children. In addition to simply reinforcing classroom teaching, Renee wanted to act as an advocate for special-needs children and their parents in navigating the public school system, where she had spent her career. She sent out a letter and resumé to all the child psychologists in her area who were known to test for special needs. Within a few short months, her calendar was completely full of tutoring appointments, many referred by the psychologists she had contacted.

Most tutoring sessions take place in the afternoons after school is out for the day, with typical hours of 3:00 P.M. to 8:00 P.M. You can arrange your schedule in 45-minute sessions beginning on the hour, with 15 minutes between for transitioning from one student to the next (and collecting your payments). You can offer a monthly rate for weekly sessions if the month's fee is paid in advance of the first session. Students will often need a break from extra study once they have met a specific goal, say taking the eighth grade Iowa Test of Basic Skills (ITBS) exam, so expect to have some ups and downs in your calendar. You will be able to take time off in coordination with school holidays.

Snags

As mentioned above, handling the business end of tutoring can be very challenging for a teacher who is used to one employer and a regular paycheck with taxes and retirement-plan contributions automatically deducted. Paying taxes and saving for retirement, collecting on time from parents, and not tutoring children whose parents can no longer pay for sessions are all serious hurdles to overcome, and often very different from the day-to-day challenges of teaching in a school.

Even though summers are vacation breaks from the school calendar, many students need to continue their tutoring sessions throughout the long summer break. You will probably be able to be as busy as you want to be throughout the year.

Pricing and Payments

Tutoring is billed by the hour or 45- or 50-minute session. Payment should either be collected in advance or at the end of every session. Rates will vary across the country, and will be dependent upon the affluence of the community in which you are working. Some special-needs families will have access to subsidies for tutoring. In general, tutoring fees fluctuate with the age of the student, complexity of the subject matter being taught, and the qualifications and years of experience of the tutor.

Sample of Hourly Tutoring Fees

Tutor Qualifications	Hourly Rate
Regular teacher with homework assistance	$50
Standardized test coaching and preparation	$75
Special education tutor	$80–$100

Special Requirements

Launching a tutoring business is a great opportunity for someone who is retiring from teaching in a school system, or even a new mother who wants to work at home. You will need the appropriate teaching credentials to be successful.

You can run this business by going to the students' homes to conduct the tutoring session; however, most professional tutors prefer to work from their own office where they can control the environment and guarantee uninterrupted time with their students. A home office can work quite nicely as a base for a tutoring business. Your students will welcome the opportunity to be in a cozy space after a day spent at school.

The Association for the Tutoring Profession is a relatively new organization that offers members networking, education, and certification at different levels of expertise and experience. Annual membership for an individual is $30—a veritable bargain.

College Consulting Services

Estimated startup costs: $250+

Estimated first-year revenue: $30,000–$60,000

This work requires credentials and solid word-of-mouth referrals to build up your clientele. You are dealing with very precious cargo—a teen's future. For those who are going through this process, selecting a college is the most important decision they will have made to date. Parents and students believe their entire future hinges on making the right decision. So before they'll trust you with something this important, you have to build a reputation for results. Start out slowly, even part time, so you are not fully dependent on deriving a full-time income in your first year or two.

There are so many iterations of how a college consulting business can be shaped and formed. The college search/selection process is just one aspect, and is the one piece that requires the most prior experience and knowledge. Much of this will depend on your previous background. The selection component is a natural progression for someone who comes from a high school guidance counseling career. But there are plenty of opportunities for other ways to enter

> **Bonus Point**
>
> Even though your focus is on the student (after all, it's the student's life decision you are advising), the real challenge is going to come from the parents. Remember—it's Mom and Dad who will be paying your fee. Often the pressure from the grownups is the most delicate issue to deal with.

this profession. Many parents can handle the college selection process but really need someone to shepherd (translation: to sit on) their children to complete the application process. Once you take the selection responsibility out of the mix, you are left with assisting the student in completing the applications; providing guidance, inspiration, and encouragement in writing their essays; editing and proofreading their essays and letters; helping them create a timeline for gathering all the necessary paperwork; and so on. For those of you with good basic financial skills, helping a parent or student complete the financial-aid package is another valued service you can offer.

In other words, you can make a consulting practice for yourself by focusing on the application process tasks, and leave the high-level selection part to those truly in the know with college campus connections. Leave the piece of this business that requires frequent trips to college campuses, hobnobbing with college admissions officers, and attending conferences across the country to the academic specialists. This approach will allow you to get started immediately and keep your startup expenses to a minimum. Of course if college selection interests you, there will be opportunities to invest the time and money in acquiring the skills and knowledge necessary to compete as you build your cash flow and clientele.

Success Story

Gary C. is a long-time practicing certified public accountant (CPA) in upstate New York who has developed a deep expertise in financial aid for college students and their families. Originally introduced to the specialty when his oldest child was applying for college, Gary became intrigued with the intricacies involved in extracting the most generous financial-aid packages from top colleges. Today Gary's CPA practice brings in a significant revenue stream providing consulting services to families going through the financial-aid process. As competition for aid and federal loans has increased over the years, his services have become even more critical to helping families get the most for their college tuition dollars.

Equipment and Supplies

The requirements for equipment and supplies for a college consultant are as varied as the options for services one can offer. Full-service consultants usually have a "personality and attributes" test they administer to help identify characteristics in their student clients that are important in the college selection process. These tests can be offered through online services and charged directly to the client. Similarly, the Internet has dramatically changed the need for consultants to have a physical library of college reference materials in the office for students to peruse. Students or parents can do all the research at their leisure from their home computers.

The one expense that should be considered is the need for a professional office space to have meetings in. You can hold meetings in an appropriately dedicated home office or den. You can also rent executive-suite conference space for a reasonable fee as needed.

Estimating the Time Commitment

During the last decade the number of college consultants has more than doubled, indicating a high level of potential in this field. As the competition for admission to top colleges has become more feverish, the value of hiring professional assistance has increased. That said, the growing number of consultants indicates that the competition is increasing, too. To project how long it will take you to ramp up a new consulting business, you will need to do some fact finding, including how many consultants are located in your particular area (some states don't have a single one) and the percentage of local high school students who go to more competitive out-of-state colleges. If the statistics are in your favor, the strength of your marketing efforts will determine how long you may have to supplement your startup income before being able to proceed on a full-time basis.

Take the time to review other professionals' websites and brochures to put together a menu of services you want to offer. You will want to create packages of services, time estimates for delivering them, and a fee structure. For example, one bundle of services could include a free one-hour initial consultation to meet the student and the parents and identify what level of support they are interested in. From there, you will be able to offer hourly consulting as needed, a multisession package including application preparation, and financial-aid assistance, for example.

Pricing and Payments

Hourly fees for college consulting range from $75 to $300. According to the Independent Educational Consultants Association, the average hourly rate is around $140. It's important to keep in mind that your level of expertise and your educational credentials (the letters M.Ed., Ph.D., or CPA after your name) will have a huge impact on the price you will be able to charge. Depending upon the depth of your services, you can plan on working anywhere from 10 to 30 hours per student. Consultants who concentrate on helping students identify schools to apply to will spend an enormous amount of unbillable time traveling to conferences and campuses each year—further justification for charging at the higher end of the fee range. Proofing essays and accumulating reference letters are less valuable but very useful services.

A full-service college consultant can expect to earn around $3,000 per student. This may be over a two-year period, encompassing both the student's junior and senior years of high school.

Special Requirements

There are three primary associations for college planners and advisors. The Independent Educational Consultants Association mentioned previously, offers an associate membership to newcomers to the profession for $300 a year. The most popular, with over 11,000 members, is the National Association for College Admission Counseling with annual membership dues of $60. The most recent on the scene is the American Institute of Certified Educational Planners Commission on Credentialing. This is the elite level of recognition. Its membership of only 200 indicates that this certification process requires a lengthy list of qualifications.

Foreign-Language Tutor

Estimated startup costs: $250

Estimated first-year revenue: $17,000–$35,000

As our nation becomes ever more international and diverse, with the global community increasingly knocking on our door, there is increasing need and desire to become multilingual. Whether for personal pleasure or career necessity, the market for foreign-language study continues to grow in the United States.

Everyone who has ever purchased a pricey audio language-study program knows how little chance there is of ever getting the CD out of the packaging and into a CD player. For enjoyment and expediency, studying a language with another person has universal appeal and is a popular way of learning to speak someone else's native tongue. Once an uncommon occurrence on this side of the pond, today one can frequent a neighborhood coffee shop and listen in on a small group gathered to converse in Spanish for a half hour. Foreign students as well as American foreign-language speakers are finding it possible to earn money teaching another language on a one-on-one or group basis.

Equipment and Supplies

You don't need to purchase any large amount of materials, you can add to your resources as you add new students. You can design a program around a required text, a series of fiction, or even an international newspaper. But it won't be necessary for these expenses to come out of pocket. You can easily arrange for your students to pick up the expense, even if it means getting reimbursed at your weekly gathering.

Estimating the Time Commitment

This is another business that is slow to ramp up, since in most cases your pupils will be pursuing something they want rather than something they need. It will take time to build a regular clientele that fills your every available hour. In the meantime, you should check out Craigslist and other potential sources of people looking for language tutoring, and use every opportunity for marketing your business.

Bonus Point

There are a variety of tutor networking websites (tutormatch.com, wyzant.com) that match students and teachers on a wide variety of subjects. You will earn at a reduced hourly rate, but you will have an established referral resource sending you business in your geographic area. The hourly rates are usually pretty decent, and your payments are processed via PayPal with direct deposit. This is a good deal for someone breaking into foreign-language tutoring.

Pricing and Payments

The average hourly rate for a foreign-language tutor is anywhere from $30 to $60 per hour. Typically, tutoring services offered by college students will be at the lower end of the range (it sure beats working in the cafeteria). More experienced foreign-language speakers, especially those who are teaching their native languages, are able to command a higher rate.

Special Requirements

There are no particular requirements for this business outside of the ability to converse in the language you are teaching.

English as a Second Language Teacher

Estimated startup costs: $100

Estimated first-year revenue: $9,000–$17,000

The opportunities to teach proper pronunciation and grammar to English speakers of other languages have grown by leaps and bounds in the last three decades. As immigrants continue to flood our shores and look for work, there is a never-ending need for those willing to help them work on their English. The demand will certainly be higher among those seeking higher education degrees and professional jobs. The beauty of this type of work is that it does not require any particular credentials or post-graduate education. It will certainly be beneficial to be someone who has studied English for Speakers of Other Languages (ESOL) at the college or post-graduate level. But it is not necessary. The prospective customers for ESOL tutoring will vary, from people who just want to converse in the native tongue of their adopted country to those who need to have excellent written skills as well.

Free training in ESOL tutoring is available to volunteers at community centers that offer these classes for free. Once you have some experience, you should be able to adapt what you have learned to a business model and start recruiting paying students of your own.

Equipment and Supplies

If you are new to teaching ESOL there are many books available on amazon.com (see the Appendix for examples) to give you an understanding of the basic objectives and methods to use. Although not necessary, there are various inexpensive supplies you might want to use in your lesson plans. Go to http://www.onlinetutoringworld.com/lessonplans to access free, complete lesson plans to help you get started. As you build confidence in your teaching abilities, you will be able to create your own lessons using photos, videos, and other visual media as the starting point for each lesson. There are no other major expenditures other than general marketing materials required to get started.

Estimating the Time Commitment

Like all the tutor options, it will take time to get your name circulated in the market-place. If you have the opportunity in your area, marketing your skills to foreign corporations in your city is an excellent idea for earning top dollar in your field. You will also need to present a highly professional appearance for this type of work, and spend time studying the culture of the corporation's home country.

You can include both private and group classes in your schedule to give you variety and increase your per-hour fee.

Pricing and Payments

The hourly rate for English as a second language tutors is on a lower scale than other tutors, since it requires less education and certification (i.e., anyone who paid attention in high school English class has the potential to do this). Rates range from $15 (working in an adult education center) to $30 per hour. Group classes can give a boost to your earnings at the same time you are offering your students a break on your fee.

Special Requirements

You must have good spelling, an excellent vocabulary, and a good ear for understanding speakers of other languages. If you teach students who are native speakers of a language you also understand and speak, this will go a long way to helping you develop a niche in this market.

Although it's not required, you may eventually want to hone your teaching skills and acquire the other benefits that come with one of the two available certification programs for ESOL teachers. You can do your research online to determine for yourself which certificate is best suited for your needs. See the Appendix for links to the related websites.

Homeschooling Curriculum Advisor and Tutor

Estimated startup costs: $500–$1,000

Estimated first-year revenue: $19,000–$48,000

Understanding the homeschooling environment is important in building your business to service this industry.

If you are a parent who has homeschooled your own children, then you are in an excellent position to transition from homeschooler to homeschool curriculum advisor and tutor. You will already have contacts in the community, know many of the parents who are homeschooling their children and are prospective customers, and have enough knowledge on which to build your business plan. If you are new to home-schooling but have an educator's background, you will have to spend time gaining an understanding of the homeschooling community. But you will have a terrific background and the credentials to command an appropriate level of respect from the lay-people in the homeschooling community.

Many parents who homeschool have strong religious convictions and choose to educate their children outside of an institutional setting in order to have strict control over the material that their children are exposed to. To work as a professional in this environment, you will either need to have similar beliefs or accept being told what you can and cannot teach.

With the number of homeschooled students increasing every year, the potential to develop a profitable business creating, compiling, and teaching curricula is growing rapidly. You will need to get a good handle on the competition in your area, if indeed there is any. Most homeschool curricula are offered through a variety of Internet-based suppliers and through vendors who attend large homeschooling conventions around the country.

Bonus Point

Many homeschooling families or groups of families will need professional support for any students with special needs. For example, a family may be able to handle basic instruction but will need support in teaching reading skills to a learning-disabled child.

Equipment and Supplies

You will likely want to explore the curricula and textbooks that are readily available on the market and evaluate them with an eye to incorporating them into your own programs. There may be opportunity for you to create your own unique materials, but this is time consuming and difficult to get compensated for. Plan on paying out-of-pocket for your own teacher's edition of any books and other materials, and billing your families for copies to be used by the students.

Estimating the Time Commitment

Even if your community has several hundred homeschoolers, keep in mind that they are a highly diffused customer base that will take a good deal of time and effort to market to successfully. You may want to consider starting out part time while keeping your regular job, or supplementing your income with regular tutoring while you build this niche business. It may take a year or two to really get underway, but once you do it is likely that you will have enough work to keep you busy.

Pricing and Payment

You should price your services at a similar level to private after-school tutors—from $40 to $100 per hour depending on the skill level and credentials required (for example, algebra versus special needs). Keep in mind that in many instances you will be working for several families, especially if you are teaching a high-level science or math, and your fee will be shared among the group. You should make advance arrangements for how and when you are to be paid. Prepayment on the first of each school month is advisable.

Special Requirements

If you are currently a certified teacher, you need the proper continuing education to maintain your certification. Since certification is granted on a state-to-state basis, this will vary according to your state's requirements. Whether or not you have certification, you will absolutely need to be on top of your state requirements to ensure that your students are eligible for passing each grade and receiving official diplomas.

Art and Music Lessons

Estimated startup costs: $250–$500

Estimated first-year revenue: $15,000–$43,000

People who choose to make their living using their artistic talents to teach others will never make as much money as well-known celebrities with similar talents. But they will get to fill their days doing something they love and sharing that enthusiasm with interested students. While it's not uncommon, especially in urban and suburban communities, to find art and music instruction within the framework of a school or academy, it is much more common to have individual teachers marketing lessons to the public at large. Whether they opt to teach private or group lessons, in their homes or the homes of their students, the weekly music lesson survives today in much the same form as it has for the past century.

Art lessons are more commonly taught in a classroom setting, but a home-based art class could be held in a teacher's home studio. Students can either come after school or on weekends. Many retirees, perhaps finding time on their hands for the first time in their lives, often take up art lessons as a way of exploring untapped talent. With efficient scheduling and good business practices, both music and art teachers can make respectable livings teaching their craft.

Equipment and Supplies

Most art and music teachers supply their teaching skills and expect their students to pick up the cost of supplies, whether paints and canvases or music books and instruments. You will need to have your own supplies or instruments in order to have the tools to teach with, but overall this line of work does not require a major investment in equipment. The estimated startup costs of $250-$500 are meant to cover basic marketing materials and local advertising, as well as art or music supplies to get your classes started.

Estimating the Time Commitment

Most music lessons are given in half-hour increments. Since most of the students are school-age children and teens, the scheduling usually begins when school lets out in the afternoon and continues into the early evening hours. With the addition of lessons on Saturdays, a music teacher can fit in a full-time work week. Once your schedule is at capacity, you can rely on word-of-mouth referrals to fill in the usual fluctuation of students.

Art lessons are most commonly taught in two- to three-hour blocks of time. You can schedule them in the afternoons and on Saturdays for school-age children. Many art teachers offer classes grouped into several weekly sessions, say six to eight. Teachers in high-density retirement areas will have more opportunities to schedule private lessons and sessions throughout the day.

Success Story

Charlotte D. started teaching children's art classes several years ago. She has turned her living and dining rooms into a teaching space and art room. During the year she offers three 10- to 12-week sessions (depending on the school holiday calendar)—one each in fall, winter, and spring. She bases her pricing on an hourly rate so she feels adequately compensated. Charlotte has written a series of articles on how to package children's art lessons at http://emptyeasel.com/?s=charlotte+Demolay. One great recommendation is to get a 20 percent deposit when the parents sign their children up for your classes. It reduces potential last-minute cancellations.

Pricing and Payments

The average cost for a private music lesson is $25 per half hour. Payment is expected on the first of the month for all the weekly lessons in that month. Keeping up with collections is probably the hardest task for a music teacher, second only to staying on schedule. Another challenge is making sure students understand how much notice is expected when a cancellation is necessary.

Art lessons, often taught in classes over several weeks, usually require payment by the student in advance of the first day of class. Spaces are often limited by size constraints and it is important to the teacher to fill as many of the spots as possible. Pricing for adult art lessons runs from $50 to $100 for a three-hour session, depending on the location and the reputation of the teacher. For children's lessons, you can base your per-class price on what other types of after-school activities charge. Keep in mind that you will be putting in time before and after the scheduled class, purchasing materials, speaking to parents, and cleaning up after the class. Charging each child $15 for each hour of class (or $30 for a two-hour class) is a reasonable fee that should yield a good income for you for six or more students. Remember that your tuition should be payable for the entire series of classes; avoid discounting for classes a student will be unable to attend, even if you know that in advance.

Special Requirements

Clearly the expectation for both the art and music teacher is that they know their craft well and are patient, caring teachers.

Knitting Lessons and Finishing Services

Estimated startup costs: $150

Estimated first-year revenue: $20,000–$43,000

The last decade has seen a dramatic return of knitting as a popular hobby. Today there are knitting stores in every town, several in any major city, and you're more likely now to see a young person with a knitting project than at any other time since the Industrial Revolution. There is big money in all things yarn, and even though many knitting stores offer classes, some novice students crave the one-on-one attention of a private teacher and are willing to pay for the time. And why shouldn't they be, when you consider the investment most knitters make today in any one individual project?

There are no formal prerequisites for becoming a knitting teacher other than a love of the craft and willingness to work with those who have less skill than you do. Since knowing how to knit is the one requirement for teaching it to others, most people who become knitting teachers and finishers (skilled knitters who literally 'finish' a project by piecing it together) have many years of knitting experience and a very advanced level of skill.

Equipment and Supplies

Similar to music and art teachers, a knitting teacher will have to have her own project and tool kit in order to demonstrate the various techniques to her students. Any true knitter will have more than one project in the works anyway, so this should not be a problem. If you have a space in your home that you can use as a teaching studio, you may want to conduct some of your lessons at home. Some knitting teachers will travel to their students' homes, making a home office or studio unnecessary. Having students come to your home is a convenience to you and will eliminate your travel time to customers.

Some knitting instructors will give their students the option of meeting them at a knitting store to learn about selecting projects, yarn, and various tools of the trade. Alternatively, you can make up a knitting basket of items you feel your students should have and sell it to each student with a markup on the cost to compensate for your efforts.

Estimating the Time Commitment

Knitting lessons are a minimum of an hour long. Depending on the attention span of the student, you could consider a longer session for certain more difficult lessons (like learning to make cable knits or socks). If you do have space in your home for holding classes, you should be able to add a few to your monthly calendar. Many public spaces, such as libraries and recreation centers, will be open to the idea of having you hold classes in their facility for a small fee. It can be difficult to earn a full-time living as a knitting teacher, and many fill open hours working part time in a knitting store, if only to get discounts on materials for their own projects.

If you have good knitting skills, adding finishing to your repertoire is another way to increase your potential revenue. Even very competent hobby knitters are skittish about finishing their own projects. This is especially true if they use expensive yarns and complicated patterns. Finishing a hand knitted item is a multistep process that requires precision, patience, and knowledge. It is a much-appreciated service and with a regular clientele of avid knitters, you should be able to add a good amount of revenue to your business.

Pricing and Payment

Knitting lessons are usually paid for at the end of each lesson. Fees are charged hourly, with $25 to $50 per hour being fairly standard across the country. The $50 per hour is more common in cities like New York and Los Angeles. Finishing garments will be billed by the project, with the same hourly rate built into the calculation. Be sure to get a deposit of at least 50 percent when the customer drops the project off with you. The last thing an avid knitter needs is a collection of unclaimed sweaters by non-paying clients.

Special Requirements

There are no formal requirements for being a professional knitter other than experience and know-how.

Part 5

Hospitality Beckons

Vacation habits may change with the times and economy, but the one constant is that Americans will still want to make something memorable from their limited time off from work. Food related activities and interests have mushroomed in the last 20 years, heavily influenced by cable television but also influenced by a greater global awareness of cuisine. Food has become entertainment as well as nourishment. Chefs of all shapes and types are treated with great respect. Many of today's celebrities come from the food world.

Even though corporate events have toned down over the last couple years, we will always celebrate life and successes. From Bridezilla to Cinderella, weddings and other important events will continue to get our attention and dollars. There are many opportunities for work related to helping people relish their event experiences.

Food Services

In This Chapter

- ◆ Why it's more critical than ever to follow state guidelines for your home-catering business
- ◆ The rise of personal and vacation chef-on-the-go concepts
- ◆ Low-cost opportunities that take advantage of increased trends in fresh produce consumption
- ◆ Branding yourself as a mobile bartender
- ◆ Combining entertainment value with food and wine classes

Home-based food services have become complicated because many states forbid selling food for public consumption if it is not prepared in a commercial kitchen. One way to get around the rigid rules and regulations of various departments of health is to prepare food in the purchasers' own kitchens. This is one reason the profession of personal chef now numbers over 9,000 people. This relatively new designation has given many individuals the opportunity to pursue careers as chefs, bakers, and so on, without the need to make a major capital investment in commercial kitchen equipment.

There are many other ways to create a business around making food or serving food and beverages. You can enjoy making a living at something you love and keep your startup costs well below $1,000. The important thing to remember is that having passion and skill for the culinary arts is a requisite of being successful in the food industry, but it is not enough. A good business plan and ability to allocate time to the business side of the venture are just as important to your future success.

Home-Based Catering Services

Estimated startup costs: $350–$1,000

Estimated first-year revenue: $30,000–$75,000

Where would America be today if not for the home-catering business started in 1976 in a basement in Connecticut? Today, the Martha Stewart media empire's humble beginning still inspires many would-be chefs to turn their love for food and celebrations into a full-fledged business. The market for catering, including large events, family celebrations, and intimate dinner parties has expanded wildly since Martha put her hand in the mix. Martha's success bodes well for anyone who loves to cook and has enough determination to add a taste for business to their passion for food.

On the cautionary side, you must study and heed your state's requirements for using commercial kitchens before you end up crying over the spilt milk of business plans gone awry. There are many opportunities for forays into the culinary field if you are willing to work within your local laws and plan your catering business to meet the rules and regulations stipulated by your health department.

Bonus Point

Take advantage of the many unmanned corporate kitchens around the country that have been without their own chef because of aggressive budget cutting in the last year. Market yourself as a freelance corporate chef who prepares meals in the office commercial kitchen on an as-needed basis.

If you can't prepare food in your own home kitchen, then prepare the food on your customer's site, in their kitchen, or in the kitchen of a commercial facility rented for their event. Many facilities contract with local caterers to handle parties booked during the year—everything from your local VFW Hall to estate homes on the National Historic Register. In addition to becoming the caterer of choice at a venue owned and operated by someone else, you can fill in your schedule with dinner parties or corporate lunches where you are completely in charge of the menu and procuring all items, and you prepare everything on-site. You can bring your favorite knives, pans, and personal spice box with you.

Equipment and Supplies

There are so many high-quality items to be had in the world of cookware and kitchen gadgets. Unfortunately, you are going to have to avoid the temptation to buy that $800 copper-clad sauté pan. Start out with your current inventory of pots, pans, and utensils. Let the nature of the jobs you land guide you to any new purchases you make. You will want to put all your startup dollars into creating an attractive website, building word of mouth about your delicious food and terrific service, and save the splurges on equipment for celebratory occasions down the road (like your company's first-year anniversary).

An investment to consider is a guide to starting a catering business ($25 to $100) that includes worksheets for budgeting jobs, setting pricing, and timelines for ensuring that all the details are handled well in advance, along with other tips of the trade. Model your organization system on someone else's. Even if you adapt it to better suit your personality quirks and unique style, copying something that works is much easier than starting from scratch.

Estimating the Time Commitment

Your success as a caterer will depend more on your business acumen than your culinary talents. Take the time to develop a complete business plan. Diligently research the market to come up with a menu and approach that will clearly differentiate you. Most importantly, structure your pricing to ensure that every event you do is profitable.

Marketing your new catering business will take an appropriate amount of flair if you want to quickly fill up your schedule. If you are going to be working from a specific facility, work on a joint "kick-off" party to announce your new business with some additional advertising dollars provided by the facility owner. Offering your services at a discount to friends and high-profile local charities is a good way to get media attention when you are starting out.

You need to build in plenty of extra time to handle the last-minute emergencies that are bound to come up as you near your events. Your customers are putting their faith in you to create the perfect occasion, which in many cases will be a life-cycle occasion of great importance to them and their entire family. Not to mention costing them big bucks. Don't be caught short on time and get frazzled before you even get to the big event. Building in plenty of time in the early stages of your business will make success much more likely in this industry.

Pricing and Payments

There are several components to generating profit in the catering business. You will be coordinating many facets of an event, from linen rental and servers to beverages and décor. Most caterers build some profit for themselves into each piece of the total party pie. Revenue from the food itself is going to be the biggest piece.

There are two different approaches to pricing your menu. The first, especially common in home-catering settings, is to present the receipts for the food totaled in an invoice with a percentage of the total cost added for your planning, supervision, and execution. This works very much like a construction general contractor's business model. Depending on the size of the event, some caterer/chefs will add an hourly fee for themselves to make sure they are properly compensated for all their time, including their shopping and clean up.

Total of all food receipts	$4,300
5 servers @ $30/hour for 4 hours	$600
Subtotal food and labor costs	**$4,900(a)**
Caterer's surcharge, 20 percent of food cost and other labor	$980(b)
Chef's time, 10 hours @ $50/hour	$500(c)
Total bill to customer (a+b+c)	**$6,380**
Total revenue for you (b+c)	**$1,480**

The second and more common way to present your bill to your customers is by calculating what your costs will be and using a multiple to create a price per guest to quote and invoice your customer. Let's use the figures from the above sample billing and covert them to a per guest invoice. Your total invoice is $4,900 + $1,480, or $6,380. If your customer was planning for 100 guests, a quote of $63.80 rounded to $65 per person would get you the revenue you need for the job with a small amount of cushion in the calculation.

Special Requirements

Many different educational backgrounds would give you a foundation for becoming a caterer on your own, including culinary training, a hotel and restaurant academic degree, or years of experience working in the food industry. There are even personal chef programs (mostly self-study) that would give you an entertainment or dinner party specialty. Of course, the industry is full of those with Martha Stewart–type backgrounds based on growing up with a parent who loved to cook and entertain.

Good marketing skills are a perfect pairing for this trend-and-style business. Of course nothing is better than being connected to lots of people who love to entertain as much as you do and have the money and lifestyle to indulge their social outlet.

Personal Chef

Estimated startup costs: $250–$1,000

Estimated first-year revenue: $21,000–$35,000

The personal chef profession originally sprang up in response to the growing trend of dining out and purchasing prepared foods that followed the growth of women entering the workforce in the 1980s. In 1991, Cindi Wallace wrote a manual and founded the American Personal and Private Chef Association (APPCA). The concept is high-end but straightforward: in this busy society, people want to eat well and healthfully but don't have the time to plan, shop, cook, and clean up for themselves. Many families with traveling spouses and children involved in all sorts of extracurricular activities cannot have family mealtime every night of the week. Yet people yearn to come home at the end of their long work day (and often after a meeting or two in the evening) and dine in the comfort of their own homes.

Enter the concept of the personal chef. Based in part on the role of a private chef who cooks most meals for one family full time, the personal chef turns cooking for others into a small business. He or she (and this is a far more female-friendly career than a commercial restaurant kitchen) accomplishes their task primarily while their customers are at work, so they act like food fairies who come in while you're gone, cook wonderful meals, and clean up so you don't even know they've been there. Only when you look in the refrigerator and freezer do you see the evidence in the meals left behind.

A personal chef plans, shops, and cooks several meals at a time for an individual, couple, or family. Some personal chefs will also plan and manage small dinner parties or even large celebrations in their customers' homes.

The main barrier to entry is the time involved in building up your income in a new business. Otherwise, anyone can become a personal chef, either with or without the proper designations.

Equipment and Supplies

Experienced personal chefs recommend newcomers use their own equipment when they start their businesses. Since you will be working in the customers' kitchens, you'll be able to use whatever appliances and kitchen utensils you find on the job, but you want to be prepared in case your customer's kitchen is not adequately equipped. You will be working on-site, so you will want to be clever about how you carry your personal items to and from your customers' homes.

Membership in either of the popular professional organizations will give you two valuable marketing tools. The first is a listing by zip code in their personal chef directory, an effective tool in bringing you leads of prospective customers in your area. The second is a website development program that will help you create your own simple website, which will be your main marketing tool to target people too busy to cook for themselves.

Estimating the Time Commitment

A personal chef's typical day includes menu planning followed by a shopping excursion to purchase your groceries and supplies. Most of your customers who work outside the home will either give or leave you a key, although many will work from home as well. After arriving and setting up in your customers' kitchens, you'll spend the next several hours preparing the meals, usually three to five entrées with complementary sides and desserts. The next task is sealing all the meals and putting them in the freezer, leaving detailed instructions for heating and serving the various items. Finally, you clean up the kitchen, leaving it spic and span, smelling of delicious ingredients, with perhaps one meal left in the oven for that evening's dinner.

Building a full schedule of customers will not happen overnight. Having other means of generating income, whether they include freelance catering or serving, will help you with cash flow while you make your career transition.

Pricing and Payments

Personal chefs price their services by the hour, with a national range from $30 to over $60, depending on location, experience, and clientele. They frequently create packages based on a number of meals and people, say 5 meals for a family of 4. The pricing is quoted both inclusive and exclusive of food cost. For example, a personal chef may charge $500 for 5 complete meals for 2 adults, including food. Or he may have a price list that shows labor only, say $275 for the same 10 total meals above with the cost of the groceries in addition.

Either way the pricing across the country is consistently within the above range.

Success Story

Chef Carlin B. became a personal chef in 1998 after reaching a point of no return in her lucrative but demanding corporate career as a project manager. Over the years she has created a well-respected reputation along with a career she absolutely loves. She manages to work only four days a week, with one of those being for office work and menu planning. She has many customers for whom she has been cooking since her first years of business, visiting most once a month and preparing 10 meals for the entire family. The most recent trend, according to Chef Carlin, is a growing request for allergy-specific meals, whether gluten-, dairy-, or peanut-free. She prides herself on tailoring her meal preparation to her customers' needs and tastes. As part of her overall business strategy, Chef Carlin has become a frequent teacher of different cooking classes, from summer programs for preschoolers to teaching and mentoring future personal chefs at the Culinary Business Academy of Atlanta.

Special Requirements

There are two competing entities that provide the personal chef designation. The original is the APPCA. Membership dues run $325 per year but come with several great benefits, the first of which is liability insurance coverage included in the dues.

Each organization has well-developed chapters at the state and local level with wonderful opportunities for networking and mentoring. In addition to sharing their love of food, personal chefs tend to be a cooperative rather than a competitive group. The chapters are terrific avenues for those new to the field to get advice and guidance from those who have been in the business for the last decade.

You can get your personal chef credentials in a variety of ways, with corresponding price tags. The most cost effective is the original home study (notice we did not say "online"—this program originated in 1991, before the "discovery" of the Internet). The cost is $505 and you can complete the course at your own pace. There are also more costly online ($895) and on-site ($1,895) options.

Vacation Chef

Estimated startup costs: $250–$1,000

Estimated first-year revenue: $30,000–$40,000

The market for vacation chefs is much smaller than for personal chefs or caterers in general, but for the more adventurous person with the right personality and skills, this niche market can offer good income and the chance to see different parts of the country and even the world.

The variations on this theme are limited only by your imagination and desire to travel. You could focus on tourists if you happen to live in a resort area. You can network with sea captains around the world and cruise the Mediterranean, shopping for provisions in Greece. You can also scale down on the glamour and expand your market by offering to be a personal chef for a group from your city taking an annual ski trip or "girls weekend." The possibilities are endless.

A vacation chef is much like a hybrid between a private chef dedicated to one family or group and a personal chef cooking a specified number of meals with responsibility for planning, shopping, preparing, serving, and clean-up.

Equipment and Supplies

Similar to that of the caterer and personal chef, your equipment needs will depend on the assignment. If you love the open seas and get hired as the chef on a weeklong sail to the Bahamas, you will need to plan menus in advance to determine whether the ship's galley has everything you need. If you end up bringing some of your favorite cookware, be prepared to share a bunk with it, since the storage on most boats is very limited.

You will need some credentials and an impressive resumé to entice people to put their vacation memories and dollars in your hands. It's great to have an appealing website, but at a minimum you will need several good references to land work in this niche market.

Estimating the Time Commitment

Combining a vacation chef business with other food-related work is the best way to get started and build a viable revenue stream. You will have to navigate the complexity of meshing a regular personal chef or catering schedule with periods of time dedicated to vacation customers. If you actually travel with a group, you can expect to have very little downtime of your own, especially if you are preparing more than one meal a day.

Pricing and Payments

Vacation chefs usually price by the day, unless they are hired for a more limited engagement. In addition to expecting any and all travel expenses to be taken care of and paid for, a daily rate for an experienced, well-known chef can be $500 or more a day. On the other hand, if you are working as a personal chef in one resort location, catering to vacationing clientele, you can expect to make an hourly rate on the high end of the personal chef scale, around $60 per hour.

Another option is to package a meal by a price per person, say brunch for 6 for $200 to $300. You can start out with more than one pricing option and see which method works better or seems more appealing to the customer.

Special Requirements

Having some formal culinary background is helpful but not necessary to develop as a vacation chef. Good marketing and connections with excellent references will be just as important for getting the attention of potential customers.

Having a personal chef certification and belonging to one of the professional organizations will be helpful as well.

Fresh and Local Produce Distribution

Estimated startup costs: $400–$600

Estimated first-year revenue: $35,000–$50,000

Everyone from the creators of the USDA food pyramid to organic food proponents has been touting the need for Americans to consume more fruits and vegetables. And the message has resonated with a large percentage of our country's citizens, who as a group have purchased at least 30 percent more fresh produce in the last year than in 1980, according to the Iowa State University Center for Agriculture and Rural Development. With the local and organic produce movements spawning everything from communal "victory gardens" to best-selling books on going local for a year comes opportunity to cash in on the trend. You need skills, know-how, and capital to become an organic farmer, but farmers need help marketing their produce and getting it to market. That's where you and your truck come into the picture.

Produce distribution is a long-standing business idea going back to the earliest days of commerce in the United States. Many farmers develop their own distribution networks through *vertical integration*, but most small and micro farmers have more than a full plate just growing their vegetables and fruits, and are grateful for partnerships with others who respect their products and want to help get it to market.

def•i•ni•tion

Vertical integration refers to one company owning different parts of production—for example, growing and harvesting food, transporting it to market, and selling it to consumers at a farmers' market or roadside stand.

There are numerous ways to structure a produce distribution business. Here we will cover two classic ideas that require limited industry experience and a small investment of capital. One idea is the roadside stand concept. Even with the proliferation of local farmers' markets in so many towns and cities across the country, these markets are limited to a small number of vendors. They also take place in early morning or weekday hours that are not necessarily convenient for the average consumer. To create a place for yourself in this chain, check out the opportunities for opening your own roadside stand. Look for a location that has high traffic but at speeds less than 50 m.p.h. for good visibility. Your job is to get up long before the crack of dawn and drive to the large, daily state farmers' market, usually on the outskirts of major metropolitan areas. Develop relationships with local farmers who bring their produce to market, and buy enough to fill your truck or van. By morning rush hour you should have your roadside stand set up with multiple displays of everything fresh and currently being harvested.

An alternate concept is to transport the produce from the farm (ideally several farms in one region) or farmers' market directly to the consumer. One form of this is the Community Supported Agriculture cooperative-style organization. You can learn more about this movement at http://www.nal.usda.gov/afsic/pubs/csa/csa.shtml. Another variation that works in dense urban centers is simply farmers' market to home delivery on a regular route and schedule.

Equipment and Supplies

Depending upon the climate of your region, you can use an inexpensive canopy tent ($150) to create your roadside stand along with a clear, homemade sign. Unless you happen to own the perfect piece of property, you will have to scout for an acceptable, low-cost location. Often a well-located parking lot works fine and the monthly rent is affordable, especially if you find an under-occupied shopping strip. You will need some tables (construction wire spool tables work well and create a good ambiance) with baskets for displaying merchandise. You will need a cash box and plastic or paper bags for packaging up the produce. You should be able to get started for an initial investment of under $400, including the canopy.

If you are going to focus on produce delivery, you can limit your investment to your vehicle expenses.

Estimating the Time Commitment

Any business related to the growing and harvesting of fruits and vegetables is going to be seasonal in most regions around the country. Weekends are going to be your best days for business, so if you have the stamina you could work six to seven days a week in the spring, summer, and fall, with a long winter break.

Success Story

One woman outside of metropolitan Atlanta has grown her fruit-and-vegetable stand from a single truck parked on the side of the road to two well-trafficked locations in affluent suburban areas. What started out as a one-person business has grown to a family enterprise, with several children and grandchildren handling the various responsibilities. It's a long day that starts long before daybreak with a truck ride down to the Georgia State Farmer's Market south of the city. Then it's back up the highway north about 50 miles to each of two locations, where the interest in eating locally grown foods has helped sustain this business from April through October each year.

Pricing and Payments

Once you establish your location, you can expect to take in several hundred dollars each day, with about a 40 percent profit margin after covering your costs. Your gross is going to depend on the density of your area, your competition, and the quality of the available produce. Your goal should be to average a minimum of $1,000 in sales six days a week to make this a viable business with enough put away for the winter break for an area with a six-month growing season. For those with shorter seasons of 20 weeks or less, you will need higher average daily sales—say, $1,500—to make this your sole source of income. You can always opt to work at other seasonal jobs during the cooler months while you build your business.

Special Requirements

There are no special professional requirements to enter this industry, but there is a definite advantage to having existing relationships with local producers. You can learn the intricacies of this business with the proper research and investment of time in exploring the competition.

Go visit other local farmers' markets to see which vendors are popular. Certain vendors always sell out before everyone else. These are the people you can learn the most from.

Bonus Point _____

The best-selling vendors are frequently the ones with the best-looking merchandise, not the cheapest prices. Research shows that the closer produce is to being ripe, the better the turnover.

Bartending

Estimated startup costs: $200–$500

Estimated first-year revenue: $17,000–$35,000

As more people have seen the benefits of working directly with the party organizer rather than as an employee of a catering company, the bartending and service professions have taken an entrepreneurial turn. There are more bartenders freelancing their services (often referred to as *mobile bartending*), and why shouldn't they? Since they bring the expertise and skills to the event, why not get paid directly? Instead of working as an employee with a low-base hourly wage plus tips, individual bartenders are finding their own customers by setting up websites and creating their own business plans.

In addition to just making a shopping list and showing up to mix drinks, you can offer more services to increase your profit on each event. These include purchasing the mixers, glassware rental, renting a bar unit, bringing your own tables and linens, and shopping for paper goods and bar snacks. Every extra you add to your package brings in extra revenue.

Equipment and Supplies

A basic bartending tool kit is the only thing you absolutely have to own to get started. You will increase your marketing results dramatically if you have your own website. Once you get cash flow, you can invest in extras like glassware and portable bar units.

Bonus Point _____

Many elite restaurant bartenders are renowned for one or more specialty drinks. Why not develop your own celebrity by adding some unique creations to your repertoire? It will help you build word-of-mouth referrals as guests talk about the special bar offerings at their friend's latest event. Create a special beverage named for your host or guest of honor, like "Gail's Glayva."

Estimating the Time Commitment

You don't need a huge amount of setup time for a beverage station, so a typical engagement is likely to be for four to six hours. Many mobile bartenders offer the setup hour as free along with supplying the tools and basic table. Base your initial business plan on working three to four days each week, something like Thursday through Sunday.

Networking with event planners, small catering companies, DJs, florists, and other event vendors will be extremely helpful in getting the word out about your business.

Pricing and Payments

The most common rate for bartenders is $25 per hour, with higher rates in major cities and for very high-end events. By adding rental items and supplies to your services, you will be able to increase your hourly rate significantly by the profit margins on these additions. Another popular business model for this kind of work is to expand your business to include other bartenders, whom you would assign to events booked on the same day. You can also expect to get paid a tip on your hourly rate, even though you are self-employed. Gratuities for events usually average 20 percent of the total compensation.

Just like a caterer, you should have a contract to use for every customer, along with a deposit requirement and refund policy in order to prevent unpaid last-minute cancellations.

Special Requirements

Most bartenders take a bartending course to prepare themselves to work in this business. There are now dozens of courses offered online, in audio or DVD versions, for under $100.

Some states have pouring licenses or other requirements, so it is important to review the laws of your home state. There may also be server penalties for serving alcohol to minors.

You do not need a license to sell alcohol, since you will structure your business to have the customer make all the alcohol purchases.

Wine-Tasting Event Host

Estimated startup costs: $250–$1,000

Estimated first-year revenue: $15,000–$30,000

Wine consumption in the United States has increased dramatically along with the number of wine producers across the country. Almost every state has its own wine country—it's not just Napa Valley anymore. Yet Americans in general still have a lot to learn about wine. If you are an above-average wine aficionado (you know, the person in your group who is always asked to choose the wine at dinner), you have a foundation to get started as a wine-tasting host. It's amazing how far a little knowledge can go when most of your peers are insecure about their abilities.

You may be thinking, "If I'm not going to open a wine distributorship or retail store, neither of which is remotely close to a low-cost business idea—how exactly can I make money in this field?" We have come up with several interesting ways in which you can earn a respectable sum putting your expertise to use.

Most wine distributors will hold wine tastings at the local wine store that buys and sells their wines, but these are limited presentations that are all about their vineyard's selections. Many people want to have a hands-on experience to learn and compare different wines. Wine tastings have become destination events for all sorts of occasions, from a bachelorette party to a fiftieth birthday celebration. Here are just a few ideas of how you can work on your image as a wine consultant and get paid for indulging a favorite pastime and hobby.

Market your services as a wine party host. Develop a package for in-home or corporate entertainment where you plan the event, select the wines to be purchased by the customer, and serve them in an appropriate setting. You can certainly network with event planners and get some help choosing venues. Create several different entertaining presentations that you can offer individually or in a series.

Many states outside of California have wine regions that would be thrilled to accommodate any tourists you might want to bring to their facilities. Design a tour and be the tour guide and designated driver. Get your chauffeur license (or hire a driver if you plan to partake in the tasting). Visitors will pay for your services as a tour guide and your "insider connections," getting them in to visit out-of-the-way, "undiscovered" vineyards. Just think of yourself as bringing a little piece of Napa or Tuscany to your hometown.

Like any hobbyist, wine enthusiasts who build a home wine cellar can get carried away and buy enough wine to last a lifetime, let alone the next 10 years. The problem is, many wines don't improve with age, but it takes education and training to identify the correct time to open a bottle. Marketing yourself as a wine-cellar specialist who helps customers solve life's wine problems can become a nice complement to your other consulting and teaching services.

Arrange an annual wine tour in France or another major wine producing country. Partnering with a local charity or your alma mater can be an easy way to get help marketing the trip to potential participants while you focus on the itinerary.

Equipment and Supplies

You need to look the part of the sophisticated wine drinker, but otherwise you don't need any particular equipment. You may want to subscribe to *Wine Spectator* to stay abreast with all current wine events both stateside and abroad.

You will definitely want your own website along with as good a marketing plan as you can afford.

Estimating the Time Commitment

The big pitfall with this type of business is spending too much time indulging your senses and not enough time on the business end of things. You will need several weeks to research what else is happening in and around your area to make sure you put together the best business plan possible. This is also a business that you could start part time, on weekends or evenings, while you hang on to your day job.

Putting in the time to write a blog, newsletter, articles for the local paper, and attracting other publicity will help the pace of growth in the first year.

Pricing and Payments

You won't have much in the way of competition from other wine consultants. This gives you the freedom to work your way into the amount you need to charge by the hour or excursion. Your required pay will also depend on the number of people who sign up for your various wine events. Wine consultants charge by the event or the hour, getting paid at an hourly rate of anywhere from $35 to $95 depending on their experience, entertainment abilities, and reputations. Alternatively, you can charge a respectable price per person, and work up to higher revenue when your events become more popular and start to fill up to capacity.

Special Requirements

There are two elite designations for wine consultants—Master Sommelier and Master of Wine. Only three people in the United States have both, and only just over 300 people have either title. Most consultants rely on their self-taught knowledge, continuing education (mostly tasting wine and visiting vineyards), and good marketing skills to promote their services.

In-Home Cooking Classes

Estimated startup costs: $250–$1,000

Estimated first-year revenue: $21,000–$35,000

By cashing in on the tail of the Food Network meteor, the in-home cooking class as education and entertainment has become an opportunity for generating revenue. Combining an interest in teaching and cooking, in-home classes can be a stand-alone business, but obviously would pair well with personal chef, vacation chef, or caterer. For years, many companies have used a hands-on cooking lesson as a team building exercise. What better way to provide an evening chock full of fun than bringing friends or co-workers together for a cooking lesson followed by a shared meal and conversation?

You will need to add your own flair and style in order to make your class not only informative but entertaining and fun. You will want to have menus to recommend but also be able to work around any particular idea or theme your host might have for the evening. Remember you are teaching new skills and at the same time designing an experience for your hosts and their guests. Making sure you do sufficient planning in order to keep the entire group engaged will be an important aspect of the evening's success.

Equipment and Supplies

Make sure that either you or your host has all the utensils necessary to properly prepare the recipes. Keep in mind that you may need some duplicate items because, unlike preparing an entire meal in sequence by yourself, you are going to be directing a group of people concurrently in making all the dishes for the evening. You will want to arrange for the host to either purchase all the necessary ingredients (perhaps you make the shopping trip to some specialty stores part of your lesson plan). Otherwise you will need to include your shopping time in your fee for the evening.

Estimating the Time Commitment

Home entertaining is often scheduled for weekends or evenings, so be prepared to work those hours. You will want to consider how much of the work you will do as part of the lesson. If you plan the menu, purchase all the ingredients, travel to the host's home, teach the lesson, and clean up while the group is enjoying their meal, you will put in a good bit of time for each engagement.

Pricing and Payments

You can calculate the price of your lesson based on an hourly rate and charge on a per person basis, using your reputation, complexity of the meal, and size of the group to maximize your revenue potential. Depending on the estimated length of the teaching component, you could charge anywhere from $50 to $100 per person, with the host covering the cost of the ingredients and any beverages.

Special Requirements

There are no special requirements for in-home cooking classes that haven't already been mentioned as suggested credentials in this chapter.

19

Travel and Tour Guide

In This Chapter

◆ Create a niche for your travel planning or tour guide business with destination specific tours

◆ Take advantage of the upward trend in foreign visitors to the United States with specialty tours of your home town

People love to travel but hate to make detailed plans far enough in advance to really put together a great trip. In the past, large travel agencies were essential for making all basic travel arrangements. Imagine Delta or Southwest airlines paying big fat commissions to travel agents for the simple task of booking a flight! But that was long before the Internet made it possible to access flight information and make reservations right from your own home computer.

Over the years, the profit margin on the traditional travel agency shrank as the opportunities for generating revenue for travel services contracted. But income-producing travel concepts haven't entirely disappeared. For many travelers, large group excursions by bus (a la *If It's Tuesday, It Must Be Belgium*) through Europe simply don't appeal. Yet many places around the planet are still considered unknown, and there are travelers who want to go there. Here's the secret to entering the travel industry as a sole proprietor in the twenty-first century: develop a specialty, either in a particular region (like Italy) or type of trip (luxury inn-to-inn cycling, wine tasting, sailing) and create something unique and affordable to offer prospective customers.

According to the Bureau of Labor Statistics, "higher projected levels of travel, especially from businesses and retiring baby boomers, will offset the loss of routine transactions. Furthermore, luxury and specialty travel is expected to increase among the growing number of Americans who are seeking out exotic and unique vacations and a growing part of travel agents' business is organizing and selling tours for the growing number of international visitors."

Travel Planner for Specific Destinations

Estimated startup costs: $250–$1,000

Estimated first-year revenue: $25,000–$35,000

def•i•ni•tion

A company that describes itself as **boutique** is small and offers exclusive, customized services to discerning customers.

Most *boutique* travel agencies are started by people who are travel lovers themselves. They have been drawn to a particular country or region and spent many of their own vacations exploring, connecting, and building relationships with natives in the destination's tourism industry.

Whether you are devoted to points east or west, there is an opportunity for you to get paid to share your connections and travel expertise with others.

Equipment and Supplies

You won't need actual equipment so much as a background of extensive travel through a particular region or continent to maintain the low-cost concept. If you have developed this knowledge base and complementary relationships through business or your own personal travel, you have the foundation on which to build a boutique travel business.

To launch a business, you need a website and contracts in place to ensure you are paid a commission by the various vendors at your customers' destinations. Let's say you have traveled extensively to Peru and have hiked Machu Picchu. You fell in love with a small hotel in the mountain region, or you have a place you have always wanted to stay but haven't been able to afford. Foreign hotels depend on American tourism and are willing to pay commissions to agents who send business their way. There is still enough of a cultural and language barrier in many places to make an American liaison highly valuable. You may have to invest in a trip or two to put all of your contractual relationships in place. Your ultimate goal is to be able to create trips for customers based on your contracts with people willing to pay you for your trouble.

Estimating the Time Commitment

Travel agent reputations take time to establish; they grow through the positive experiences and feedback of happy customers. To break into this industry, you may have to keep your day job while you build your reputation creating great trips for members of your church, synagogue, or alma mater. With time and effort, you can expand your services to include individual trip planning, organized group travel for third parties, and expand the services you offer to include all or some of the following:

- Reservations for airlines, ground transportation, and transfers to and from accommodations

- Hotel, apartments, and villa bookings

- Completely escorted tours

- Sightseeing with native guides and drivers

- Custom event planning

- Travel insurance

- Special event planning and staging

Pricing and Payments

Travel agents make money by putting together packages at a price that exceeds their costs. With respect to the hotels and other tourist services you offer through your website, expect to earn between 10 percent and 15 percent of the sale depending on the magnitude of your buying power with a particular vendor as well as the going currency conversion rate.

A conservative projection of revenue is 10 percent of the value of the travel that you book for customers. This gives you an idea of just how much travel services you have to sell in order to make the transition to running a travel business on a full-time basis.

Special Requirements

To open a travel agency, you need formal approval from suppliers or corporations, such as airlines, ship lines, or rail lines to extend credit on reservations and ensure payment of your commission. To gain approval from the Airlines Reporting Corporation and the International Airlines Travel Agency Network, an agency must be financially sound and employ at least one experienced manager or travel agent.

The National Business Travel Association offers three types of designations for corporate travel professionals: Corporate Travel Expert, Certified Corporate Travel Executive, and Global Leadership Professional.

Experienced travel agents can take advanced self-study or group-study courses from the Travel Institute, leading to the Certified Travel Counselor designation. The Travel Institute also offers marketing and sales skills development programs and destination specialist programs, which provide detailed knowledge of regions such as North America, Western Europe, the Caribbean, and the Pacific Rim. With the trend toward more specialization, these and other destination specialist courses are increasingly important.

Tour Guide for Group Trips

Estimated startup costs: $250–$1,000

Estimated first-year revenue: $25,000–$35,000

Many tour guides are employees of large travel companies that handle every single detail for week- to three-week-long trips. The companies that sell these A-to-Z comprehensive travel packages are numerous; many are longtime family-owned businesses that have loyal customers who come back each year for their main vacation planning.

Several of these companies initially started out with the founder as not only the planner, but also the tour guide. Tauck Travel, founded by Arthur Tauck in 1924, has this history on its website:

> *The area's fall foliage was in full display, and Arthur savored the colors as he lunched at the Wigwam Restaurant on the Mohawk Trail, just east of the Berkshires. Given the beauty of the foliage, Arthur (Tauck) was surprised to notice that the restaurant's only other patrons were traveling salesmen like him. He concluded that there were no leisure visitors enjoying the scenery because few outsiders knew the area well enough to travel through it without guidance. As Arthur later reflected on this insight, an idea grew in*

his mind. He possessed the expertise necessary to show people the beauty of New England he'd discovered on his travels. Intuitively he sensed that vacationers would gladly attempt a travel adventure if they could sign on with a knowledgeable guide.

What corner of the world do you love and know like the back of your hand? Would you like to share that experience by showing others the beauty of the region first-hand? Read on to see how you can actually make money arranging the details and escorting others to your favorite destination.

Equipment and Supplies

There are many prerequisites to becoming a tour guide, but most of these are intangible skills and innate personality attributes. People who make great tour guides truly enjoy being with others and get tremendous satisfaction creating memorable travel experiences for others. You need to be tactful, patient, diplomatic, and understanding. Your customers will be people who are venturing out of their comfort zones and want to combine travel with relaxation and fun. They are depending on you to take care of all arrangements down to the last detail, so their vacation is not only packed with excitement but also completely care-free.

Your marketing startup costs should include a website and printed brochure with photos of your destination.

Estimating the Time Commitment

There are literally thousands of variations on the tour guide theme—so many places to go, physical activities (sailing, cycling, walking, hiking), cultural possibilities (theater, music, museum tours, architectural tours, folk art excursions), and personal-development interests (cooking, wine tasting, painting, writing). You should focus most of your startup planning on narrowing down your menu of trips based on your interests, contacts, and market research on potential customers. There are many people doing this kind of tourist business, but with endless travel options and the predictions for the strength of the industry at large, you should be able to find a niche market that works for you.

You will want to reach out to *"step-in" tour guides* on the destination side of your journey to assist you with the details involved.

Once you decide on the overall scope of your trip, you'll have many details to take care of.

def•i•ni•tion

In the travel industry a **step-in guide** is a local guide who joins a tour for a local sight-seeing excursion. He or she takes over a part of the tour, sharing specific knowledge and training. For example, a experienced whitewater rafting guide who comes on for just that part of an outdoor trip is referred to as a step-in guide.

You'll spend most of your time planning trips and marketing to prospects. Since you will be making your revenue from a commission structure on the price of your packages, you will need to project how many trips of what length you need to schedule and book in order to make a go of doing this full time.

Pricing and Payments

Your fee structure should be similar to a travel agent's, with an expectation to earn 10 percent of the travel revenue you sell. Starting out, you may want to concentrate more on average pricing to expand your potential market. Many week-long trips are priced at an average of $3,500 to $5,000 for all-inclusive packages. The only additional cost to the customer is airfare to and from an arrival airport, tips, and personal spending. There is so much information on other companies who use the Internet as their main marketing tool that you will have a wealth of competitor pricing and packages to study in your startup phase.

Success Story

Jacqueline G. came from Belgium to the United States in 1995 to pursue a career in medicine. But her heart has always been in traveling the world. She now spends her time traveling between her home in the United States and France and Belgium. Check out her company website at www.frenchescapade.com.

Let's use a simple example to calculate how you might earn $30,000 for yourself in the first year of business. With an average package price of $3,500 to your customers, you would need to sell $350,000 worth of travel, or 100 individual packages in order to reach your income goal for the year.

Special Requirements

Becoming a tour guide is something you can learn. Since you will be physically accompanying your customers on the trip, you will need to have the ability to handle last minute glitches and emergency situations. This is the biggest selling point for a tour guide: you are there with your customers to solve any problem that may arise. A high degree of organization and time management are both important characteristics of a good tourist guide, in addition to a true passion for travel and the area to which you are leading your customers. For some people, the trip you escort them on may be their very first trip abroad and the dream of a lifetime. That is a responsibility you will need to deliver on—*100 percent of the time*—to succeed as a tour guide.

It will always be an advantage to be able to speak the language of your tour destinations. If you are not confident in your language skills, you can always hire an interpreter to accompany you or do business with English-speaking vendors abroad.

Tour Guide for Foreign Visitors to Your City

Estimated startup costs: $250–$1,000

Estimated first-year revenue: $25,000–$35,000

"Travel agents might … find success in organizing groups of foreign visitors to their home markets."—*Forbes* magazine, October 2007

With the rise in the value of the Euro and other foreign currencies against the U.S. dollar, our country has seen a tremendous rise in foreign tourism. Many of us live in cities and other regions that attract millions of visitors each year. For anyone who has an interest in interpreting the history and culture of their home or other areas of interest for tourists from other lands, there is a large gap in most markets for businesses catering to foreign visitors. Granted, most local chambers of commerce have some kind of outreach, but business ventures designed to reach out to groups of foreign visitors and guide them to our known and unknown attractions are few and far between.

The opportunities in this area will vary depending on where you live. Your first order of business is to uncover just how many visitors there are annually to your area. (They can be Americans from other parts of the country.) Another great source of information will be any and all guidebooks about your area. Use these to figure out what kind of tour packages you would want to put together. Can you do a walking or biking tour? Can you rent Segways and have access to public byways for your tourist group? Use your imagination and your best hosting vibe to scout out popular, unique, and downright secret places to offer as part of a one-day or multiday touring package.

Equipment and Supplies

Depending on your business plan, you might need access to a 15-passenger van or motor coach in order to provide transportation and deliver a cohesive tour. You can rent either one with reasonable advance planning and build the cost into the price you charge your customers.

You will need to budget for marketing and building a website that appeals to both English-speaking customers and speakers of other languages.

Estimating the Time Commitment

You will need to spend most of your startup time planning and researching. Your first task will be to determine what special niche market you want to tap. If you or your family are recent immigrants to the United States, you may have a natural path to creating tours especially for those visitors from your homeland. You will have an even greater advantage if you speak the language of the groups in your target market.

You will need to schedule thoughtfully to make sure you build in time to plan and market along with acting as a tour guide. Many foreigners who visit our country come for several weeks and try to explore several different regions and states. Keep this in mind and be sure to offer packages of one, two, or even more days.

Pricing and Payments

Your pricing will depend on the costs associated with visiting the well-known tourist attractions of your area and the market rate for similar types of travel options. Look for packages that other travel companies have assembled for your region and use this information to help you decide what to include for your customers and how to price your packages.

Special Requirements

The National Federation of Tourist Guide Associations was formed in 1998 to provide a national umbrella organization to already existing state and local tourist guide groups. Individuals interested in U.S. tourism or in the tourism business can join for $50 per year. The mission of the NFTGA is to help guides improve their understanding of trends and challenges in local and national tourism.

Chapter 20

Event Planner

In This Chapter

- ◆ Event planning for weddings and other family occasions
- ◆ The logistics of planning events for corporations
- ◆ Managing the details of the right invitation
- ◆ The profit side of fundraising events

The basics of event planning require strong organizational, planning, negotiation, and people skills. But there are a thousand small details that must be considered along the way, and the effective event planner should be calm and ready for anything. This includes the tenacity to anticipate those details in the least obvious places: inspect bathrooms on a spontaneous site visit for cleanliness and supplies, walk through the kitchen and the service corridors behind your meeting space to consider noise levels, find out if and when the property last renovated, and interview a venue's management team who will handle your program (such as the bell captain, spa manager, and others), before signing a contract.

—Rob Hard, event planner consultant

Once a concept for the rich and famous, the event planner has become a common participant in making the arrangements for major life celebrations. The primary occasions for using an event planner are weddings, with bar and bat mitzvahs a close second. Weddings have become big business and mega events for people of all ages and social classes. An event planner not only alleviates much of the stress from worrying about all the details, large and small, but also sells his or her connections to various party vendors as a major benefit to the customer. Using a planner can actually lower the overall cost of an event, even with the money paid to the planner herself.

In addition to personal celebrations, event planners are frequently involved in orchestrating corporate events. An overlooked market for event-planning services is the nonprofit world, where often an organization's most significant fundraising for the year is tied to an elaborate gala or multiday happening. Depending on the size of the invitation list and the price tag for the affair, even the details of creating and managing the invitation list can be a single task delegated to its own special coordinator.

The opportunities in this profession are not limited by geographic location or population density. There are few barriers to entry and the startup costs are virtually nonexistent.

Individual Celebrations

Estimated startup costs: $250–$1,000

Estimated first-year revenue: $40,000–$60,000 and up

If you love throwing parties, making decisions on every level, and coordinating lots of moving pieces into one coherent dramatic experience, individual event planning may be the perfect business for you. It helps to have good taste, an eye for beauty, and a long list of contacts. Your job will be to help the hosts come up with a workable budget and stick to it. Your level of involvement will vary with each event and the personality of each host. Some people will hand over every decision to you; others will want to be a part of each and every choice. You need the tact and diplomacy of a travel guide and the decisiveness of General Patton. Every event has at least one if not more crises that require someone to call the shots, and you will be surprised at how readily people will step aside and let you take charge. Your customers will expect a perfect, glitch-free occasion that their guests will remember forever. If you are planning someone's wedding, you are dealing with what many believe is the defining moment of their entire existence.

You can decide what specific services you would like to offer. Do you want to specialize in weddings, teen-oriented events, parties in certain types of venues? If you live in a less populated area, you may have no option but to do any type of event planning that comes your way. You will be expected to coordinate everything from the venue, music, flowers and décor, alcoholic beverages, and gifts for the bridesmaids and groomsmen, to orchestrating the order in which everyone enters the sanctuary for a wedding ceremony. Even if a task seems of the utmost personal nature, if something goes awry you will be held responsible no matter who was in charge of it.

> **Snags**
>
> It really is up to the event planner to run an event that goes off without a hitch. Remember, every event is a marketing extravaganza for you. Everyone in the room is a potential customer, or critic.

Equipment and Supplies

You will need a great website that conveys how in-the-know you are about everything to do with organizing a spectacular event. Otherwise, the only equipment and supplies you need to get started are an address book of vendors and a fool-proof calendar system to keep your schedule on track.

Since you may be working with multiple moving parts as you plan events—and more than one event at a time—this would be a good time to buy and learn a software program like Microsoft Project ($175 from discount sources). It won't be sufficient to have your commitments blocked out on your calendar. You will need to manage different components of different events, all in different stages of completion. You will likely be working with several different people, both on the customer side and the vendor side. You want to make sure you have all the tools you need to stay on-track and on-schedule with your planning details. All deposits for event space, catering, and so on will be paid by requesting an advance payment from your customer to prevent you from having cash flow issues in the early stages of your business.

Estimating the Time Commitment

You need to be highly organized, which can be very time consuming. Your to-do list will become your best friend in this job. Your ability to efficiently check items off your list is the ultimate test of your event-planning mettle. Most weddings, even low-budget ones, begin planning a year in advance. You will absolutely want a detailed contract for every customer, outlining what you will deliver and when, and what is expected of them as the host. Be sure you have read every contract you ask your customer to sign with each vendor, from the venue to the bartender. You are essentially acting as your customer's agent and are responsible for protecting them from getting into a situation that may be problematic in the future. Never ask your customer to commit to anything you would not commit to yourself.

Since you will have to be planning several events concurrently throughout the year, you will want to ensure that your time commitment to each customer is clearly communicated in the contract. For example, you cannot work on a flat-fee basis and be expected to have an hour-long meeting every week with someone whose wedding is 12 months away. You also don't want everyone calling you at all hours day and night; most issues, even important ones, can be solved during regular business hours.

Pricing and Payments

Event planners usually charge a flat fee and get a commission or price break from the vendors they hire for the occasion. Some get paid a percentage of the total cost of the event. Maintain your integrity by avoiding working on a percentage from your customers and getting paid commission by the vendors. From the customer's perspective, you want to stay away from an impression that you are making more the more they spend. That represents a true conflict—an event planner is supposed to help the host get the most value for the party dollars spent.

Special Requirements

According to the U.S. Bureau of Labor Statistics, having a Bachelor's degree improves opportunities for winning work as an event planner, along with some prior experience. Strong written and verbal communication skills along with excellent interpersonal skills are absolutes in this profession. You will also need solid quantitative and analytic skills to put together and stick to budgets and to understand and negotiate contracts.

Corporate Events

Estimated startup costs: $250–$500

Estimated first-year revenue: $50,000–$70,000

The corporate event planning industry has stronger ebbs and flows depending on the state of the economy than private entertaining. People will still pull out the stops for a wedding even in bad times, but the entertainment budget of a corporation is the first to get the axe when times get tough. There will be good times in the future, and when spending picks up there will be opportunity for new corporate event planners. In the meantime, there will still be business and medical conferences, workshops, and summits where industries come together to exchange ideas. Each of these happenings is within the realm of corporate events, and they still need someone to take the reins and plan the details.

Corporate events include entertaining occasions for customers or employees, conferences, and training seminars. As the event planner you will be expected to handle all the details of the day, evening, or multiday event. A corporate environment will be much higher pitched than an individual one, and expectations will be high. This is not an ideal setting for on the job learning, unless you start out working as an employee for either the corporation or an event-planning company. You need to be able to work under pressure, multitasking many variables simultaneously in order to meet expectations.

Equipment and Supplies

Similar to the individual event planner in the previous section, you will need a very good tool to keep track of the different stages of the multiple events you will be handling. A sharp-looking website and professional marketing materials will be critical as well.

Estimating the Time Commitment

Event planning requires you to be prepared to work long hours up to the event and almost nonstop for the duration of the event. It will be important for you to know how much time to budget for each job in order to make sure you have the time in your schedule for handling more than one customer at a time. You will definitely want to stagger events so they don't overlap or run up on each other too closely.

The ideal situation is to target events that are recurring in nature; the annual Spring Product Debut, Christmas Party, Tax Update Seminar, and so on. The more recurring jobs you land, the easier your workload will get. You will still want to change things up every year to keep it fresh, but after one year on the job, there will be so much less of a learning curve the following year. This carries over to the life years of an event as well. If you are coming on board as a successor event planner, and your predecessor was a good professional, there is hope that there are files and prior-year notes for you to use to get a jump start learning the ins and outs of the job.

Pricing and Payments

It is most likely that your pricing structure will be dictated to you in a corporate setting. The customer may have preferences or requirements to be invoiced on an hourly basis, request quotes based on a flat fee, or use a cost-plus structure for budgeting purposes. If this event has been done in the past, there is likely to be an amount in the budget that will include your fee as well as the expenses for the event.

It is common in corporate events to charge anywhere from $50 to $100 per hour. If you are asked to quote on a cost-plus basis, it will depend on whether you have a fixed budget to work with or are expected to bring the event in at a lower cost than budgeted. In the latter case you will want to make sure you have something in your contract that ensures you don't lose out for bringing the event in below expected cost.

Since most event planners are hired well in advance of the event date, it is important to include how frequently you are to be paid in your contract. If the job is significant, you should arrange to be paid no less than monthly in order to match your earnings with the time you are spending on the project.

Special Requirements

Include plenty of time in your schedule for networking with other corporate professionals as a mainstay of your marketing plan. The more people who know about your services and know you, the more work will come your way. Producing an event is a very public project, and no corporation wants to tarnish their reputation or professional image with a poorly managed event. Your professional references are an important part of your marketing strategy.

The Convention Industry Council (CIC) offers a Certified Meeting Professional certification that is recognized throughout the industry. Several universities offer Bachelor's or Master's degrees with majors in meetings management.

Invitation Designer and Coordinator

Estimated startup costs: $1,000

Estimated first-year revenue: $20,000–$45,000

Unique wedding invitations have a big appeal to anyone planning a special event. The mood and tone are set with a formal invitation, which today usually is preceded by a save-the-date card. If you can create a collection of impressive, one-of-a-kind designs, you also have an opportunity to bundle place cards, programs, menus, thank-you notes, and other accessories in an order for one event.

Weddings are not the only occasion you will have a market for, nor are invitations the sole product. Baby announcements are another avenue for continuing your relationship with the newlyweds. And just think of all the built-in marketing: you get paid for each piece mailed to someone on the wedding or birth announcement lists. The word-of-mouth concept is taken to another several levels as your product takes on a marketing life all its own.

Equipment and Supplies

Your customers will be looking for complete packages, so you will have to have all your ducks in a row by the day of your launch. You won't want to inventory all your paper stock, but you will want relationships with reliable vendors who can ship you everything you need at a moment's notice. You will need an extremely professional website and the means to update it frequently. Most of your first customers will find you on the web, so make sure your search engine optimization is top notch.

You will be shipping finished products to your customers. Since your products are extremely date sensitive, you must have dependable fulfillment resources and quality packaging materials to ensure you are able to deliver on time. Ultimately, not missing a deadline is equally important to a gorgeous, perfectly crafted end product.

Estimating the Time Commitment

The startup phase for this kind of business will likely be in the four- to six-month range, so be prepared to keep your current job or go without revenue for at least that period of time. If you have local contacts for helping you market your business, with event planners, photographers, venues, and other vendors for weddings, you will have the means for early promotional activities. Locating a major charity that could use some pro-bono designing for their upcoming events would be an excellent way to spread the word about your talents and form helpful relationships.

Pricing and Payments

Printing is always priced by the piece with a minimum quantity required. You may start out with a minimum order requirement of $100 for an order of 25 invites, and consider raising this as your business gains momentum. It is much easier to work on fewer larger orders as a solo freelancer. Most invitation suppliers include the blank outer envelope in their per piece pricing, but have additional per piece fees for all other add-ons, such as printing return addresses, envelope linings, insert envelopes, and response cards and envelopes. Today there is even a market for custom postage stamps that coordinate with the invitation graphics.

Special Requirements

Most invitation designers have art or graphic design backgrounds and have held jobs in marketing and promotion.

You will already need to possess the skills required to design high-quality printed materials, in addition to computer equipment and software for producing the designs.

Developing and Coordinating Nonprofit Fundraising Events

Estimated startup costs: $250–$500

Estimated first-year revenue: $29,000–$60,000

It is arguable that the recession has hit nonprofits even harder than their corporate counterparts. The last two years have seen traditional sources of charitable funding become the Dust Bowl of this century. Nonprofits have reacted to their new reality in two different ways. Some have put their fundraising events on hiatus, unwilling to risk advancing the expenses for a major event in the current economic climate. Others have had no choice but to follow through with their annual events with extra vengeance. With corporate and government grants evaporating, nonprofits are more dependent on successful fundraising events than ever before.

There is an endless variety of fundraising events held in every corner of the country every year. Some of the more popular varieties include the high-styled gala, live and silent auctions, walks from 3 to 60 miles in length, and multiday cycling events. This is just the tip of the iceberg. Event management for nonprofits has become a business niche all of its own, with players ranging from large companies that handle events like the three-day Walk for the Cure (to raise money for Breast Cancer research) in 20 cities each year to your local museum's annual art auction. Each event has its own extensive list of details that must be handled, with expectations and high hopes that this year's event will best those that have preceded it.

You will be responsible for handling any and all of the tasks involved in putting on the event, such as venue selection, food choices, all production details, entertainment, contract negotiation, transportation for all participants, lodging, conference services, and emergency back-up plans for all obvious potential pitfalls.

Equipment and Supplies

You won't need specific equipment to get started, but you will have to have some relevant prior experience at a supervisory level before an organization will hire you to handle its events. This can be previous work for an event planner or even events handled as a volunteer. In fact, one way to get hands-on experience in this industry is to work with a local nonprofit on a volunteer basis. If you demonstrate strong skills and ability, this will often lead to paying work.

Estimating the Time Commitment

The time commitment will vary with the type and size of each event. You can plan a gala in 90 to 120 days. A multiday walk or cycling event can take a full year of planning, with contracts required to be negotiated at least a year in advance. Major event dates are often coordinated over a year ahead of time, so there is usually plenty of time to handle the advance details. You may also be responsible for handling several smaller events leading up to the main one, such as a kick-off event and publicity opportunities. As you approach the date of the main event, you will be working around the clock to ensure that no detail has been left unturned.

Pricing and Payments

Nonprofits frequently contract out their event planning in order to save money on a full-time employee. Beware of this when negotiating your own contract for event planning services. Working on an hourly basis will be to your advantage, but it may not be possible to manage this. Most nonprofits work on a fixed budget and only sign contracts for fixed fees. Before you sign up, make sure you talk with prior-year event planners or volunteers to get a clear understanding of everything involved.

You can expect to earn from $25 to $75 an hour depending on the size of the event and the organization. Bigger nonprofits have deeper pockets.

Special Requirements

See special requirements for corporate event planners. For working with nonprofit entities, you need to have a desire to contribute or give back to whatever cause your event is related to, because you will probably be working long hours for less money than you would in a corporate setting. You also are more likely to work closely with untrained, well-meaning volunteers who require a greater level of appreciation and patience.

Part **6** Business Goods and Services

Our final part deals with low-cost startups that market to other small businesses and leverage experience from previous jobs. We outline the basics on taking a professional career and moving it to a home-based office. These ideas are for all those who love what they do but need to be in an environment other than corporate America. Another major opportunity in the next several years is being part of the maturing virtual office world. Now that working from home has become accepted, using the Internet to connect with other home-based businesses is how companies of the future will conduct business with one another.

Chapter 21

Professional Services from Home

In This Chapter

- ◆ Credentialed professionals hanging out their shingles with a home office
- ◆ Supporting the growing small business sector with coaching, consulting, and personnel recruitment
- ◆ Contract professionals in the not for profit environment

Small businesses love to work with independent professionals, and even prefer it when they work from home. Where you might think the prestige of an office is a necessity, your potential clients will think, "*Yes!* A good professional who knows his stuff and doesn't charge me for any fancy offices!" So for all you corporate types who are still ingrained with the expensive image and branding that went along with your big firm perks, you don't need it.

First of all, make it your practice to meet with your clients at their offices or places of business. They will love you for it. No, you won't want to bill separately for your travel time. But no one down in accounting is going to be calculating your chargeability stats, either. You will still get the respect that comes with a professional pedigree and previous big firm experience, but you will have a lot more direct contact with your clients. If you are truly a people-person, then you are in for a pleasant surprise—you will love your new modus operandi as a solo practitioner.

CPAs, Financial Planners, and Attorneys

Estimated startup costs: $1,000

Estimated first-year revenue: $60,000–$80,000

By nature, CPAs and financial planners are cost-conscious individuals who were some of the first professionals practicing from home offices, long before the advent of the Internet and its connectivity. With all the technology available to today's professional, from sophisticated tax software, QuickBooks, video and teleconferencing, to document generating and digital storage packages, it is more cost effective than ever before to operate as a home-based professional. (See our next chapter on virtual assistants for how you can hire out everyday tasks and focus on tasks that make you money.)

Solo professionals working from home offices perform the same work they would in any office. The main difference will be the size of the accounts you work with; the wealth of individual clients is by nature on a smaller scale than those of the large, high-priced downtown firms. The challenge for most professionals considering a leap to their own firm is the idea of working in isolation, independent from colleagues and the safety net of administrative support. We can't say this concern is unwarranted, because large firms do provide great training, mentoring, and resources. But you can create your own personal replica of all of these aspects of a good professional practice right in your own home office. Read the personal story on the next page to see how easily it can be done.

Equipment and Supplies

CPAs, financial planners, and attorneys all require state licenses that must be renewed at least biannually. Continuing education requirements are important to keep up and comply with at a cost of a few hundred dollars a year. Sometimes more than one professional license is needed if you set up your own firm, so you need to check with your state boards to be clear on exactly what you need.

Although you can operate just fine with one computer, either desktop or smaller, you will need to keep your technology current in order to maximize your productivity. The professional software programs you will need for your business usually require state-of-the-art machinery to run them. If you have a five-year-old computer you've been using to surf the web and download music, you probably need to upgrade.

Success Story

Gail R. has been a CPA for 25 years, most of which were spent owning her own home-based small firm. After leaving the largest CPA firm in the United States, she started her practice in an 8 × 12 back room of her home. At the time she was the only person from the large firm to branch out on her own. Many of her colleagues expressed envy but total fear at the thought of practicing without the support of the firm.

To counter this potential pitfall, Gail made a priority of staying in touch with her former co-workers for all the years she ran her practice. They were always willing to assist her when she needed support answering tough tax questions. She also built her own network of other professionals, including a tax attorney and two other CPAs with different expertise, all with their own solo practice. These professionals were her go-to people when she needed to confer with others—which was often. Being on her own was never "isolating" the entire time she was in practice for herself.

The biggest challenge in launching a solo professional practice is deciding what to do yourself and what you should contract out. If you happen to be a tech geek, you may have everything you need to spec your own computer setup. If tinkering with your PC is not your favorite pastime, connect with a local (or virtual) tech company (a possibility for your first client) to handle this side of things for you. This is a good idea for marketing collateral and website development as well.

Estimating the Time Commitment

If you have been working in your field for a number of years, you'll probably have a few clients from the day you open your doors, either from personal or business relationships. Most professional firms forbid moonlighting, so you won't have an opportunity to build business on the side while you continue on your job. There are limitless options for networking with others in your business community. You will grow faster and start out with much better financial results if you define a specialty area or two and focus on these with your marketing.

Snags _____

One of the most common detours new solo professionals take is starting out by accepting any and all interested prospects as clients. Most take years to learn this valuable lesson: not everyone is your client.

Whenever you start out in any business, it is so hard to turn away work. This is especially true for professionals, because all you have to sell is your time. If you are not working, why not pick up a project even if the pay is lower than your expectations? You can easily get bogged down with lower paying and demanding clients. Learning to say no will build your practice faster than anything else you can do.

If you are fortunate enough to have clients lined up on your first day, you are on the fast track to having a full-time business. If you are starting from scratch, you will still have a rapid growth outlook if you have a good marketing plan and stick to it. In the beginning there are always opportunities to pick up some freelance work through a placement agency or on contract with a larger firm to keep cash coming in.

Pricing and Payments

There has been a great deal of debate regarding pricing by the billable hour in the legal, accounting, and financial-planning professions. In fact, the advent of the asset-management fee, based on a percentage of clients' portfolios, became popular in part because of a shift away from hourly billing in the financial-planning industry. Although the arguments for pricing per project or deliverable have merit, the reality is that the most lucrative way for a professional to charge is by hourly rate. The downside of quoting a fixed or project fee is ending up with much more time to completion than expected and not enough compensation to make a profit. It's a big risk. Most of your clients might secretly complain about your fee, but if you do good work, they will pay it and come back for more.

Average billing rates for solo practitioners depend upon geographic location and the local marketplace, years of experience, and areas of expertise.

Current Average Hourly Fees for Professionals

Description	Average Hourly Rate
CPAs	$175
Attorneys	$265
Financial planners	$175

Special Requirements

All these professions require the proper education, examinations, and experience of their individual licenses. The continuing education requirements are rigorous and the work is demanding. That said, having your own professional practice is extremely rewarding.

You can belong to myriad professional organizations as a lawyer, accountant, or financial planner. The most common are the American Institute of CPAs, the American Bar Association, and the National Association of Personal Financial Advisors.

Recruiters, Coaches, and Consultants

Estimated startup costs: $250–$1,000

Estimated first-year revenue: $50,000–$75,000

Each of these professional jobs could easily fill a book with details about starting a home-based business, but for the sake of expediency we have grouped them together. As different as each is from the other with respect to skills, background, and customer needs fulfilled, there is commonality in how to establish independent home offices.

You can target all three of these professions to individuals, businesses, or a combination of both. Your primary market as a home-based version will be small companies where the owner/operator can use help with both leadership development and the successful expansion of his or her business. One thing that sneaks up on the small business owner is just how lonely it can be at the top, even if the heap you're on top of is a lot smaller than General Motors.

Your customers will be business owners searching for support and comradeship from outside professionals. Some fully acknowledge the need for mentoring and guidance and seek out organizations that market to this need specifically, such as the Executive

Committee. But the vast majority of entrepreneurs happen upon a *consigliore* through chance. This is your opportunity to develop your brand as a potential partner to the business owner, either through helping them recruit quality employees for key positions, coaching them toward accomplishing objectives and goals, or providing the big picture perspective that most CEOs need to move their companies to the next level.

def•i•ni•tion

Consigliore is Italian for counselor or advisor. The term has gained popular usage in this country from the film *The Godfather*.

For the purposes of this chapter we are defining these professions as follows:

◆ **Recruiters** are professionals who locate, interview, and present qualified applicants to employers with job openings to fill.

◆ **Business coaches** work directly with a company's leader or entire management team. They create an individualized development process that builds a leader or team's capability to achieve short- and long-term organizational goals.

◆ **Business consultants** have some similarities to business coaches, with the addition of a technical area of expertise on which they normally build their approach to solving specific management problems. For example, many business consultants have in-depth information and technology knowledge that they apply in developing solutions to communications and reporting issues within a company.

Equipment and Supplies

There are credentials for recruiting, coaching, and consulting that will bring you more activity on your website, but these professions do not have the state licensing requirements of the legal or accounting professions. Your marketing investment will need to take the bulk of your startup capital; a website will be helpful more for credibility than for leads to prospects. These professions require a solid reputation and word-of-mouth referrals, such as, "Coach Amy really helped me turn my business from barely surviving to thriving."

You will need to stock your office with about $200 of basic office supplies and updated communication equipment.

Estimating the Time Commitment

Your networking and existing connections to the community will be key in accelerating the process of winning projects and bringing in revenue. Ideally, if you have been doing this work as an employee, you may have some clients that follow you and hire your small company. It will take a good nine months to a year to reach a full-time schedule.

Some opportunities will lend themselves to working on several jobs at the same time; others will require more concentrated effort. You will need to weigh your options for each job and fashion your proposal or bid according to what is best for the customer's situation and for your business. Recruiting tends to be very project-oriented, filling a specific opening in a company's personnel structure. Coaching is an ongoing service delivered with a series of meetings (either in person or by phone) over a longer period of time. Consulting falls in between these two, with some assignments being short-term and goal-specific and others requiring more of a process approach.

> **Bonus Point**
>
> In challenging economic times, many small business owners reach out for someone to help them keep their company afloat. Consider positioning yourself as a turnaround expert, who can help a business owner make the decisions necessary to meet the challenges of a downturn. This is the kind of help people will pay for in trying times.

Pricing and Payments

Recruiting fees are most commonly based on a percentage of the annual salary of the position being filled. The typical fee is 10 to 20 percent of the first-year salary. This gives a higher per placement fee to a recruiter placing employees higher up the food chain. Although this is expensive for a small business to bear, the recruiter's value proposition is much more accepted today than ever before. Most small businesses simply do not have the personnel to attend to the details of an HR department. And even though the fee is expensive, finding the right person is much cheaper than making a wrong choice.

Coaching and consulting are often fee-based arrangements based on an hourly rate for the service provider. Fees in the range of $100 per hour and up are commonplace for coaching and consultants, depending on the size of the companies they work with and their reputation for delivering results.

Special Requirements

To operate at the level of third-party business advisor, customers will expect you to have a Bachelor's degree, with an M.B.A. a definite plus.

Fundraisers and Grant Writers

Estimated startup costs: $250–$1,000

Estimated first-year revenue: $30,000–$65,000

Fundraisers and grant writers help nonprofits access revenue streams from donors. Fundraising professionals focus on corporate and individual giving programs. They create and implement programs from a year-end letter writing campaign to carefully orchestrated corporate outreach involving high-level contacts both within their own boards and from the community at large.

A grant writer's expertise involves crafting well-written grant applications to public and private foundations and some corporations for major dollars. Grant writers are expected to not only write well but also to know the grantors well enough to identify new sources of funding for their customer organizations.

A fundraising consultant or grant writer can be brought in for a one-time project or for a more strategic role in assisting the executive director and organization's board of trustees in developing or revamping an overall program for giving and/or grants.

Equipment and Supplies

As a freelance fundraising consultant or grant writer, your previous work experience is going to be your most important asset. Your investment, in addition to marketing your services, will be in a well-organized and detailed press kit presenting your qualifications. Any savvy nonprofit executive director will expect to see …

- One or more documents that convey your ability to craft the necessary components of a successful grant proposal or fundraising campaign.

- Solid references from reputable organizations.

- Grant award letters and reports of results from a recent fundraising campaign that you designed and managed.

◆ Educational background in a field related to the mission of the organization, such as art, health, or education, or several years of experience with—and successful results for—organizations with similar programming to the prospective customer.

Estimating the Time Commitment

The length of any given assignment will depend on the nature of the work (strategic or project-based) and the size of the organization's fundraising goal or grant award. It will also vary with the maturity of the organization's development; a long-time entity will have some staff in place to implement your recommendations. Smaller, more fledgling organizations will need more of your time.

You may win contracts with certain organizations that simply cannot afford to add a full-time development director or grant writer to their staff, but do have a part-time position. Others will want you to train them to do more of the future development work on their own. Either way you will have meetings to attend, several different personalities to deal with, organizational history to learn, and strategies to devise. Each assignment will require your full attention, and you should be able to use past experiences to guide you in scheduling your work.

Pricing and Payments

Grant writers charge between $25 and $50 per hour based on the size of the project and their experience. Fundraising consultants usually fill more executive-level positions and can earn a much higher hourly rate. There has been some negative publicity in the last 15 years about fundraisers who earn a percentage of what they raise for an organization. Most respectable fundraising professionals will not work on this type of commission structure.

Special Requirements

There is no specific degree or license required to be a professional fundraiser. The Association of Fundraising Professionals (AFP) is the professional association of individuals responsible for generating philanthropic support for a wide variety of nonprofit, charitable organizations. Founded in 1960, AFP (formerly the National Society of Fund Raising Executives) advances philanthropy through its nearly 30,000 members in more than 200 chapters throughout the world. The AFP has a strong local chapter network throughout the country with membership that varies between $25 and $75 depending upon the chapter location.

Chapter 22

Virtual Office Providers

In This Chapter

- ◆ Providing basic office support virtually
- ◆ Catering to high-level executives
- ◆ Using your technical expertise to develop a virtual business

> In looking at home-based business opportunities in 2009, a Virtual Assistant would be at the top of the list in terms of income opportunities. From the testimonials received from our program graduates, they are leaving corporate settings and enjoying their own thriving businesses within 12 months of startup.
>
> —Craig Cannings, co-founder of VAClassroom.com, Training Center for Virtual Assistants

Perhaps the biggest boost to the world of virtual assistants came from a previously unknown author, Timothy Ferriss, in his best-selling book *The 4-Hour Workweek*. Ferriss championed the concept of setting up a business that generates income for the founder even though his business plan is to only work four hours a week after the business is up and running. The catch—the virtual assistant steps in to fill the gap and do the actual work. Although Ferriss was working mostly on a model that used assistants located on the other side of the globe, the idea of working virtually as someone's office assistant is not only workable, it's downright brilliant. It's much easier to do most of the work without getting any of the credit if you can do it from the comfort of your own home office, without anyone shouting down the hall for you to open the mail and fetch the coffee!

The virtual office assistant is a dream come true for many people who provide valuable services to executives, keep the paperwork moving, and actually get tasks accomplished.

Companies and individuals are employing office assistants who work remotely or from a home virtual office. You merely have to define your strongest skills and determine which marketing avenue is going to be the best for your new company. With so many 50- to 60-somethings cut loose by large corporations in the last decade, there is a large market of former executives stirring up work for themselves who need your help to deliver the goods they've promised. Read on for the details of how to make this work for you.

General Secretarial and Administrative Work

Estimated startup costs: $250–$500

Estimated first-year revenue: $25,000–$50,000

Secretarial work is a keystone of the virtual assistant job description. Duties involve phone reception, scheduling appointments, handling travel arrangements, troubleshooting problems for your virtual bosses and their customers, and drafting and finalizing documents such as letters, contracts, and other types of general correspondence.

Very few assistants who have been in the marketplace for less than 20 years really understand the level of service required by a fast-paced executive. This creates an ideal situation for office administrators with 10 or 15 years left until retirement who would love to slow down the pace and give up their daily commute.

The duties of a secretarial and administrative virtual assistant would include word processing; data entry; database management; transcription; bulk mail services; travel arrangements; Internet research; event and meeting planning; expense tracking and expense-report compilation; screen and send e-mail, faxes, and regular mail; create and maintain electronic mailing lists and address book; and maintain company website.

Equipment and Supplies

Virtual assistants need to have a soup to nuts home office with all the up-to-date communication equipment including phone, fax, e-mail, and instant message. Most of your deliverables will be digital files returned to your client for printing, and so on. If you should get the request for bulk printing, you can decide at the moment whether it's worth the cost of a better printer for your office or whether you want to outsource it to a print shop. With your existing home computer equipment, you should be able to outfit your office within the $1,000 startup budget.

Estimating the Time Commitment

It will take time to get to know each of your customers in order to map out your time commitment to each one and as a whole. Many virtual assistants suffer from the same long-hours syndrome that happens to most small business owners. The days start early and end late, and weekends are just extra time to get caught up. Once you get established and put your marketing plan into action, you should pick up business pretty quickly.

One aspect of your marketing plan must be to let everyone you ever worked with know you are now available as an independent contractor. Being a virtual secretary or administrative assistant is likely to attract the business of a former boss who has never been able to adequately replace you. Starting your business with a good client out of the gate will go a long way to curbing your anxiety in the first year of operation.

You will also want to send out e-mail announcements about opening your business to everyone you know, mail postcards to local businesses in your area, visit some office parks and distribute your business card, and join some local networking groups. Word-of-mouth marketing will help you jump-start your business.

Pricing and Payments

Virtual assistants providing administrative and secretarial duties charge anywhere from $25 to $75 per hour, depending on the type of skills they use for a client. For example, bill basic word processing at the lower $25 per hour, but database and website management and updating should command a higher price per hour.

Special Requirements

Professional virtual assistants recommend setting up a PayPal account for ease in collecting from clients potentially located around the world. Since there is a strong possibility that you'll be dealing with people you will never meet, getting paid up-front in the form of a retainer is strongly suggested.

The International Virtual Assistant Association has memberships for $125 a year and provides many opportunities for support and networking along with a listing in their membership directory.

Although many virtual assistants offer secretarial services, as more people with diverse backgrounds and skills enter the ranks, virtual assistants who specialize in such areas as marketing, graphic and web design, IT support, or even translations are becoming more common.

The Virtual Assistant Networking Association is the largest membership base of virtual assistants online today, with over 10,000+ registered members.

Executive Assistant

Estimated startup costs: $250–$1,000

Estimated first-year revenue: $40,000–$60,000

Those readers who have been executive assistants will understand why this job description merits its own special section. The relationship between a high-powered executive (or someone who used to be one) and his or her assistant is much more intimate and intense than a broader secretary or administrative assistant. An executive assistant establishes a bond with an executive boss that crosses a line to greater interdependency. As an executive assistant, you have to be prepared to be available not quite 24/7, but almost.

The main difference between working for a high-level executive and other professionals is that you will be expected to deliver results rapidly and consistently. When your executive client calls or e-mails you for assistance, he or she wants it done now. Right now. It is more difficult to have several clients when you are working with someone at this level. The expectations are great, and a client's focus is on what he needs, not what your workload might look like. If you are accustomed to working in this type of environment, you will be able to make the transition to handling these tasks virtually as long as you don't overcommit to too many clients at one time.

Equipment and Supplies

You will need a complete office setup similar to the one described in the virtual assistant section.

Estimating the Time Commitment

You will need to establish some boundaries with your clients in order to have time to develop more than one client at a time. Also you may need to limit client access after a certain hour in the evening and on weekends. Many high-level executives work 24/7, but you may not want to be on call every minute of every day.

Pricing and Payments

Executive assistants make a high salary in a corporate setting. There is every reason for you to expect to be paid at the higher hourly rate of the virtual assistant pay scale.

Special Requirements

Secretaries and administrative assistants today perform fewer clerical tasks and are increasingly taking on the roles of information and communication managers. They are often responsible for tasks that used to be handled by managers and professionals, including spreadsheet design and compilation, direct correspondence, maintaining databases, and generating presentations, reports, and documents using desktop publishing, PowerPoint, and digital graphics. Many of these functions require special training and classes to develop competency.

Microsoft Office Specialist

Estimated startup costs: $250–$750

Estimated first-year revenue: $40,000–$60,000

It takes a special administrative technician to take the path of developing application expertise along the road of her career. People with advanced skills, quick minds, and the ability to meet deadlines don't come along every day. If you have on-the-job and other training from previous jobs and possess strong spreadsheet and database skills, you are a highly marketable commodity.

Number-crunching isn't the only software application that managers and self-employed professionals are clamoring for. There are desktop-publishing projects and many other kinds of specialty web-based digital files that can be updated remotely by anyone with the proper user ID and password. There is nothing more difficult than putting together a well-organized, smoothly-working end product created by a software package (intricate spreadsheet or PowerPoint presentation) while working in the middle of a bustling office environment with its never-ending distractions. This gives a virtual assistant with high-level software skills a wide-open opportunity to attract well-paying projects and develop a loyal clientele. You can deliver a great end product with greater efficiency than could ever be achieved in a corporate setting.

Equipment and Supplies

To launch a business as a virtual Microsoft Office Specialist you need a relatively new computer and ownership of Microsoft Office Professional Software. You will also need all the requisite telecommunications equipment.

Estimating the Time Commitment

If your skills are top-notch, the first place to look for potential customers will be former employers and co-workers who already know of your legendary software skills. Even with your specialties you may want to offer a variety of services to fill up your schedule. After you have a good customer base, you can become more discriminating about the work you choose.

It is always difficult to judge how long a particular complex document is going to take to compile. You will want to stand by your hourly rate to make sure you get fairly compensated for your efforts. Once you have a working application, you can price your updating projects for the same customer based on a fixed rate. To balance your cash flow, it is a good idea to look for new development projects as well as those that will have the same customers coming back on a regular basis.

Pricing and Payments

Competency with specialty software applications and the ability to deliver complete, on-time projects are skills that will garner top dollar in the marketplace. There are many opportunities on the web for you to check out the competition. In general, a range starting at $50 to $75 per hour and up will be feasible for this type of work.

Special Requirements

Becoming a Microsoft Office specialist requires that you pass an exam offered through the Microsoft Authorized Testing Center. Designations are available for Microsoft Office 2003, Microsoft Office XP, or Microsoft Office XP products. Each specific MS application has its own special certification: Word, Excel, PowerPoint, Access, Outlook, and Project.

E-commerce websites like guru.com and odesk.com provide web-based marketplace environments where businesses in need of service providers and freelancers looking for work can come together for mutual benefit. Many of the posted job listings are from companies with immediate needs. This is a good way to interact with potential customers, especially early on when you are developing a regular clientele.

23

IT Services

In This Chapter

♦ The enormous growth of the number of websites bodes well for web designers and developers

♦ Hosting and maintaining websites is a great money maker

♦ The iPhone is driving the next growth spurt for software application development

♦ Computer selection and system design comes of age in the twenty-first century

The history of humanity is the history of being part of a group, having a group mentality, and the Internet makes a whole other set of those groups possible. And they don't have to be physically proximate to you, you can create content for people who are physically distant.

—Professor Rebecca Grinter of Georgia Tech's College of Computing

The Internet may be over 15 years old, but it is still the California Gold Rush, the Colorado Silver Rush, and the dot.com boom combined and multiplied tenfold. Never in modern history, before or since the personal computer was invented, has one single phenomenon opened up horizons in quite the same expanse and time frame. We get excited about something new invented to improve the World Wide Web, like DSL access making us forget we ever nicknamed it the "World Wide Wait," and we think we've peaked out. And then something new like wireless comes up and we fall in love all over again.

Since the dot.com bust, the careers of individual CIOs have taken an unrecoverable nosedive. Chief information officers may still have a place in multibillion-dollar operations, but for the average company, and certainly for the small business, there is no longer a key spot for a $150,000-a-year employee to shepherd us through the computer labyrinth. There are too many qualified vendors to whom we can outsource in a much more cost-effective manner. The Internet has become the frontier of the New Economy—heretofore unknown entrepreneurial concepts that have gained momentum using the interconnectedness of cyberspace.

So the answer to the question, "How do the entrepreneurial masses get to 'them thar hills'?" is obvious. You must have a web presence to fulfill today's vision of a twenty-first-century business. Older marketing techniques are still in play, but they are being superseded by the marketing techniques abounding in cyberspace.

Accordingly, the market has driven down the prices of website design and development from the exorbitant levels of 10 years ago ($100,000+) to less than $1,000. This has opened the market to millions of customers who can now afford to have a web presence. The natural cycle of growth in customers creates the opportunity for more vendors. Website design, development, hosting, and maintenance are entering the phase that personal computers experienced in the 1990s. Everyone wants them and the market is huge, so falling prices are compensated for by unlimited volume.

In the meantime, while website businesses become the norm, application design for iPhones, Guitar Hero, and other hot-hot-hot games and applications remain avenues for get-rich-quick opportunities. For those preferring a slow and steady approach, there is still money to be made in freelance computer system procurement, installation, and maintenance. Once the exclusive territory of the classic disorganized tech school graduate, IT services have become increasingly professional. The compensation is still excellent for those who have the discipline to develop systematic approaches to their work and the marketing savvy to compete with strong competition from companies like the Geek Squad.

Website Design and Development

Estimated startup costs: $250–$500

Estimated first-year revenue: $25,000–$40,000

Many people are attracted to the idea of investing a minimal amount—say $500—in acquiring everything they need to know to design and maintain their own website. But if you read the popular blogs of the day, you are easily persuaded to delegate the tasks that are important to the success of your business and better done by someone else.

Website design and maintenance involves creating a blueprint of the overall look and details of a company's website, from scratch. A design company will spend time with the owner of a business asking questions specific to the image, branding, and mission of the company. Once the information has been collected and a concept has been formed (in much the same way an advertising campaign is mapped out), a website design firm will draw up plans for the pages of a website. With approval from the key players, the plan will be executed, a site will be launched, and the company that designs it may continue to bring in a regular monthly income from hosting and updating the site.

There is a special skill set to creating a website, and it can be done using a variety of software for a corresponding gamut of prices. Many talented and successful web designers have a background in graphic design, marketing, or information-system engineering. The industry has spawned a homegrown variety of web designers as well; individuals who have taught themselves a web design application and found a niche in the marketplace.

Equipment and Supplies

Many good software packages are available for designing and hosting websites. You will want to select one that works for you and that is teachable to your customers. In today's market, many customers want to be able to update their own website without having to pay their website designer.

What makes a web hosting startup low-cost is the ability to lease out the servers for your business from datacenters. This concept is referred to as *cloud computing*, where the datacenter gets paid for the usage of its computers' power, hard drive storage, and systems maintenance. The server may be in Utah with users all over the world connecting via the Internet. Cloud computing also makes it possible to have parallel systems with affordable backup, because everything is communicated over the Internet.

def•i•ni•tion

The term **cloud computing** refers to a computer system where the user can upload software to a shared computer system. In effect, it is just like the way computers used to run, with a huge mainframe in the bowels of the bank operation center.

Estimating the Time Commitment

This is a competitive market with a lot of customers in need of the product. The good news is that you cannot begin to quantify the market based on new business starts or population demographics given today's trend of one person creating a network of multiple interconnected websites. The graph below shows the total number of domain names reserved on a cumulative basis from 1995 to January 2008.

Graph of number of websites 1995-2008.

(Courtesy of news.netcraft.com/ archives/web_server_survey)

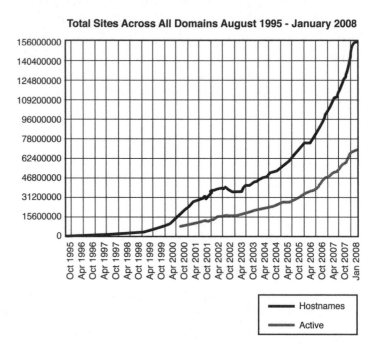

Total Sites Across All Domains August 1995 - January 2008

The length of each job will vary with each customer, their specific needs, and the number of pages they want to include in their site. It also depends on which market you decide to tap into. There are still companies that need big beautiful intricately designed sites, as well as other small startups looking for a turn-key web presence for less than $1,000. Moreover, this type of business is ideal for building a virtual *back office* of others to do the work if your forte is marketing and sales. Since all the work is behind the scenes and performed offsite, there is unlimited potential to delegate the design and building responsibilities to someone else anywhere in the world.

def•i•ni•tion

Human resources, accounting services, and the technology required to manage a company itself are considered the **back office** of a company.

Success Story

Trent P. owns a web-design business in the northern suburbs of Atlanta, Georgia. He has good IT skills, but his passion is meeting people and marketing his company's services. He joined a networking group that met early mornings for a weekly breakfast, and found that this worked really well for connecting with a market of small independent business owners in need of website design and hosting. It worked so well that he multiplied his effort in several weekly face-to-face networking groups and found that his business grew steadily in relationship to the number of meetings he attended each week. He was able to manage the growth by outsourcing the actual design and development to other IT contractors who worked virtually from their own home offices.

Pricing and Payments

Pricing of websites varies depending on the level of graphic design and whether the site is for marketing purposes or is also a sale portal for product or services. Many companies have interactive websites that have the potential to provide customers with the ability to communicate with a business via the Internet (such as to schedule appointments online).

Many companies that target the mass market of website customers offer fixed price solutions starting as low as $750 for a four-page site. As part of your business plan, you will need to project what market you plan to focus on and the size and shape of your basic website offering. Based on these parameters, come up with a time budget and calculate the amount of time it will take you to get a website up and running. Then apply your desired hourly rate and come up with minimum and standard quotes for the specific sites you plan to market.

Snags

It's fine to offer a "loss leader" product with the hope of getting the prospective customer to upgrade for more options. But make sure you can make a decent profit on whatever basic models you offer to the public. If you end up with a majority of your business at the lower end of your pricing menu, you will be stuck working at lower pay and have to re-create your offering in midlaunch.

Since you have the opportunity to market to virtual customers, your website will have to include the ability to take payment via credit card or bank draft. The most common payment method for web development is to get 50 percent of the price upon the signing of the contract with the balance paid upon getting the site online. (Yes, you need a contract to protect your ability to collect after the work is completed.) Some developers will accept the balance in monthly payments over three to six months' time, predicated on having a charge card or bank account to bill automatically for the monthly payment.

Special Requirements

You still need a business license even if your business is completely virtual.

The World Organization of Webmasters (WOW) is a leading organization in providing certification and educational resources to web professionals in all phases of their career. For $69 a year, benefits include webmaster tools and techniques; prospective employment networking; web professional certification and education programs with online training options; and security, marketing, and Internet law information relevant to Internet commerce.

Reseller Hosting and Web Maintenance

Estimated startup costs: $250-$300

Estimated first-year revenue: $20,000–$30,000

Dozens of free or very inexpensive hosting sites are available to the small business owner. The challenge is understanding how everything fits together and how to get the most for your dollars, as small as they might be. For most solo business owners, maintaining a website is like many administrative tasks. It is absolutely necessary to have it, but it's hard as the dickens to keep up with it as a nontechnical, one-person company.

This creates a niche for creating a business that maintains websites and takes responsibility for choosing the hosting platform (like godaddy.com). Often this is another service area that a web-design business can offer customers. Or it can also be bundled with other media maintenance such as Facebook, Twitter, or a blog. We go into more depth about the terrific potential in the growing field of virtual social marketing in Chapter 24. As a web-hosting company you are expected to provide the following services:

- Shared or dedicated web-hosting services
- Corporate e-mail
- Domain registration services
- Continual uptime

Equipment and Supplies

Reseller hosting allows a company to set up an account with a host originator (like yahoo.com) and resell its allocated bandwidth (available capacity to transmit data on the Internet) and hard drive space. The reseller buys the services at a wholesale price and sells it to customers at a profit. For example, a reseller may pay yahoo.com $10 a month for a site, and charge their customer $85 per month including ongoing maintenance and a certain amount of updating and monthly statistical reports that give the owner information on their web traffic.

As a reseller you are able to start a web-hosting business for minimal upfront costs. You can actually sign a monthly or annual contract with a hosting company for as little as $50 a month. Everything you need to get started is included in the monthly fee.

Estimating the Time Commitment

Attracting and setting up new customers' websites is going to be the most time-consuming aspect of this business. There will be times when technical crises cause you to spend extra hours on the job, along with regular maintenance required periodically to keep your system fine-tuned. You can outsource most of this work, even to low-cost labor pools on the other side of the world. This is also an economical means of keeping someone on call 24 hours a day.

Pricing and Payments

Reseller hosting fees depend on the size of the website (required bandwidth and storage capacity) and amount of web traffic. In any case, you should set your margins so that what you bill your customer is calculated based on what your costs associated with their website are.

By having a merchant credit card account, you should be able to arrange for monthly automatic payments which will greatly reduce your costs and time commitment for invoicing and collections.

Special Requirements

There are no particular requirements or organizations specifically for web hosting and maintenance.

Software, Game, and iPhone Applications

Estimated startup costs: $400-$500

Estimated first-year revenue: $20,000–$30,000

With the introduction of the iPhone, the ante has been raised for producing software applications for Apple's latest big hit product. Many freelance programmers have made a career from creating game software or writing code for others working from home. These are all very much still viable options in our world of computing. As more of the Internet becomes accessible via cell phone, a whole new universe of possibilities opens up for writing software for computer-based programs and translating them for use as cell phone applications.

Equipment and Supplies

You don't need special equipment, just the program to write the software for games and phones, depending on the project. What you need to be successful, besides good timing and luck, is an understanding of a need to be met for a large segment of the web-using population.

The Apple Software Development Kit costs around $200; this gives programmers the code they need to create new applications for the iPhone.

Estimating the Time Commitment

The amount of time it will take you to launch a program-writing business will depend on the type of work you have previously done. If you have worked for companies that paid you for your programming skills, there is a great likelihood of being hired on a contract basis to assist them on various projects.

Pricing and Payments

Demand is high, especially for U.S. personnel. A June 2009 study of freelance software developers conducted by odesk.com (a marketplace for online work teams) showed freelance hourly rates up by 35 percent in mid-2009 over the same time frame for 2008. The hourly pay range goes from $20 to $50 per hour. Many people who are creating game and iPhone applications are working for themselves with the hope of a much bigger payoff. The amount can't be projected; it will depend on the timing and response by consumers.

Special Requirements

Many e-commerce sites give programmers and software developers the opportunity to post resumés or look for others seeking their services. These include odesk.com and guru.com.

Computer System Installation and Maintenance

Estimated startup costs: $250–$500

Estimated first-year revenue: $40,000–$50,000

There has been a great deal of consolidation in the marketplace of small firms servicing corporate networks. Along with the outsourcing of formerly lucrative chief information officer jobs, those large companies and firms have shifted away from the small computer services firms to more corporate, better-branded service providers such as Geek Squad.

Yet there is still a tremendous amount of business for computer technicians who are willing to develop a sound pricing structure and service smaller but ever-needy businesses with a computer network. There are no longer the same lucrative markups on equipment sales; most computer installation and network maintenance companies will develop specifications for new systems and equipment, source the computers and peripherals at companies like Dell or HP, add a small markup for their planning and purchasing time, and make the bigger portion of their revenue on the time involved in the installation. Once a business has acquired the equipment from a systems provider, they're likely to purchase a monthly maintenance contract to make sure the system stays in perfect running condition and all updates are properly downloaded on a regular and timely basis.

It helps to have a technical or academic degree in computer science, but it's by no means required. Many of today's computer technicians come from a wide variety of backgrounds and fell into the field by taking some indirect route.

Equipment and Supplies

The cost of running an IT-maintenance company has dropped dramatically in the last decade, going a long way toward removing cost of startup as a barrier to entry. With a relatively new laptop and access to web-based programs that allow you to interface (literally take over and work remotely) with your customers' networks on a moment's notice, you can service customers from any location, day or night.

Success Story

Bill F. led an adventurous young-adulthood, traveling and working his way around the globe. After returning to his hometown roots and starting a family, Bill got involved with his brothers in a computer installation and service business. Each brother has his specialty; one handles marketing and sales; another, business administration; and Bill has been trained in the technical end. He oversees the installations and maintains the systems; his personable approach to business and zest for life solidifies his company's relationship with customers. The brothers have been in business for over 12 years, and have done hundreds of installations and keep dozens more up and running on a daily basis.

Estimating the Time Commitment

Installing a new network is time consuming; it is also most frequently handled after business hours. Thus, this work will definitely require some evenings and weekends in order to accommodate the needs of your customers. Certain maintenance services must be done after hours as well, although oftentimes this can be performed from a remote location (like your own home office).

Depending on the size of the customer's network (number of workstations) and the sophistication of the software, it is common to have service contracts that include weekly, semimonthly, or once-a-month service calls. The length of the call will also vary with the size of the network, but initially you should plan on two calls per day and give yourself the morning or afternoon to make sure you take care of all maintenance required. This is also your opportunity to have one-on-one contact with your customer and to sell upgrades or more equipment. You can take emergency calls from other clients, but you should make it your policy to focus your attention on the customer you are visiting.

One of the critical selling points of this type of service is making yourself available to respond to a customer emergency. In today's business world, few businesses can function when their computer systems are down. Word-of-mouth referrals are going to be critical to your success. If you are there for your customers when they really need you, you will never lack business.

Pricing and Payments

Even though a monthly maintenance contract is usually quoted with a monthly fee, the pricing of the service is based on an hourly rate for the computer technician's time. Most IT companies bill at least 30 minutes of travel time for each visit. The average rate being charged today is $125 per hour. One pricing option that many IT companies use is a graduated scale of rates based on window of response time. For example, if the customer wants a guaranteed response within 24 hours, the hourly rate is $150. Those who are willing to wait up to 48 hours might be billed $115 per hour.

Bonus Point _____

One IT company specializing in fax server equipment and software has made a niche of large banking and accounting customers. These are businesses that cannot afford to be without a working fax. The IT company has made a profit center from offering "insurance" on the fax equipment, selling a separate maintenance contract that guarantees replacement of any component that fails with same-day service. In order to manage this, the IT company has to inventory parts or have access to vendors able to ship the part at a moment's notice.

Special Requirements

One warning to new IT companies is to make certain you review your state sales tax laws with respect to taxing labor as well as the sale of equipment and software. Each state is different, and you don't want to get caught not collecting sales tax when it needs to be included on your bill. You are liable to the Department of Revenue for any tax that should have been remitted. It is almost impossible to go back to a customer after the fact and collect the 6 to 8 percent due. And you certainly can't bill the customer for any penalties that accrue on the unpaid taxes.

Chapter 24

Marketing Services

In This Chapter

- Social marketing as the new frontier of corporate marketing strategy

- Why public relations and marketing consulting are still critical to business strategy

- Graphic design and copywriting expand into the website domain

- Search engine optimization remains the driving force behind success in Internet-focused marketing efforts

- Why direct mail and e-mail advertising still have an important place in a marketing plan

"From the heart of the Dirty South, Hardy Wallace, from Atlanta, GA, is Murphy-Goode's new 'Wine Country Lifestyle Correspondent'!" This quote was recently added to the Murphy-Goode Winery website to welcome the winery's newest employee, Hardy Wallace. Hands-down a plum job for any human being on the planet, Wallace, who had been writing for his blog on wines, landed the job by winning a contest sponsored by Murphy-Goode. The challenge was to get the job of "lifestyle correspondent" by creating a grassroots campaign using social media and thus get the most people to vote for him.

All of the topics included in this chapter represent the various pieces of the broad concept of marketing. Each section describes specific tasks that make up the activities that help businesses bring their product or service to the marketplace. As modes of communication ebb and flow, so, too, do the applications of marketing.

Take copywriting, which until recently was confined to the printed word, whether in newspaper advertising, glossy marketing collateral like brochures and press kits, or the script for radio and TV commercials. Today the Internet is rapidly replacing older modes of communication and shifting the focus of marketing to blogs, websites, webinars, and online video. The same skills that sold products to the generations of consumers who came before us are still applicable prerequisites of successful marketing, albeit in different formats.

Another major shift in marketing in the twenty-first century is that many products and services today are marketed globally. English is now spoken by the citizens of many foreign countries and messages conveyed in today's marketing platforms are heard around the world. Virtual work environments allow people of all nationalities to come together to work on projects, buy products and services from each other, and share information without any geographical boundaries. The savvy marketing professional is constantly at work adapting the principles that help businesses add value to their companies to the newest marketing trends.

Social Marketing

Estimated startup costs: $500–$650

Estimated first-year revenue: $40,000–$50,000

It's official. Adults are creating Facebook accounts at the rate of 250,000 per day. As consumers struggle to learn the ins and outs of social media, marketing professionals of all specialties are turning their attention to the social media as well. These networking tools include Internet sites like Facebook, MySpace, and other interest-specific sites for pet lovers, knitting fanatics, home beer brewers, and much, much more.

According to a 2008 study released by Wetpaint (a DIY social networking site) and the Altimeter Group, brands most engaged in social media during 2008 experienced higher financial success rates than those of their nonengaged peers. To determine this relationship, the study focused on 100 companies from the 2008 BusinessWeek/ Interbrand Best Global Brands survey. The results?

"Those brands that were the most engaged saw their revenue grow over the past year by 18 percent, while the least engaged brands saw losses of negative 6 percent."

The only barrier to entry is having the knowledge to implement an effective social networking campaign on behalf of a customer. These are learned skills and they do not require a college degree (see the previous Hardy Wallace story). Many people learn by creating their own accounts in the various media. Another quicker path to becoming a professional is to take a class or attend a seminar or conference.

The graph below shows the enormous growth in social networking opportunities over the last two years.

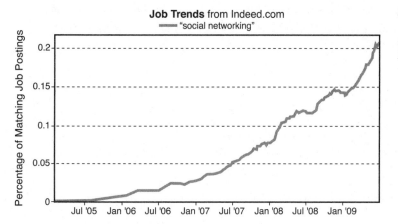

Social networking job trends.

(Courtesy of Indeed.com, Job Posting Website)

Equipment and Supplies

This is a minimal cost startup. The best investment you can make is taking a course to help you learn the tricks of the social networking trade. VAClassroom.com offers a comprehensive 8-session program for $397. You also get listed in its directory of trained virtual assistants with a specialty in social networking. The skills you should concentrate on learning include:

- Video editing

- Online-presence management

- Social network account set-up and maintenance

- Blogging and maximizing content for greater placement

- Identifying opportunities for your customers to engage in online networking

- Brand-reputation management

Estimating the Time Commitment

The best way to position yourself for rapid growth is to use your social networking skills to market your own business. It will help your growth tremendously if you narrow your focus by industry, target audience, and other relevant criteria. If you work at your marketing efforts diligently, you'll avail yourself of on-the-job training and get known in the online communities of your choosing.

In addition to online networking, create local opportunities for yourself by joining a couple of networking groups that meet in your area. Many job opportunities are available through job boards and other job listings, and you can do plenty of work on a contract basis while you build your business.

Bonus Point _____

Social networking is an ongoing process. Most freelance social networkers contract with half a dozen or so customers for a period of six months to a year in order to demonstrate results, like increased customers and sales. Make sure you are tracking your progress and communicating results to your customer on a regular basis.

Pricing and Payments

It is perfectly acceptable to charge $40 to $75 an hour for your services. You can arrange to be paid on retainer at the beginning of each month. Use a contract with your customers. Be sure to clearly outline customer expectations and how you are going to measure the outcomes of your work building brand recognition and reputation for your customers.

Special Requirements

A marketing degree and background in the field will be extremely helpful to you in developing strategies and methodologies for achieving results for your customers, but it is not necessary. This work is also well-complemented by quantitative skills to capture data for reporting results.

Public Relations

Estimated startup costs: $250-$350

Estimated first-year revenue: $35,000–$65,000

A public-relations consultant (also referred to as a publicist) builds and maintains a publicity campaign for a company, brand, product, or individual. Efforts are targeted to multimedia formats in order to spread interest among the general public or specific demographically defined audiences.

Working in public relations can be described as face-to-face social networking. A publicist keeps his customer out in the public eye, creates brand recognition, buzz, public interest, and recurring opportunities for public appearances and speaking engagements. A publicist might identify community awards that his customer would be eligible for and actually nominate the customer for consideration.

The classic activities conducted by publicists include composing press releases, using market research to determine which media outlets most successfully attract a specific audience, and—most importantly—developing and maintaining strong relationships with key media personnel to ensure clients get the coverage they need in order for the publicity efforts to be successful.

Although their expertise is not limited to any one medium, today's public-relations consultants have to be adept at all kinds of social marketing (see previous section) and be just as capable of arranging an online podcast as a standard publicity tour.

Equipment and Supplies

Your computer and home office will have everything you need to get started using your PR skills to promote your most important client—your new consulting business. Perhaps your biggest hurdle is conveying the economics of your value proposition; many businesses don't consider hiring PR support because they believe they can't afford them. If you can change this perception and publicize the affordability of your services, you should be able to engage all the clients you need to have a successful PR firm.

Estimating the Time Commitment

Theoretically, you should have a rapid launch since you have better tools than most to get the word out about your business. Many PR consultants take on one or two pro-bono clients in order to demonstrate their abilities to the community at large. Much of the work done by a good publicist occurs in networking after business hours, so long days and evening commitments are common. In your startup phase you are likely to put in extra time to yield positive results for your early clients. This will build client loyalty and get your client noticed, which is a direct win in getting attention for your new firm.

Pricing and Payments

Pricing is based on hourly rates of $50 to $100 per hour. The protocol in this industry is to package services priced with a monthly retainer. This allows you to match the fee with the reality that you will be working for your clients many days during the month, not just one or two days. A lot of maintenance work is involved in keeping clients in the public eye. If you are mounting a major campaign, you will want to make sure you increase your monthly retainer for that period to make sure you get properly compensated. You don't want to do a lot of work in a condensed period, only to be terminated before you have had a chance to recoup fees based on a monthly retainer.

Special Requirements

Many public-relations professionals have degrees in various aspects of communications, but it is not necessary as long as you have strong written and verbal skills and enjoy all kinds of networking.

As a public-relations consultant, joining various organizations is key to staying connected with other professionals in your field. The Public Relations Society of America boasts the largest membership of PR professionals with 32,000 members. The dues, which fluctuate by chapter, are all under $100, and benefits include extensive resources and educational and conference opportunities.

Marketing Consultant

Estimated startup costs: $250–$1,000

Estimated first-year revenue: $50,000–$80,000

A marketing consultant is a generalist, bringing together all the components of an overall marketing plan to create a systematic strategy with a single purpose: increasing customers' sales. Where a publicist concentrates on the "soft" aspects of a business like branding, public image, and message, the end-game of marketing is much more concrete—selling more and increasing revenue.

A marketing consultant creates an action plan for communicating the uniqueness of a product or service, with the goal of getting customers to buy. She focuses the client's attention on the specifics of the marketing strategy and overcomes any hesitation or doubts on the client's part in order to launch the marketing plan with full force.

Equipment and Supplies

All you need to get started is a basic home office setup and marketing materials for your own company, which you will be able to do for yourself quite cost effectively.

Estimating the Time Commitment

The ramp-up period for a new marketing consulting business will depend greatly on the state of the economy and your existing reputation in the marketplace. Unfortunately, marketing budgets have been slashed in the recent economic downturn, so crafting a unique message will be critical to landing jobs.

On the positive side, many more businesses today realize that even in bad times they must continue to market their products. Many companies will be looking for a fresh approach to add more bang to their marketing buck. With the opportunities presented by the Internet, some small marketing firms are adding hourly consulting and coaching to their service listings. But most marketing professionals prefer longer engagements that allow them to bring their creativity, brainstorming abilities, and connections together to implement a plan for increased sales and market share for their customers.

Pricing and Payments

Marketing consultants price their services similarly to publicists, using a monthly retainer over a specified period to execute a complete plan. Position your pricing according to the market in your region. Most marketing consultants charge between $100 and $200 per hour. Some offer fixed pricing for basic introductory services, and publish these fees on their websites.

Bonus Point _____

Fixed pricing is a win/win for both marketing consultant and customer. By charging fair prices for introductory services, the consultant eliminates the "free consultation" offering, which is often a big loss leader when the prospect doesn't buy. With a decent fixed fee for a limited deliverable, you are actually getting paid to court the customer. What can be more winning than that?

Special Requirements

Marketing professionals typically have a degree in marketing and years of professional experience in well-regarded local or national firms. The American Marketing Association offers memberships at $225 per year.

Graphic Design

Estimated startup costs: $250–$1,000

Estimated first-year revenue: $35,000–$50,000

What has been lost to graphic designers in the efforts of many to "go green"— the decline of print advertising and the shift from marketing collateral to online marketing—has been compensated for by incredible online growth in the last several years (see graph in Chapter 23) and the need for good graphic design for web-based applications. Although there are significant differences in the craft of designing for the web versus print, a great deal of graphic design skill is still required to build the front end of an attractive website. Granted, there are also quite a few technical aspects of building a website in addition to the design—but if you have the creative talent to handle the graphics, you can learn or outsource the technical side.

Even if you have been doing graphic design for many years and prefer to create tangible printed collateral and packaging, you will have to apply your skill set to web design if you want to make a go of it as a solo graphic design firm.

Equipment and Supplies

Most graphic designers use Apple computers and peripherals in producing their designs and deliverables. These can be pretty pricey, so if you don't already have a system you need to think about how you are going to get one. You will also want to consider financing the purchase either with a credit card or existing line of credit in order to keep your startup costs to the $1,000 limit. You can purchase supplies as you are hired for specific jobs, with no need for inventory.

Estimating the Time Commitment

If you are willing to apply your graphic design skills to web design, your business will ramp up much more quickly. This is obvious from the number of job postings on Internet job boards and the fact that a Google search for graphic design immediately brings up hits related to web design. There is a huge demand for Internet design right now, as discussed in the web-design section of Chapter 23. Again, forming a partnership with someone with the IT skills to do the back end of the sites while you focus on doing the design work you love is a perfect way to tap into what's hot in the marketplace and follow your bliss.

Pricing and Payments

Graphic design pricing is quoted either by the hour or on a fixed price basis depending on the project. Designers will use fixed pricing for jobs that are frequently part of a customer's request for services, such as logo or letterhead design. You can have multiple logo prices, for example, $250 for logo updating, $650 for simple logo creation, and $1,000 for more complex logo design. Hourly rates for graphic designers range from $45 to $85 for small design firms.

Special Requirements

Graphic designers are usually degreed and trained in computer-aided design tools. The American Institute of Graphic Artists (AIGA) is a professional organization with the mission of fostering graphic design as a craft, strategic tool, and cultural force. It has 22,000 members nationwide; membership dues are $230 to $315 a year.

Copywriting and Web Content Developer

Estimated startup costs: $250–$500

Estimated first-year revenue: $30,000–$40,000

Copywriting, the function of communicating the value of a product, service, or brand to potential customers, has had an incredible resurgence and huge growth along with the number of websites, blogs, and online media sites in the last three years (see the graph in Chapter 23). Being able to write well has always been a valuable tool in the world of marketing; with new sites coming online every day, the need for web content has never been greater.

Many of the opportunities for copywriting on the web are for short, succinct articles that include enough key words to draw traffic. Although the better-written articles and blogs certainly get the most attention, there is plenty of work to be found in this arena.

Equipment and Supplies

Copywriting requires a simple computer system and straightforward word-processing software. Unless you are responsible for the layout of a publication, like an online newsletter, you can get by with the least expensive of computers to start this very low-cost startup business.

Most copywriters have degrees in English, journalism, communications, or marketing. It is possible to hone your writing skills from another background and turn yourself into a writer if you have enough talent and drive.

Estimating the Time Commitment

If you focus on answering job board postings for copywriters, you can stay very busy but you might end up on the lower end of the pay scale. A lot of the online postings for writers advertise payment per article from $5 to $20 each. You would have to write a great many articles to make a decent living if you only tapped into the online job board marketplace.

Many copywriters charge $50 per hour and some can demand even more. Finding higher-end work will require more marketing effort, but the likelihood is that the quality of the customer and assignment are likely to be worth the extra effort.

The writing assignments will vary in length and your time commitment per job will fluctuate accordingly. The more you have to research a certain topic, the longer it will take you to write about it.

Pricing and Payment

If possible, stick to the hourly rate for your billing. It's what's most common in the industry and the best way to get the best fee for your services. For web content paid per article, make sure you fully understand the nature of any assignment in order to determine whether it's worth your time.

Special Requirements

Many copywriters have degrees in English or communications. There are no formal requirements to work in this field.

Search Engine Optimization

Estimated startup costs: $250-$350

Estimated first-year revenue: $50,000–$70,000

Search engine optimization (SEO) is a technique used to maximize the number of hits a website or blog gets using key word–identification techniques. Just like its name conveys, this is a technical field, but most companies that offer SEO to customers use a traditional marketing approach. Once the very leading edge of web-based marketing, SEO has become a more competitive profession, but the growth of the Internet continues so rapidly that there is still plenty of work, especially for freelancers. In fact, SEO companies were some of the first to recognize the potential for a virtual office approach to business.

Success Story

Stacy W. had a successful corporate career in advertising and direct marketing that led her to the Internet side of marketing by 1995. After having children, Stacy decided to launch her own company specializing in SEO services. A pioneer in the marketplace, Stacy used her excellent customer-development skills to parlay her small company to rapid growth. She soon realized the SEO work was perfect for other highly experienced marketing professionals who were ready to leave corporate America and work from home to spend more time with their young families. Stacy built her company as a virtual office, with several part-time freelancers like herself handling customers as account managers. Since its inception in 2001, her company has grown steadily, affording her flexibility in her own lifestyle as well as the satisfaction of enabling her team to have the same.

Equipment and Supplies

This work can be done with a basic home office setup for a sole freelance business. It can also be expanded to a multiperson operation with cost-effective web-based software and phone systems.

You need to have an SEO background in order to hit the ground running with this. If you don't, then plan on investing some up-front time learning the trade. You may find a more seasoned SEO professional desperate for help and willing to train you. The potential of this work over the long term of your career makes the investment in training very worthwhile. There are affordable (less than $300) web-based training classes and certification programs available. See the Appendix for a listing of links to some of these sites.

Estimating the Time Commitment

There is great demand for SEO skills, so this is a startup that should move rather quickly. You can advertise worldwide through a website, but should also have great results with more traditional networking. With other new businesses being more website-dependent than ever—and your customers increasingly savvy about the great need and benefits of SEO services—this profession is one of the best to launch right now.

Pricing and Payment

You can structure SEO pricing with an hourly rate or monthly retainer. This is a front-loaded service, with many more hours being delivered in the beginning. If you go the monthly retainer route, you will definitely need to price your first 3 to 6 months at a premium, with perhaps a hefty upfront fee for the first 30 days. Average monthly retainers run in the $2,000 to $3,000 range, even for small business customers.

According to the indeed.com job board site, the hourly rates for SEO have climbed by 30 percent since the beginning of 2009. If you combine account management, SEO strategy, and web analytics (a summary report of web traffic statistics written for the client's management team) with your SEO offering, you can bump your hourly rate considerably, to the high side of the $50 to $125 per hour range for a startup consultant.

Bonus Point

There is definitely great efficiency in billing all clients on the same day, despite the signing dates of their contracts. Not only do you get to bundle your administrative tasks all in one day, but everyone is on the same collection cycle as well.

Since you are offering web-based services, there is no reason not to use a green approach to your payment requirements. You can e-mail a monthly retainer invoice on the first of each month for the services to be rendered for the next 30 days.

Special Requirements

As we stated above, experience in SEO is a must for this work, with a marketing background a definite plus. If you are more of a behind-the-scenes person, you'll find a great deal of work as another small business's back-office techie.

Direct Mail and E-Mail Advertising

Estimated startup costs: $250-$350

Estimated first-year revenue: $30,000 and up

Direct and e-mail marketing are still viable professions in spite of the rapidly changing media environment. Surprisingly, direct marketing employment and salary trends are higher than e-mail marketing. The fact that e-mail marketing is so closely associated with spam e-mail has tainted this field somewhat. Spam is not only seen as the devil in the world of e-mail, it's flat-out illegal. A company may be ringing its death knell if not extremely careful with its e-mail campaign.

There is still a great deal of opportunity for creating e-mail campaigns to a company's online subscribers and a website's members. Once the target audience is established, there are still three major hurdles for e-mails with marketing messages:

1. How do you ensure the e-mails will be read by a significant percentage of recipients?

2. Can you craft a call to action that moves readers from their inbox to the marketing company's website?

3. What will you use to measure the effectiveness of your e-mail campaign?

Equipment and Supplies

You don't need special equipment, but having a portfolio or samples of work will go far in helping you win jobs. Creating e-mail samples is cost-free, and printed direct-mail samples can be mocked up if you are new to the field, or borrowed from previous campaigns if you have prior mailing experience.

Success Story
It may seem that direct mail is for the older end of the baby boomer generation, but even young people still use postal mail pieces to spread the word about their businesses. Take Angela in Hudson, Wisconsin, who used a simple postcard mailing to generate some local interest in her new graphic- and web-design firm when she opened it in 2005. Small and simple in scale, Angela was pleased with the positive response she got from local business owners interested in meeting her to talk about her design services.

Estimating the Time Commitment

Mailing services are essentially about selling a project and a marketing method. There will be customers who seek you out to help them with a mailing project they have decided to do. Many other potential customers will need proposals and presentations showing them the benefits of mailing and the way you will measure *ROI* (or eROI as the case may be).

def•i•ni•tion

ROI stands for return on investment, which is a ration that measures the amount of money generated by the value of a particular investment of funds. For example, if you spend $1,000 on an e-mail marketing campaign, and you generate at least $5,000 in net revenue (sales less direct-mailing costs), then your ROI for this project would be 5 to 1, or $5 of revenue for every $1 spent on the mail campaign (5:1 in ROI notation).

Pricing and Payment

Direct and e-mail marketing hourly rates are in the $30 to $50 range. Naturally if you are offering a mail campaign as part of a comprehensive marketing plan, the rates you can charge will be higher (see section on pricing in marketing consultant). You need a contract since a campaign will require several phases of planning and execution, and your payment schedule should be structured accordingly.

Special Requirements

You will need experience in creating and implementing a mail campaign and delivering results, in addition to the ability to generate reports on the analytics of the results.

Chapter 25

Goods Resellers

In This Chapter

◆ What you need to know about multilevel marketing programs

◆ The best way to make money selling on eBay

◆ The ins and outs of importing products for sale

◆ The challenges of selling your own art

◆ Turning your collecting hobby into a business

Our national gross domestic product (GDP) has been moving to a service-based economy for a long time now, but many people still make their living selling products to businesses and consumers. The Internet has made this process so much more accessible and cheaper to anyone with regular access to a computer. Many people have found themselves starting a side business selling items on eBay only to end up with a full-scale e-tail business in a matter of months.

You can create a business selling things you've purchased going to closeout sales, large gift markets, traveling abroad for unique imported items, even selling your own arts and crafts. It takes a great deal of research and marketing skill to identify items that will sell well and the best, most cost-effective way to bring them to market. But many ordinary folks are creating these businesses to provide part- or full-time income for their families.

Multilevel Marketing

Estimated startup costs: Variable*

Estimated first-year revenue: Variable*

* You are more likely to lose money in an MLM business than to make any profit at all!

Multilevel marketing (MLM) refers to a hierarchal commission structure that provides a strong incentive to not only sell product to consumers but also to recruit other product users into the sales force. In this way, the company builds a sales team in a pyramid format, and the commissions earned grow exponentially as a team member expands the number of people in his particular sales group (who then add more people to their sales team, and so on).

There are many success stories within the framework of MLM. Usually a minimum purchase is required in order to acquire product inventory. Success in this arena requires the same fortitude as selling door-to-door. The American landscape has hundreds of MLM opportunities, with many well-known companies. Others are less known by name but sell popular consumer products, like health supplements and diet foods.

We have included this section in the book because, in a down economy, the concept of becoming part of an established sales company has its appeal, and there are relatively low barriers to entry. Many people will be tempted by this type of business. A great deal of information is on the web, including academic and journalistic articles. We highly suggest you read them and educate yourself, and approach any MLM proposition with a healthy skepticism and appropriate caution.

Equipment and Supplies

As stated above, most MLM companies have a minimum purchase requirement—not only a starter kit, but required quarterly purchases in order to stay in the program. If you sign on with a MLM company, make sure you like the product, because you will be buying it. Lots of it. You will also need a larger space for a home office, since you will need to store your inventory.

Estimating the Time Commitment

It will take a long time to build a loyal customer base—at least a year or two. Once you start selling a good bit of product and are making some profit, you can attract others to the idea of joining your sales team. If you function like a good sales manager and keep your team focused and on-target, you have the makings of a successful MLM startup. It can be done.

Pricing and Payment

Since you are actually working as a sales rep for another company, you will have strict guidelines for pricing your product. You will be expected to pay for product at the time of its shipment to you. You will collect from customers when and where you deliver product to them.

Special Requirements

A strong sales background and product knowledge will be important to your success as an MLM participant. No matter how good something is, nothing sells itself. Not even over the Internet.

eBay Sales

Estimated startup costs: $1,000

Estimated first-year revenue: $20,000–$40,000

Yes, it is possible to make a living setting up an e-store using eBay. It allows you the space to retail your products and eliminates the costs associated with a) a brick-and-mortar location or b) your own e-commerce website.

However, selling on eBay still has costs associated with it, and if you don't already have a clear understanding of what is actually involved, that is the first thing you will have to learn. Many people learn the ropes by listing their own used items, like an alternative to a yard sale and more money than giving things away to Goodwill. This is a great way to downsize (your life), declutter (your stuff), and make money (your goal) all at the same time.

Estimating the Time Commitment

Selling your own used items is a great way to get a handle on the many intricacies of this Internet icon. Not only will you learn the process of selling, you should use the experience to learn about the "what factor,"—as in, what sells. You will have to work at all aspects of the sale: setting it up, learning how to get your photos uploaded, what days work best to close a sale (a big discussion topic for the regular eBayers out there). Take the time to really study the eBay site, looking for:

1. How merchandise is priced relative to your local market.

2. How fast things sell.

3. What you might want to sell.

If someone is selling guitars, how does the pricing compare to your local music store? How does it compare to other eBay sellers' prices? And being able to push through a lot of product will make the difference between selling on eBay as a hobby and selling on eBay as a business. Selling on eBay is going to take many of the same characteristics for success as selling a product anywhere, including product knowledge, being able to relate to your customer base, and great customer service.

It will take at least a year to get to the point where your income is at a level that can fully support you. Remember, your sales volume is your first tier benchmark; you also have to have a good profit built in to make money.

Pricing and Payment

There are many pricing models for selling product. The best ones tend to be those that have 100 percent markup, meaning you multiply your cost by 2 to get to the price you will sell it at. Here's an example to help you calculate this:

1. You buy a classic baseball card for $100.

2. You sell the card for $200. You have $100 gross profit.

3. You close out the sale and pay the fees associated with PayPal, eBay, and so on. Let's say those come to $20.

4. Your net profit is $80.

5. Be sure to add shipping (at cost) and sales tax as required to your customer's invoice.

Special Requirements

Many how-to manuals have been written by currently successful eBay sellers, and they're available on the web. Make use of these resources, and be sure to contact anyone you know who is already doing eBay sales.

Retailing Imported Specialty Items

Estimated startup costs: $1,000

Estimated first-year revenue: $20,000–$30,000

Another way to turn your love of travel into a marketable business, in addition to selling travel concepts as we discussed in Chapter 19, is to find inexpensive, nonfragile products unique to a region and import them into the United States for sale.

Consider several qualities when identifying products you think will sell well. First, if the region from which you will be importing is infrequently traveled, the products are from local *cottage industries* with a limited availability in the United States.

Second, the cost of the items, the shipping costs, and the currency exchange rate must come together in a way that makes it possible for you to make a profit.

Up until the last 15 years, the only way to market these products was to bring them physically to the potential buyers. You could do this through a retail location, a booth in a consignment store, or by attending festival-like, open-air markets on weekends. Today you have the additional options of eBay sales and other Internet-based outlets. You can also supply other retail establishments with your products, but this will not have as high a profit margin.

def•i•ni•tion

Cottage industries are small-scale businesses that can be carried on at home by family members using their own equipment. Most common examples of cottage industries are regional products that are hand made in the home like clothing, baskets, pottery, and folk art.

Equipment and Supplies

The main cost of starting up an import business is the cost of purchasing your beginning inventory. Unless you buy a relatively small quantity, you will have a hard time keeping this business low cost. You also need enough space in your home to store the items in an organized fashion. There's no better way to lose money on inventory than to warehouse it in a way that makes it difficult to know what you have, or where it is.

One way to counter the inventory cost and storage issues is to start small and buy items that don't take up a lot of space, like jewelry. Most of the jewelry sold at local art festivals today is imported from other parts of the globe. The items may be designed by the person selling them, but they are usually crafted and imported from a foreign land to keep prices down.

Snags

Carl Z. (not his real name) started a side business importing ceramics from southern France. In the late 1990s, with the exchange rate in the United States' favor, the items sold well at comparatively good prices. Carl expanded his business, adding linens and other specialty items. He loved going to France on his shopping trips. (Who wouldn't?) Things went well as long as he kept his investment at hobby levels, but early success inspired Carl to start doing it full-time. Several trips later, Carl had a large inventory, a warehouse with retail space, and his own truck. However, a rising Euro made it difficult to buy items at a good price, and it became more difficult to sell much volume at higher prices. After a couple of years, Carl was forced to close his doors and file for bankruptcy protection.

Estimating the Time Commitment

It takes time to build a retail business, no matter what your outlet for sales may be. This is what makes the eBay model so appealing: you can start out part-time with very little investment and work up to enough business to quit your day job. The same is true for an e-commerce site. Even if you have the greatest products, people have to find you and you need to establish your reputation in order to have enough sales to generate a decent cash flow.

Pricing and Payments

Just like with eBay sales, have a pricing model that allows you to mark up your items 100 percent. Otherwise it will be very difficult to make money. If you don't have a profit built into every sale, you will lose money and it won't take long to get in deep. You're not truly running a business if you are not pricing your goods to make money.

Special Requirements

It is great to have a business background when starting a retail company. With so many details to handle, it would be to your advantage to know what to expect instead of being surprised by unanticipated events.

Another big plus to starting an import business is having a relationship with someone on the other side of the transaction who can represent you to the product vendor. This often improves credit terms, as you have a built-in element of trust with an existing relationship. Those with family members living abroad may have the good fortune to arrange an expansion of a foreign business on U.S. soil. If you have siblings in business in India, and you start importing goods purchased from their company, you are effectively helping them expand into the U.S. market. Cash-flow terms with foreign vendors can make or break an import business, and no one will provide you better terms than your own family.

Selling Your Arts and Crafts

Estimated startup costs: $1,000

Estimated first-year revenue: $25,000–$35,000

Many of us have craft hobbies. We may have a talent for making our own specialty items, like knitted hats and scarves, quilts, pottery, or photos and paintings. While our loved ones and dear friends may treasure any homemade gifts, selling these items on the open market is another story, let alone actually making money at it.

Many people have taken their arts and crafts on the road and made a business from selling their work at various art locations around the country. The most popular outlets for selling art are weekend art festivals. Many large metropolitan areas have several during the year, while smaller cities and rural areas usually have at least one yearly county fair. There is some kind of romantic appeal about making a living in this fashion, but a closer look at the concept begs the question—"Can you really make money doing this?"

Equipment and Supplies

Many working artists don't have much money to invest in their art, so they make inexpensive products intended for "mass market" appeal. This is often the dividing line between crafts and more expensive art. You will need to create a sizeable inventory of items to take with you to any festival you might attend. There are a lot of expenses just to get somewhere, including travel, packing materials, display booth and counters, a merchant credit card account, and lodging and food during the event itself.

Estimating the Time Commitment

The festival months are seasonal. Unless you live in a temperate region, like the Southeast, your travel and work time will be limited to May through September. It will be hard to get yourself to more than one festival each month unless they are within a couple hours of your home. You have to pack up your inventory, load it onto a truck or van, drive to the festival site, unload, set up your display, and then man the display for the festival hours, usually 9 A.M. to 9 P.M. in the summer.

This is a time-intensive business, and for most artists and crafters it is a labor of love.

Pricing and Payment

Pricing will depend on the material cost as well as the amount of time you have invested. One artist on the Eastern Shore of Virginia takes found objects like shells and creates keepsake items with the names of the local towns on them. She only sells them for $8 a piece, but she can make six an hour and the materials don't cost her anything.

Taking the investment of time and money into account, someone participating in this type of business would have to make at least $4,000 per festival (before expenses) to make it a profitable venture. Other outlets for selling your items include consignment marts, art league shops, websites, or local neighborhood shows.

You will need a merchant credit card account for processing credit cards. Since you will be in areas away from home, taking personal checks is too great to risk. All you need is one bad check to cancel out all the profit you made for your efforts.

Special Requirements

You need to have some art or craft talent to exploit in order to make items that will appeal to a mass audience. The more local the flavor of your work, the stronger the likelihood your work will sell.

Collectibles

Estimated startup costs: $1,000

Estimated first-year revenue: $15,000–$25,000

There is an infinite world of collectibles and how people sell and trade them. It's impossible to name the thousands of different things people collect as hobbies and investments. Everything from vintage cars to gold-plated cigarette lighters is part of somebody's collection.

If you own a collection of some kind, this is a great place to start developing some skills in trading collectibles. People who collect things not only take pride in owning the items but also in learning about all the details and hidden stories. Before the advent of Facebook and other social networking via the Internet, collectors formed their own clubs of a sort, meeting up at conventions and exchanging photos and correspondence about their latest acquisitions. They also buy and sell from each other, refining their collections for various specialties. For individuals who are good at negotiating and trading, and at recognizing a particularly interested fellow collector, there are opportunities to develop a business as a middleman, acquiring special high-priced pieces expressly to resell to another collector.

Equipment and Supplies

There are extensive libraries that chronicle the various items in different kinds of collections, and it helps to have access to these books to authenticate certain purchases. Having the knowledge base of a lifelong collector is helpful as well. You will also need a digital camera for photographing items to exchange with interested buyers, decent home office equipment, and room for your collection.

Estimating the Time Commitment

It's possible to leap into collecting mode and learn a lot about a certain type of item in a short period of time, but if you're thinking of earning money trading collectibles, you probably already have experience with your own collections and know the usual buyers and sellers.

Knowing the market value of an item is a very important piece of the collecting transaction. This knowledge, usually based on recent sales of comparable items, is not readily available. You need to be in-the-know on pricing in order to ensure that you don't overpay and get stuck with an item that is really not as valuable as you were led to believe.

Pricing and Payments

Prices for collectibles are set by the cost, the quality of the item (how close it is to perfection), and the activity level of the marketplace. Two or more individuals both looking for the same item to add to their collection are going to drive prices to an inflated level. You may be sadly disappointed if your purchase is overpriced because of a fabricated demand.

There are books and a few online databases that are sources of market value information. The key is to keep abreast of the most recent sales in the marketplace. Be sure to review the available pricing resources for the items you are buying. Attending conferences with other interested parties is another good way to keep current with pricing information.

Special Requirements

There has been a lot of activity in the last year or so from people selling or attempting to sell collectibles as a way of raising capital in tough times. These situations lend themselves to others who see the chance to insert themselves into the market and become a liaison, helping those who want to sell find others who want to buy.

Having good insurance on your collectibles is important to protecting them. A typical homeowner's or renter's policy will not come close to covering the value of a special collection. Work with your insurance agent to make sure your items are properly appraised and insured against future loss or damage.

Websites and Resources by Chapter

Chapter 2, "How Low Is Low-Cost?"

SCORE   Counselors to America's small business; free business consulting by experienced, retired business executives:
www.score.org

Small Business Development Center (SBDC)   These centers are funded by the U.S. Small Business Administration (SBA). There are several centers in each state (usually affiliated with a state university), each offering free business seminars and individual coaching to new startups and entrepreneurs:
http://www.sba.gov/aboutsba/sbaprograms/sbdc/sbdclocator/
SBDC_LOCATOR.html

Chapter 3, "Do Your Homework"

Locally owned printing shop locator   Resource for identifying an owner operated print shop in your area:
http://www2.allegranetwork.com/allegraprint/index.php

Servicemagic.com   Servicemagic.com is a website that can be used by consumers to find local service professionals for various home service needs, such as home repairs and maintenance, and home remodeling projects. Independent service professionals meeting the servicemagic.com criteria have the opportunity to pay a monthly fee to be included in the website's referral database. Check out competitors' pricing and see if this lead-generating service is for you: http://www.servicemagic.com/servlet/ServiceProfessionalRegistrationServlet

Bureau of Labor Statistics   Resource for data, tables, and details on hundreds of industries and professions: www.bls.gov

Commercial Insurance Quotes   This site will match you with commercial insurance companies in your area for a quick response: http://www.netquote.com/nq/s-business.aspx

Loan Payment Calculator   http://www.bankrate.com/calculators/mortgages/loan-calculator.aspx

Business Networking International   Networking groups for small business owners: http://www.bni.com

E-mail marketing services   Outsource the task of tracking all customer e-mail addresses and use as a resource for e-mail marketing: www.constantcontact.com

Free and inexpensive marketing techniques for startups: http://www.michaelhartspeaks.com

Search engine optimization information http://www.searchenginejournal.com/55-quick-seo-tips-even-your-mother-would-love/6760/

Chapter 4, "Nuts and Bolts of a Home-Based Business"

Article on Voice over IP phone systems www.entrepreneur.com/technology/newsandtrends/article203150.html

Free conference calling service   www.instantconference.com

QuickBooks Software Links http://oe.quickbooks.com for online software; http://quickbooks.intuit.com for software packages

Paying Taxes

For Federal Tax information: www.irs.gov

For State Tax information: http://www.irs.gov/businesses/small/article/0,,id=99021,00.html

Self-Employment Tax Calculator

http://www.bankrate.com/calculators/tax-planning/self-employed-business-tax-calculator.aspx

IRS pamphlet on independent contractors versus employees

http://www.irs.gov/pub/irs-pdf/p1779.pdf

Article about payroll services

http://smallbusiness.yahoo.com/r-article-a-2034-m-2-sc-52-payroll_services_buyers_guide-i

National Association of Self-Employed

www.nase.com

Chapter 5, "Housework"

Article on how to start a cleaning business

http://www.entrepreneur.com/startingabusiness/businessideas/startupkits/article41426.html

Online certification courses for green cleaning

http://www.greencleaninstitute.com

Cleaning startup manual

http://www.smallbizbooks.com/c/s/00049.html

Carpet and Rug Institute

http://www.carpet-rug.org

Carpet-cleaning equipment source

http://www.carpet-cleaning-equipment.net/startup_kits.shtml

National Air Duct Cleaners Association   Air-duct cleaning certification: https://www.nadca.com/training/trainingschedule.aspx

Blog about carpet-cleaning business

http://baneclene.blogspot.com

Professional Carpet and Upholstery Cleaners Association
http://www.pcuca.org

Environmental Protection Agency   Recommendations for cleaning air ducts:
http://www.epa.gov/iaq/pubs/airduct.html#Summary

Air-duct cleaning equipment
http://www.giind.com/PDF_Docs/Brocductwho2.PDF

Chapter 6, "Outside Work"

Lawn care startup manual and information
http://www.lawncaredirectory.com

Equipment needed for landscaping business
http://landscaping.about.com/od/helpforconsumers1/tp/cutters_traps.htm

Marketing for lawn care companies
http://www.synergeticmarketingsales.com

Lawn care blog
http://lawnchat.com

Association Pool and Spa Professionals
http://www.apsp.org

Pool business statistics
http://www.aquaticnet.com/media-statistics3.htm

Great website for pool industry data and information
http://www.pkdata.net/PKData

Article on the pool business
http://www.entrepreneur.com/businessideas/1214.html

Pool business startup resources
http://www.poolcaredirectory.com/freedayone.html

Chapter 7, "Concierge Services"

Article on how to be a concierge
http://www.entrepreneur.com/startingabusiness/businessideas/startupkits/article37930-6.html

Guide to starting a personal concierge business:
http://www.fabjob.com/personalconcierge.asp

Home-maintenance checklists
http://www.mgservicesonline.com/default/index.php?option=com_
content&task=blogcategory&id=100

U.S. Government Census statistics on vacation home
http://www.census.gov/hhes/www/housing/census/historic/vacation.html

Property management FAQs
http://www.ibiblio.org/london/agriculture/general/1/msg00098.html

Property management courses
http://education-portal.com/property_management_courses.html

Chapter 8, "Home Resale Services"

Home staging training and information
http://homestagingresource.com

International Association of Home Staging Professionals
http://www.iahsp.com

Real Estate Staging Association
http://www.realestatestagingassociation.com

American Society of Estate Liquidators
www.aselonline.com/index.html

Article on Estate Sales   http://couponing.about.com/b/2009/06/22/
hiring-a-professional-estate-sale-service.htm

Home inspection tool source
www.professionalequipment.com

American Society of Home Inspectors   This site has lots of great information
about the home inspection profession. Be sure to check out the tabs for "Becoming a
Home Inspector" and "State Regulations":
http://www.homeinspector.org

Home inspector insurance resource
www.targetcapital.com

Home appraiser association and resources for certification
http://www.appraisalinstitute.org

Real estate appraisal article
http://www.ehow.com/how_2214759_start-real-estate-appraisal-business.html

Chapter 9, "Interior Home Renovations"

Referral network for interior home professionals
www.servicemaster.com

Article on building a carpentry business
http://money.cnn.com/2008/01/23/smbusiness/carpentry.fsb

To purchase a complete kit of tile installation tools   http://www.tiletool.net/tool_kits.asp

Certified tile installation classes
www.tilecareer.com

Tile Council of North America, Inc.
http://www.tileusa.com

Ask the Tool Man forum
http://www.ceramic-tile.com/Ask_standard_registration.cfm

Great site for everything tile
http://www.ceramic-tile-floor.info/ceramic-tile-installation/install-your-tile

Sound system and wiring pricing
www.geeksquad.com

Infocomm International   An audio-visual professional organization:
www.infocomm.org

Chapter 10, "Interior Design Services"

Feng shui consultant training
http://www.thefengshuitrainingcenter.com

Feng shui information and blog
http://openspacesfengshui.com

Kitchen design resource and idea website
http://www.kitchendesignersideas.com

Google SketchUp software site
http://sketchup.google.com/industries/archdesign/interiordesign.html

Article on trend toward hiring professionals for home improvement projects
http://www.kitchenbathdesign.com/print/Kitchen-and-Bath-Design-News/
New-Survey-Sees-Move-Away-from-DIY-Projects/2$5012

Faux paint product website
http://www.fauxpaintingproducts.com/site/1417279/page/45030

Discussion of pricing faux finishing
http://www.gofaux.com/fauxcost.html

Pittman, Rebecca. *How to Start a Faux Painting Busines*s. New York, Allworth
Press, 2003

International Decorative Artisans League (IDAL)   An organization dedicated
to the promotion and preservation of the art of stenciling and related decorative
painting:
http://www.decorativeartisans.org

Ralph Lauren Faux Painting training program
http://www.ralphlaurenhome.com/rlhome/products/paint/sponging_howto.asp?step=1

Information and links related to the reupholstery repair business
http://www.encyclopedia.com/doc/1G2-3434500942.html

Articles on window replacement business growth trends
http://www.free-press-release.com/news/200805/1211569015.html;
http://products.construction.com/Manufacturer/Distinctive-Window-Treatment-Plus-
NST150852/products/Window-Shades-NST16290P

Article on how to price services for interior design
http://www.dezignare.com/newsletter/fees.html

Blog on starting your interior decorating career
http://www.blogcatalog.com/blog/starting-your-career-as-an-interior-designer-the-
business-of-interior-design

Sources of custom closet components
http://www.easyclosets.com;
http://www.plusclosets.com

Online magazine about the closet design business
http://www.closetsmagazine.com

Chapter 11, "Exterior Design Services"

Example website and pricing packages
http://glorydesign.blogspot.com

Gardening tips and ideas
http://www.gardeningtipsnideas.com/garden_tools

Software for landscape design
http://www.homedesignersoftware.com/products/landscaping

Association of Professional Landscape Designers
http://www.apld.com/members/search.asp

Article on hardscaping
http://www.articlegallery.net/Art/90296/96/Hardscape-Installation-Patio-Design-Pool-Decking-Retaining-Walls-Fireplaces-in-Houston-Texas.html

Website that inspires contractors to build a professional hardscaping business
http://www.hardscapemagazine.com

Website with discussions on how to bid a hardscape job
http://lawnchat.com/?p=539

North American Deck and Railing Association
http://www.nadra.org

Chapter 12, "Personal Services"

National Association of Professional Organizers (NAPO)
www.napo.net

E-books on office organization and decluttering
http://www.lotusbridge.com/e-books/index.html

Association of Image Consultants International
http://aici.org

Article on business support service startup
http://www.entrepreneur.com/startingabusiness/businessideas/startupkits/article41392.html

Chapter 13, "Personal Health"

Blog for personal training business consultant
www.rickmayo.com

Nutritionist website with pricing information   http://www.blairgiles.com/service.php

American Dietitic Association   The world's largest organization of food and nutrition professionals:
http://eatright.org/cps/rde/xchg/ada/hs.xsl/index.html

Massage therapy supplies
http://www.massagesupplies.com

Chapter 14, "Child Care"

Steelsmith, Shari. *How to Start a Home-Based Day-Care Business.* Guilford, Connecticut, Globe Pequot Press, November 2006

Database on licensing requirements of child-care settings by state
http://www.daycarehotline.com/how-to-start-a-daycare/index.htm

National Resource Center for Health and Safety in Child Care
http://nrc.uchsc.edu

Bureau of Labor Statistics on Child Daycare Services
http://www.bls.gov/oco/cg/cgs032.htm

Table of 2005–2006 statistics for percentages of children in home-based child-care centers
http://nces.ed.gov/programs/coe/2008/section1/table.asp?tableID=857

Daycare curriculum
http://www.adaycare.com/buy.html

Baby nurse training
http://www.thestorkstopshere.com/Index.html

Childbirth and Postpartum Professional Association   An association for childbirth professionals with programs for certifications:
http://www.cappa.net

Education Resource Information Center An online digital library of education resources and information:
http://www.eric.ed.gov

Article on the cost of special needs child care
http://www.care.com/special-needs-p1145-cost-of-care-qxid%7C0811261515.html

Chapter 15, "Elder Care"

Chauffeur's licenses by state
http://search.dmv.org/dmv/chauffeurs-license

Blog about the elderly need for transportation
http://www.timegoesby.net/weblog/2006/01/elder_transport.html

Senior relocation training and certification
http://www.moveseniors.com/syllabus.htm

Bureau of Labor Statistics, U.S. Department of Labor *Occupational Outlook Handbook, 2008–09 Edition*, Personal and Home Care Aides:
http://www.bls.gov/oco/ocos173.html

National Association for Home Care and Hospice Certification Program
http://www.nahc.org/education/home.htm#ol

Chapter 16, "Pet Care"

Pet Sitters International
https://www.petsit.com

Salzburg, Kathy. *How to Start a Home-Based Pet Care Business, 2nd Edition.* Guilford, Connecticut, Morris Book Publishing, LLC, 2006

The World of Professional Pet Sitting **magazine**
http://www.petsitters.org

Pet care industry statistics
http://www.americanpetproducts.org/press_industrytrends.asp

Article on starting a pet-sitting business http://www.associatedcontent.com/article/3824/starting_a_petsitting_business_pg2.html?cat=3

Article on pet grooming and training opportunities
http://www.associatedcontent.com/article/211983/learn_the_dog_grooming_
business_in_pg2_pg2.html?cat=31

Dog grooming supply resource
http://www.sitstay.com/dog/supplies/servlet/CategoryDisplay?catalogId=10001&storeI
d=10001&categoryId=23203&langId

Martin, Mark W. and Talbot, Ret. *The Complete Idiot's Guide to the Saltwater
Aquarium*. New York, Penguin Group, September 2009

Article on starting an aquarium maintenance business
http://www.aquarticles.com/articles/management/Aquariumpros_Maintenance_
Business.html

Article on saltwater aquarium startup
http://petcare.suite101.com/article.cfm/no_better_time_to_go_
marine#ixzz0Ne38ofSn

Chapter 17, "Teaching and Tutoring"

Article on how to become a college planning consultant
http://www.entrepreneur.com/startingabusiness/businessideas/startupkits/
article190442-2.html

College admission assistance services
http://www.college-admission-essay.com/pricechart.html;
http://www.collegedirection.org/collegeselection.html;
http://www.businessweek.com/magazine/content/06_25/b3989109.htm

The American Institute of Certified Educational Planners
http://www.aicep.org/becoming.htm

Association of the Tutoring Profession
http://www.myatp.org/History.htm

Tutor Marketplace Websites
https://www.wyzant.com/tutorsignup.aspx;
http://www.my-tutor.com/rates.html

English as a second language tutoring blog
http://www.esltutoringblog.com

Homeschooling curriculums and resources
http://www.homeschool.com

Chapter 18, "Food Services"

Bartending course
http://www.bartendingcollegeonline.com

Culinary business education
http://culinarybusiness.com/entertainmentcooking

How to become a freelance chef article
http://freelancepro.blogspot.com/2007/10/how-to-become-freelance-chef.html

Starting a catering business
http://www.ehow.com/how_4733024_start-homebased-catering-business.html

Personal chef insurance resource
http://www.personalchefinsurance.com

Chapter 19, "Travel and Tour Guide"

French Escapade   Personnally guided tours of France, Belgium, and other select destinations, with a focus on very small groups:
www.frenchescapade.com

Guided tours of Scotland
www.mini-tours.com

Group travel seminars
http://www.groupuniversity.com/Home.html

Information for travel professionals
http://www.leisuregrouptravel.com/tool.php

Example of a tour guide business for a specific city
http://www.washingtonwalks.com/index.shtml

Chapter 20, "Event Planner"

Article on how to start an event planning business
http://eventplanning.about.com/od/eventcareers/a/fees_5.htm

Bureau of Labor Statistics Occupational Outlook Handbook, 2008-09 Edition, Meeting and Convention Planners   Data, tables, and details about event planning business:
http://www.bls.gov/oco/ocos298.htm;

Convention Industry Council   Organization that facilitates the exchange of information among professionals in the meeting, convention, and exhibitions industry:
http://www.conventionindustry.org/aboutcic

Website with information on what people are paying for wedding planners
http://www.costhelper.com/cost/wedding/wedding-planner.html

Chapter 21, "Professional Services from Home"

American Institute of CPAs
www.aicpa.org

American Bar Association
http://www.abanet.org

Article about attorney billing rates
http://www.lawmarketing.com/pages/
articles.asp?Action=Article&ArticleCategoryID=7&ArticleID=907

National Association of Personal Financial Advisors
http://www.napfa.org

Article/White paper on executive coaching
http://www.theexecutivecoachingforum.com/ECFCompetencyModel905.pdf

National Association of Home Based Recruiters
http://nahbr.org

Website by fundraising professional Tony Poderis   Includes resources and advice for the freelance professional fundraiser:
http://www.raise-funds.com

Chapter 22, "Virtual Office Providers"

Virtual assistant training programs, certification, and networking forums
VAClassroom.com

Website of information and networking opportunities for virtual assistants
http://www.vanetworking.com

Chapter 23, "IT Services"

Article on increase in freelance software developer pay rates
http://www.odesk.com/blog/2009/05/freelance-software-developer-rates-up-35-in-the-united-states

World Organization of Webmasters
http://webprofessionals.org

Web development pricing schedule
http://www.stanford.edu/services/itrates/sharedservices

Chapter 24, "Marketing Services"

American Marketing Association
http://www.marketingpower.com/Pages/default.aspx

Articles on providing freelance marketing services
http://advertising.about.com

Article on freelance copywriting
http://www.flixya.com/post/soft666/1671745/A_Day_in_the_Life_of_a_Freelance_Copywriter

E-book manual on running your own public relations firm
http://www.fabjob.com/publicrelations.asp

Article on how publicists work
http://entertainment.howstuffworks.com/publicist.htm

Article on correlation between social media marketing and business success
http://www.readwriteweb.com/archives/new_study_finds_correlation_between_social_media_and_financial_success.php

Article on e-mail marketing
http://www.bizreport.com/2009/08/five_reasons_you_should_be_testing_email_marketing_campaigns.html

Article on growth of social media
http://www.bizreport.com/2009/06/for_marketers_social_takes_over_direct_mail.html

Website for search engine optimization consultant
http://patrickfbruce.com/Content/23/Internet_Consultant_Fees__Value_of_SEO_
Consultant

Website that provides tips and information about searching the web
http://searchenginewatch.com

Graph of trends in search engine optimization consultant salaries
http://www.indeed.com/salary?q1=Seo+&l1=

Chapter 25, "Goods Resellers"

Skip McGrath Auction Seller's Resource   eBay sellers 'how to' site:
http://www.skipmcgrath.com

Article on turning clutter into cash   http://ezinearticles.com/?Thrifty-Retirement-
--Turn-Clutter-Into-Cash&id=2631878

Professional education course on selling goods on eBay
https://www.mypescpe.com/open/cpe/eBay-Business-at-Your-Fingertips.
cmc?&view=12C

Article on the basic principles of multilevel marketing
http://www.cscs.umich.edu/~crshalizi/notebooks/multilevel-marketing.html

Index

Q-R

organization and efficiency experts, 136

painting businesses, 94

personal celebration event planners, 242

personal chefs, 219

personal shoppers and wardrobe consultants, 138

personal trainers, 148

pool and hot-tub services, 57

produce distribution, 223-224

projections, 26-30

public relations consultants, 286

recruiters, 257-258

secretarial virtual assistants, 264

SEO services, 293

social marketing services, 284-285

software development, 278

special-needs child-care, 170-171

summer camp programs, 168-169

travel planners, 234

upholstery and drapery business, 115

vacation chefs, 222

vacation concierge, 69-70

web content developers, 291

web-hosting companies, 276

website design and development, 272-273

window blind sales and installation, 117-118

window cleaning, 59-60

wine-tasting hosts, 228-229

yoga teachers, 153

ROI (return on investment), 296

S

salary expectations. *See* revenue expectations

sales (goods resellers), 297-306

arts and crafts, 303-304

collectibles, 304-306

eBay sales, 299-300

import businesses, 301-303

multilevel marketing, 298-299

sales tax, 39-40

search engine optimization. *See* SEO services

seasonal flower installation, 63

secretarial virtual assistants, 264-266

selling homes (home resale services), 79-90

appraisers, 88-90

estate sale facilitators, 83-85

inspectors, 86-88

staging services, 80-83

senior transition management, 180-182

Senior Transition Society Council, 182

SEO (search engine optimization) services, 293-294

shoppers (personal shoppers), 138-140

sitters

babysitting, 165-166

dog and cat sitting, 186-188

hospice and hospital caregivers, 182-184

snow removal services, 64

social marketing services, 284-286

software development, 278-279

sole proprietorships, 16

solo approach, 28-29

special requirements

after-school academic tutoring, 200

after-school programs, 168

alteration and tailoring businesses, 145-146

aquarium set-up and maintenance, 196

art and music lessons, 210

arts and crafts sales, 304

attorneys, 257

baby nurses, 164

babysitting, 166

bartending, 228

business coaches, 260

catering services, 218-219

collectible sales, 306

college consulting, 203

computer system installation, 281

consultants, 260

cooking lessons, 231

copywriting, 292

corporate event planners, 246

CPAs, 257

dietitian and nutritionist, 152

direct-mail marketing, 296

dog and cat sitting, 188

dog grooming, 192

doggy daycares, 190

e-mail marketing, 296

eBay sales, 300

elder companions and aides, 178

elder-care concierge services, 176

ESOL (English for Speakers of Other Languages) tutors, 206

estheticians, 158

executive assistants, 267

financial planners, 257